Charles Larpenteur

Fort Union

Forty Years a Fur Trader

on the Upper Missouri

The Personal Narrative of
CHARLES LARPENTEUR
1833–1872

HISTORICAL INTRODUCTION BY
MILO MILTON QUAIFE

Introduction to the Bison Book
Edition by Paul L. Hedren

University of Nebraska Press
Lincoln and London

First Bison Book printing: 1989
Most recent printing indicated by the first digit below:
3   4   5   6   7   8   9   10

Library of Congress Cataloging-in-Publication Data
Larpenteur, Charles, 1807–1872.
    Forty years a fur trader on the upper Missouri: the personal
narrative of Charles Larpenteur, 1833–1872: historical introduc-
tion by Milo Milton Quaife; introduction to the Bison Book edi-
tion by Paul L. Hedren.
    p. cm.
    Reprint. Originally published: Chicago: Lakeside Press, 1933.
(Lakeside classics)
    "Bison Book"—T.p. verso.
    Bibliography: p.
ISBN 0-8032-2888-0 (alk. paper).—ISBN 0-8032-7930-2 (pbk.: alk.
paper)
    1. Larpenteur, Charles, 1807–1872. 2. Fur traders—Missouri
River Valley—Biography. 3. Fur trade—Missouri River Valley—
History—19th century. 4. Frontier and pioneer life—Missouri
Rivery Valley. 5. Missouri River Valley—History. 6. Missouri River
Valley—Biography. I. Title.
F598.L332   1989
978'.02'0924—dc19
[B]   88-38637 CIP

Reprinted from the Lakeside Classics edition published in 1933 by
R.R. Donnelley & Sons Co., Chicago. The Publisher's Preface to
that edition has been omitted.

The University of Nebraska Press is grateful to Marvin L. Kaiser,
who provided a copy of the book for reproduction.

Contents

v

Contents

Introduction to the Bison Book Edition
By Paul L. Hedren

Close associates remembered fur trader Charles Larpenteur (1807–1872) as intelligent, vivacious, unusually
well informed, and well read. Superiors appreciated his
honesty and aggressive handling of company business.
Detractors thought of him as vain and cynical, as one
capable of bearing a timeless grudge. Modern historians
applaud his "roving eye" that captured in journals and
a reminiscence the drama, personalities, and complex-
ities of the Upper Missouri fur trade.

Although Charles Larpenteur embodied many admi-
rable personal qualities, it is clear from his writings and
from the views of contemporaries that he barely rose
beyond middle-management responsibilities in the fur
trade. In his 1843 history of Fort Union, bourgeois Ed-
win Denig referred to Larpenteur simply as the retail
storekeeper. John James Audubon visited Fort Union in
1843 and noted in passing that Larpenteur "opens the
gates when the bell rings at sunrise." Audubon's travel
mate Edward Harris offered a comparable glimpse of an
ordinary man, observing but not elaborating on a quick
trip "north of the fort to search for shells and impres-
sions of leaves." We gain the impression that Larpenteur
carried out decisions but seldom made them.

Larpenteur's middle-level stature becomes one of the
more appealing aspects of his legacy. He was neither an

uninitiated nor an uneducated common hand, nor was he, except at the very last, a head man. Instead, he walked comfortably in all circles, befriending and re-membering hunters, masons, interpreters, Indians, smiths, fellow clerks, boatmen, and bourgeoisie; and his journals and memoir provide matchless insight into the multiple castes of the western fur trade.

A wiry Frenchman, Charles Larpenteur was deter-mined to pursue a career in the fur trade. In 1833 he was employed by William Sublette and Robert Campbell as a laborer on their expedition to the annual rendez-vous. This indoctrination was an eye-opener. Moreoever, the "one sober man in camp" caught Campbell's per-sonal attention. Larpenteur was soon invited to continue with Campbell and Sublette to the Upper Missouri River, where they intended to establish a post in opposition to John Jacob Astor's Fort Union.

After taking a considerable financial beating on the Upper Missouri, this trading partnership sold out to the American Fur Company. Fort Union bourgeois Kenneth McKenzie spotted hard-working Larpenteur during the brief existence of Fort William, and invited him to clerk at the Astor post. For the next decade Larpenteur dem-onstrated tireless devotion to the American Fur Com-pany. But when the opportunity to manage a company post of his own never materialized, he struck off inde-pendently. Regrettably, he struck out too. After suffering through an unusually harsh and profitless winter in 1848–49, and a physical breakdown that he labeled a "great derangement" to his nervous system, Larpenteur bailed out briefly to Baltimore.

Recuperation was spontaneous, and for the next sev-eral decades Larpenteur continued a personal quest for a niche in the Upper Missouri trade. As an independent trader and agent, he operated posts and wintering houses on the Missouri from Nebraska to the Great Falls of Montana and on the Yellowstone nearly to the future townsite of Billings. But profits for his underwriters and himself were always elusive and by the 1860s he was once again back in the employ of the American Fur Company at the ageless Fort Union.

Larpenteur had already witnessed great transitions in the fur business. At Fort Union he participated in a final saga of the old trade, and he witnessed the dawning of a new and tension-filled era of soldiers and conflict. In 1867 proud old Fort Union was demolished by the U.S. Army. Larpenteur gravitated to the new Fort Buford and attempted to sutler among the Indians and soldiers at that post. Even that was thwarted in 1870 by a governmental decree allowing but one sutler per military reservation.

In 1871 Larpenteur packed out of the Upper Missouri country for the last time. Although fortune forever eluded this capable Frenchman, his accomplishments in one last ambition reserved his place in the annals of the American fur trade. Larpenteur never elaborated about journal-keeping in *Forty Years a Fur Trader,* but like other literate nineteenth century individuals he faithfully maintained a daily account for many, and perhaps even all, of his years on the frontier. When he retired to a small farm near Little Sioux, Iowa, he commenced writing his personal narrative. He grieved over the death of his twelve-year-old son and his health broke; yet with journals at hand he produced a chronicle of his life and adventures.

Larpenteur finished his personal history in mid-June

1872 and bundled it off to Dr. Washington Matthews, an army surgeon and good friend at Fort Buford. He asked Matthews to help put the foolscap pages into shape for publication. The doctor made a clerical copy of the manuscript and returned the original to Larpenteur. Matthews was typical of a class of army officer emerging about this time with an unquenchable interest in documents and knowledge of this sort. But before much could be done to polish and shape the narrative, Larpenteur died and the project was put aside.

In the next several decades Matthews's stature as a soldier-ethnologist grew. His curiosity led him to study disappearing native communities and it brought him into close contact with other scholars with similar interests. One of them, Elliott Coues, had also been an army doctor, but by the 1890s his attention had shifted to matters of history and exploration. In 1897 Matthews gave Coues the Larpenteur manuscript.

Coues was instantly intrigued by Larpenteur's fur-trade history. He quickly sought out surviving family members, who lent the first copy of the manuscript as well as original journals, notebooks, and other papers that could be useful to background and editing. Coues found the manuscript in need of grammatical recasting, a requirement Larpenteur himself had certainly realized when he sent it to Matthews in 1872. Coues wasted little time editing the memoir. Ultimately, how much of *Forty Years a Fur Trader* is Larpenteur's and how much is Coues's has never been determined. Coues explained his editorial approach in an introduction that closed with a caveat noting how he "simply helped the author to express himself; the sense and sentiment are his own, if the style is not."

Bison Book Introduction

Today this two-volume first printing of *Forty Years a Fur Trader*, published in 1898 by Francis P. Harper of New York City, is commonly called the "Coues edition." Beyond a strong editorial influence, Coues contributed copious annotations on matters of geography and personality. He obviously took great satisfaction in preparing Larpenteur's narrative. "Thus has been realized," he noted, "the desire of the author's heart, a quarter of a century after it ceased to beat." The 950 copies of this first edition have long since disappeared, and today even the dingiest specimens command premium prices on the antiquarian book market.

In 1933 an academic historian, Milo Milton Quaife, republished *Forty Years*, combining Coues's two volumes into one. Like Coues, Quaife recognized impressive qualities in Larpenteur's story. But at the same time he took serious objection to Coues's editorial practices, brandishing them as the sort which "no careful scholar would permit himself to indulge." In preparing the new edition, Quaife excised all of Coues's laborious and often superfluous annotations, he corrected certain capitalizations, and he added a limited number of his own explanatory footnotes. It is this "Quaife edition" that is herewith reprinted by the University of Nebraska Press as a Bison Book.

In 1962 *Forty Years a Fur Trader* appeared in a third edition, this from Ross and Haines of Minneapolis. Ross and Haines combined Coues's two volumes into one but otherwise reprinted verbatim the 1898 Harper version in an edition limited to 1500 copies. Like its predecessors, this printing is also very difficult to locate.

Notion of a fourth printing of *Forty Years a Fur Trader* would probably startle its author. And Larpenteur would probably be equally bemused by the character of his revered Upper Missouri country in this century after his departure. The once wild river was long ago tamed by the dams of the Pick-Sloan project, and the great lakes created behind those numerous concrete and earthen barriers have inundated much of the Upper Missouri's fur trade heritage. The passage of time has played its own havoc on other sites, where perhaps the river did not. Forts Clark, William, and McKenzie, for instance, are desolate fields today bearing but limited testimony to their former trading prominence.

Remarkably, some of Larpenteur's world has a physical context in this new century. The Fort Laramie countryside he passed as he headed to rendezvous, and Fort Benton, the American Fur Company post at the head of the Missouri River navigation, bear structural and aesthetic remains that would be familiar to our Frenchman.

Most remarkable of all, perhaps, is the recent rebirth of Fort Union Trading Post at the confluence of the Yellowstone and Missouri Rivers. There, under the careful charge of the National Park Service, Charles Larpenteur is remembered. Moreover, many of the fort's structures—the walls, the great stone bastions, the Indian trade house, and the lavish Bourgeois House that Charles called home during his final tenure—have been carefully reconstructed. Nearby, original army buildings at Fort Buford also retain a nineteenth century charm that Larpenteur could find comfortable.

But most significantly, it is his memoir *Forty Years a Fur Trader* and his journals that are Charles Larpenteur's greatest legacy. Journals from the 1830s, '60s, and early '70s survive. His style lacked pretension (which was Coues's opinion at the start), yet the journals have a faithfulness and vitality that add measurably to our understanding of the upper river trade. To the good fortune of fur trade scholars and afficionados, retired National Park Service historian Erwin N. Thompson has transcribed and annotated these journals. Their publication will be a great addition to fur trade literature.

Making *Forty Years a Fur Trader* again available is equally laudable. Sandwiched into Larpenteur's narrative is insight into the mechanics of the American Fur Company and details on those countless little wintering houses and subposts that comprised the trading network in Indian country. And he gives us a no-holds-barred look at the social milieu of the trade. We applaud the business acumen of Kenneth McKenzie, grimace at the calculated murder of Fort Union's Deschamps family, and sneer at the arrogance of rival trader Malcolm Clark. Larpenteur gives us a commoner's tale that is extraordinary, noteworthy most of all for its forty-year duration.

Erratum

P. XVI: Quaife wrongly states that from 1763 to 1803 the Missouri country belonged to Spain and that in 1803 Spanish Louisiana passed from Spain to the United States. Although Spain had, indeed, received the Louisiana Territory from France at the Peace of Paris in 1763, the secret Treaty of San Ildefonso, signed in 1800 between Spain and France, retroceded Louisiana to France. Therefore, the United States negotiated with France, not Spain, for the Louisiana Purchase.

Historical Introduction

THE life-record kept by Charles Larpenteur is one of our most important sources of information concerning the fur trade of the Upper Missouri in the nineteenth century. To sketch for the reader the historical setting of his journal, is the task of the present introduction.

Its logical starting-point is the discovery of the mouth of the Missouri by Jolliet and Marquette on their memorable voyage of western exploration in 1673. They were much impressed by the sight of the turbulent, muddy current of the Missouri, and with them originated the idea that by ascending the great river a water route across the continent, and thence to the golden wealth of the Indies, might be found. Within a generation of its discovery, the lower course of the river had become familiar to the French, and by 1717 they had mapped it as far as the vicinity of present-day Sioux City. Two decades later the La Vérendrye, working westward from Lake Superior, reached the Mandan villages of central North Dakota, where sixty years later Lewis and Clark were to spend the winter of 1804–05.

Historical Introduction

From 1763 to 1803 the Missouri country belonged to the King of Spain, and its governmental and commercial center was Spanish St. Louis. Until about 1790 the Spaniards made little effort to add to the knowledge of the Missouri which their French predecessors had gained, but during the next few years repeated and diligent efforts were made to explore the Upper River and open the route to the western sea which over a century before Jolliet and Marquette had speculated upon. Although they did not realize this ambition, before the year 1800 they had charted the river for 1800 miles, and had obtained from the natives a fairly accurate idea of its remaining course.

Thus matters stood when in 1803 Spanish Louisiana passed into the possession of the United States. One of the earliest acts of President Jefferson, following the acquisition, was to despatch Captains Meriwether Lewis and William Clark upon their famous expedition from St. Louis across the continent. In three years' time they were back again, having successfully achieved their mission and written their names high on the roll of the great explorers of the earth.

Their reports of the country they had traversed, and of its surpassing abundance of fur-bearing animals stirred the St. Louis merchants to a prompt renewal of trading enterprises to the Upper River. The first important expedition was led by the enterprising Spanish merchant, Manuel Lisa, who in 1807 ascended the Missouri and the Yellowstone as far as the mouth of Big Horn River, where he established Fort Manuel. Returning to St. Louis the following year, he joined with other merchants in organizing the Missouri Fur Company, with William Clark as resident St. Louis agent. The new organization in 1809 sent a formidable expedition, 350 strong, up the river, to establish a line of posts and garner the wealth in furs which seemed awaiting them. They erected Fort Lisa in North Dakota a few miles above the mouth of the Big Knife, and in the summer of 1810 a post was established at Three Forks, Montana. The hostility of the Blackfeet soon compelled the abandonment of the latter, however, with consequent loss of the anticipated profits, and this disaster led to the dissolution of the Company.

Meanwhile, John Jacob Astor of New York, perhaps the greatest figure in the history of the American fur trade, had entered upon the scene, determined to reap his share of the fur harvest of the Northwest. Rebuffed by the St. Louis merchants when he sought to become a partner in their company, in 1808 he organized the American Fur Company, and laid plans for the great Astorian enterprise whose promising beginnings were cut short by the disasters attendant upon the War of 1812.[1]

Although the successors of the Missouri Fur Company continued to operate for some years after the War of 1812, a more important renewal of trading activities on the Missouri was signalized by the organization in 1822 of the Rocky Mountain Fur Company by William H. Ashley and Andrew Henry. Henry had been associated with the older Missouri Fur Company but Ashley was a new-comer to the trade. On March 20, 1822, he published in a St. Louis newspaper an advertisement for one hundred "enterprising" young men to serve him at the source of the Missouri for terms of one, two, and three years. The plan was to establish headquarters at Three Forks, and from this center trap all the adjoining region

[1]The Astorian enterprise has been productive of much historical literature. Some of Washington Irving's best-known books deal with its history, to which two former volumes in *The Lakeside Classics Series* have been devoted: Alexander Ross's *Adventures of the First Settlers on the Oregon* . . . , published in 1923, and the same author's *Fur Hunters of the Far West*, published the following year.

for a period of three years. For several years the Rocky Mountain Fur Company conducted its activities in the Upper Missouri and Great Salt Lake regions, and in 1826 Jedediah S. Smith, David E. Jackson, and William L. Sublette succeeded to the ownership of the Company. Ashley, Smith, and Sublette are three of the greatest figures in the fur-trade annals of the mountain area. The success of the Company was such as to inspire the American Fur Company and other competitors to enter the field, and the bitter rivalry for the trade which ensued both demoralized the natives and threatened the profits of the traders. Under these circumstances the Rocky Mountain Company voluntarily dissolved in 1834. In the dozen years of its existence it had written an important chapter in the history of the fur trade and in the annals of North American exploration. Its members had discovered the South Pass and the Great Salt Lake, and had explored the Great Basin, as well as the sources of the Platte, Green, Yellowstone, and Snake rivers. They had crossed the deserts of Utah and Nevada, and the Sierras to California, and had traveled by land from San Francisco northward to the Columbia.

Foremost in the field of its competitors was the American Fur Company, which in

1822 established a Western Department at St. Louis. For a few years its efforts were confined to the Lower Missouri, but in 1827 it absorbed the rival Columbia Fur Company and with this amalgamation accomplished it invaded the field of trade on the Upper Missouri. Its leader in the field was Kenneth McKenzie, builder of Fort Union in 1829, who figures so prominently in Larpenteur's narrative. Although the Rocky Mountain Fur Company bowed to the new rival in 1837, the profits of the trade were such that other competitors were constantly in the field, an ever-changing procession of traders, whom the Great Company fought, browbeat, or absorbed as circumstances and opportunity might dictate.

Into such a field of endeavor eagerly entered young Charles Larpenteur in 1833. His experiences and activities from then until his final withdrawal in 1871 are the theme of the present volume. The narrative has recently been characterized by a competent scholar as "probably the most valuable contemporary document extant" dealing with the fur trade of the Missouri River region. Its human qualities will be evident to the reader, who will find himself alternately thrilled and shocked by the ever-shifting panorama of scenes of daring and horror. The recital is one of "nature in the raw," and its perusal will bring little pleasure to those who shrink from the realities of life.

The keeping of a journal seems to have been a lifelong custom of Larpenteur, and in the comparatively brief period which elapsed between his retirement from the active affairs of life and his death, he applied himself diligently to the task of composing his autobiography. Within less than a year it was finished, and after some vain efforts to procure its publication in Sioux City, on March 1, 1872, he invoked the aid of Dr. Washington Matthews of the U. S. Army in bringing it out. Before anything material was accomplished Larpenteur died. A quarter of a century later when Dr. Elliott Coues was actively engaged in editing works on the early history of the trans-Mississippi country, Matthews turned over to him the copy of Larpenteur's manuscript which the author had sent to him so long before. Coues also procured the original manuscript copy from A. L. Larpenteur, a nephew of the author, and various of the original journals and other material from the widow, who was still living at the old home near Little Sioux, Iowa. Coues proceeded with his customary diligence to edit the journal, which was published the following year by Francis P. Harper of New York in a two-volume edition of 950 copies.

Although Dr. Coues was a man of wide learning and high scholarly repute, some of his editorial practices were not in harmony with the principles of historical scholarship. In particular, in his editing of historical documents he exercised a freedom which no careful scholar would permit himself to indulge. The consequence follows that one never knows, when reading a document which Coues has edited, how closely the original record has been reproduced, or in what way it has been altered by the editor. Probably the usual motive which animated such alterations was the desire to supply the reader with a smoother and more readable narrative than the original document presents. This would be laudable enough if the editor took the care to inform the reader what manner and degree of alterations he had introduced into the author's narrative.[2] It departs from scholarly standards when alterations are introduced without informing the reader that the editor, rather than

[2]This was done by the present writer in editing George Rogers Clark's *Conquest of the Illinois*, *The Lakeside Classics* volume for the year 1920.

the author, is responsible for these portions
of the narrative.

In the case of Larpenteur's journal, the
means remains for checking Coues' proce-
dure, since the original manuscript of Larpenteur is preserved in the library of the
Minnesota Historical Society at St. Paul, to
which it was presented by A. L. Larpenteur
in 1901. Comparison of the published narrative with it discloses[3] that Coues pretty completely revamped the language and literary
construction of the latter. The advantage
to the general reader is evident, for instead of
the labored style and awkward orthography
of the original, he is given the graceful,
smooth-flowing narrative which is before us
in the present volume. For the serious stu-
dent of history the matter has, of course, a
different aspect. He will much prefer to con-
sult the journal as it was actually written by
the author; and he will learn for the first time
from the present introduction, that in preparing it for printing Coues revamped and mod-
ernized it with great editorial freedom.

[3]The present writer has not seen the original. The
comparison has been made, in response to his request,
by Miss Grace Lee Nute, Curator of Manuscripts of
the Minnesota Historical Society, and Dr. Theodore C.
Blegen, Secretary and Superintendent of that institu-
tion, and the statements made above are based upon
their reports.

Historical Introduction

The text as here presented is an almost literal reprint of the narrative as printed by Dr. Coues, only a few changes in capitalization, and the correction of a few obvious errors having been made. Instead of the voluminous and frequently much-too-rambling footnotes supplied by Coues, the editor has appended a much smaller number and quantity of his own. The map, designed to aid the reader in following the narrative, has been prepared under his direction.

As for the author, Charles Larpenteur, Dr. Matthews described him to Coues as "a small, wiry man of distinctly Gallic type. . . . He was very intelligent, vivacious and witty in conversation, full of anecdote and reminiscence, and unusually well-informed for a man in his position." He was a man of unquestioned integrity, respected even by those who disliked him personally. That he was proud, and quick to resent an offense against his sense of dignity is apparent from his own narrative, in which he does not hesitate to speak plainly about the shortcomings of his associates. One of the men thus criticized, Captain Joseph La Barge, has left a like piquant estimate of his critic. He observes that Larpenteur, "although very long in the Indian country, was never a man of high standing there, and proved a

Historical Introduction

failure in whatever he undertook. Like all such men, he nursed the delusion that the world was in league against him, and he took advantage of the opportunity offered by the preparation of his memoirs to even matters up. . . . Larpenteur was probably an honest man in his business relations, but never an able man, and his attempts to account for his own deficiencies by attributing them to the rascality of others, does not add to the value of his memoirs as historical material." Quite possibly this estimate, like some of Larpenteur's own, is overdrawn; some support, however, it seems to find in the author's own recital of his career, who freely confesses his ultimate failure in life. In any event, he was a very human man, he passed the years of his active career in a stern and turbulent environment, and he had the discernment to realize that its story would command the interest of future generations, and the industry to preserve for us the record of it. For this service we are greatly indebted to him.

M. M. QUAIFE

Detroit Public Library
   October 1, 1933

MAP OF
LARPENTEUR COUNTRY

Forty Years a
Fur Trader

Forty Years a
Fur Trader

—

Chapter 1

(1807–33)

MY PARENTAGE AND EARLY LIFE

IN order to inspire the reader with confidence in the veracity of my writing—for it must be borne in mind that I write this book for true and faithful information of the public—I thought it would be well to give him an introduction to myself, before entering on the journey.

I was born in France, in the year 1807,[1] five miles from Fontainebleau, on the border of the beautiful Seine, 45 miles from Paris. My father, who was neither rich nor poor, but a great Bonapartist, left France for America immediately after the battle of

[1] The inscription on his tombstone indicates that he was born May 8, 1803; but the statements contained in the following pages point to 1807 as the correct year.

Waterloo, thinking that the American government would make some attempt to get Napoleon off the island of St. Helena; but after conversing with several individuals, and particularly with Commodore Porter, he found that the government would countenance no such attempt. So the project was abandoned—I say the project, for it had been started by the many French officers who were at the time in Philadelphia. Louis XVIII having issued a pardon, most of them returned to France. My father returned after an absence of one year, during which he found the American government and the country to suit him. So he sold all his property and left France in 1818, with a family of four children—three boys and one daughter, I being the youngest son. In his travels in America he had chosen Baltimore as his future residence. Having landed at New York we came to Baltimore, where he purchased a small farm of 60 acres, five miles from the city. This farm belonged to some French who had been forced to emigrate by the massacre of St. Domingo, and was established by Monsieur La Bié Du Bourgh De Berg [sic]; it was well supplied with fruits, but the soil was poor and stony, and this lad got sick of it. Hearing much of the fine rich soil of Missouri, I determined to try my luck in the Far West—for at that time it was considered quite a journey to St. Louis.

So at the age of twenty-one I determined to leave home, and started with a gentleman by the name of J. W. Johnson,[2] who had been a sutler at Prairie du Chien, and had a large number of negroes whom he was taking to Missouri. I assisted him as far as Wheeling, where he took a steamer, and I went across country on horseback alone.

[2] John W. Johnson was a Marylander whose elder brother, Rinaldo, had married a sister of John Mason, U. S. Superintendent of Indian Trade from 1806 to 1816. Through this connection, in 1808 Johnson secured the appointment of factor for the new government trading house on the Des Moines River (modern Fort Madison, Iowa). The factory was destroyed in September, 1813, as the result of an Indian siege, and upon the establishment of Fort Crawford (at Prairie du Chien, Wis.) in 1816, Johnson was appointed factor at that place, where he remained until the government factory system was abolished in 1822. Some time later (precise date undetermined) he removed to St. Louis, where he seems to have been established about the year 1828, the probable year of Larpenteur's removal to the West.

Johnson was twice married, first to a Sauk woman at Fort Madison, by whom he had three daughters; second, to the widow of George Gooding, a captain in the Fifth U. S. Infantry prior to his retirement in 1821. The date of Johnson's death is unknown; he was living as late as July, 1850, when he deeded a lot in St. Louis.

That is 43 years ago.[3] I had a fine trip of 22 days. I remained two years about St. Louis in the capacity of overseer for Major Benjamin O'Fallon,[4] a retired Indian agent, with whom I had a great deal to talk about Indians and Indian countries, which finally induced me to try the wilderness.

My first trip was up the Mississippi to Des Moines Rapids, the year previous to the Black Hawk War of 1832. At this time there were two stores at Keokuk—not yet called by that name; one of them belonged to an individual named Stillwell, and the other to Mr. Davenport, who was afterward

[3] Apparently written in 1871, which would indicate 1828 as the year of Larpenteur's migration.

[4] Benjamin O'Fallon was a son of Dr. James O'Fallon of Ireland who came to America before the Revolution, served as surgeon in the Continental Army, and in 1790 married Frances Clark, youngest sister of General George Rogers Clark. He died three years later, leaving two young sons, John and Benjamin. John became a captain in the War of 1812, and in 1816 was a member of the force which built and garrisoned Fort Howard, at Green Bay, Wis. In 1818 he resigned his commission and settled at St. Louis, where he became wealthy, and a noted philanthropist. Benjamin accompanied him to Green Bay in 1816, and accompanied or followed him to St. Louis, where Governor William Clark, his uncle, appointed him Indian agent on the Upper Missouri. His later years were passed at his home near St. Louis, where he died in 1843.

murdered on Rock Island.[5] I came up to the place in a small steamer called the *Red Rover*, commanded by Capt. Throckmorton,[6] who is still alive and has made many trips up this river—as fine a gentleman as I ever knew. On the way up I became acquainted with Mr. Blondo,[7] interpreter for the Sac and Fox Indians. He took a great fancy to me, and nothing would do but I must go with him to his farm, seven miles up the

[5] The murder of Colonel George L. Davenport in his home on Rock Island, July 4, 1845, was one of the notorious crimes of the period. He had served ten years in the regular army before coming to Rock Island in 1816. Here he became a notable trader and merchant, influential both with the red men and the white. He helped to lay out the city of Davenport, which bears his name. In 1833 he built on Rock Island the fine residence in which he was murdered, and which is still preserved. See *Dict. Am. Biog.*

[6] Captain John Throckmorton was one of the earliest steamboat captains on the Upper Mississippi. In 1832 he commanded the *Warrior* which figured in the destruction of Black Hawk's followers in the tragic battle of the Bad Axe. Dr. Matthews informed Coues that he had a steamboat on the Upper Missouri as late as 1870 or 1871.

[7] Maurice Blondeau, whose career is sketched in *Wis. Hist. Colls.*, XX, 356–57. He was a member of a French family having early trading connections at Mackinac. His farm, seven miles above Keokuk, where he entertained Larpenteur, was developed about the year 1820. He died at Burlington prior to the Black Hawk War of 1832.

rapids, and remain there until the boat got over the rapids, which it was supposed would take a long time, as the river was very low. I consented, got a horse caloh [calesh], and we started. The improvements consisted of a comfortable log cabin, and Blondo was indeed well fixed for the country at the time. After some little time he took me into the village and introduced me to several of the leading men, of whom a great many were drunk, and toward evening he got so drunk himself that he frequently asked me if I did not want to "smell powder," but as I never felt like smelling powder as he proposed, I declined, not knowing why he used the expression. After the spree the old gentleman was very kind, took me all over the half-breed reservation—as fine country as I ever saw—and finally remarked that he would give me all the land I wanted if I should happen to make a match with his niece, Louise Dauphin. That was said after I had given up the idea of going on to Prairie du Chien, where I was bound; but, thinking myself too young, I declined all overtures, although I confess that I came very near accepting the offer, for Louise was one of the handsomest girls I ever saw —it cost me many long sighs to leave her, and more afterward.

𝔐𝔶 𝔓𝔞𝔯𝔢𝔫𝔱𝔞𝔤𝔢 𝔞𝔫𝔡 𝔈𝔞𝔯𝔩𝔶 𝔏𝔦𝔣𝔢

After two months' residence at the rapids I returned to St. Louis, with full determination to see more of the wild Indians. General Ashley,[8] who was then carrying on great beaver trapping in the Rocky Mountains, was in the habit of hiring as many as 100 men every spring. They were engaged for 18 months, to return in the fall of the following year with the furs. Not long after I came from the rapids General Ashley's party returned from the mountains with 100 packs of beaver. A pack of beaver is made up of 60 average beavers, supposed to weigh 100 lbs., worth in New York at that time from $7 to $8 per lb. It is impossible to describe my feelings at the sight of all that beaver—all those mountain men unloading their mules, in their strange mountain costume—most of their garments of buckskin and buffalo hide, but all so well greased and worn that it took close examination to tell

[8] General William H. Ashley, whose operations are here described, was one of the notable figures in exploiting the fur trade of the Upper Missouri and Rocky Mountain areas in the years subsequent to the War of 1812. Among other exploits he was the first to descend Green River, which to the present day has been navigated only a few times. He made his home at St. Louis, and after withdrawing from active participation in the fur trade became active in political life, serving in Congress several terms. See *Dict. Am. Biog.*

what they were made of. To see the mules rolling and dusting is interesting and shocking at the same time; most of them, having carried their burdens of 200 pounds' weight for about 2,000 miles, return with scarcely any skin on their backs; they are peeled from withers to tail, raw underneath from use of the surcingle, and many are also lame.

William Sublette[9] and Robert Campbell had attended General Ashley on several trips to the mountains—Campbell as clerk, mostly on account of his health; he had previously been clerk for Keith and O'Fallon. Sublette was a farmer near St. Louis, but was more for trapping beaver than farming.

The sight of all this made me determined to take a trip of the same kind. The journey to the Rocky Mountains at that early period

[9] William L. Sublette was born in Kentucky in 1799. In early manhood he removed to Missouri and soon thereafter engaged in the fur trade. He was an associate of General Ashley (later, his successor in the trade), and an active opponent of the American Fur Company. His partnership with Robert Campbell, here noted, began about the year 1832. Campbell was an Irishman, who like Josiah Gregg, sought the western plains in search of health. He served under General Ashley for several years and upon the latter's withdrawal from the Indian trade, became a partner in the Rocky Mountain Fur Company. He lived in St. Louis the latter half of his life, where he was long a prominent and prosperous citizen. He died in 1879.

was considered very hard, and dangerous on account of the Pawnees and Blackfeet. While trapping that summer William Sublette had been badly wounded in the shoulder in a fight with the Blackfeet.[10] But not all this danger, and the hardships to be endured on such a trip, could prevent me from engaging, in the spring of 1833.

I first provided myself with a good recommendation from Major Benjamin O'Fallon, who was well known for his integrity, and would give no one a recommendation unless he deserved it. Provided with this document I next made application to the American Fur Company, which was then carried on by P. Chouteau and Co.[11] J. J. Astor was still in the company. Mr. J. B. Sarpy was at the time the person who engaged the men. As I was young, well dressed, and not a bad-looking lad, but did not seem to be very robust, he remarked that he did not think I would answer for his purposes. I then showed him my document from the major,

[10] The battle of Pierre's Hole in 1832, described by Washington Irving in Chap. VI of his *Adventures of Captain Bonneville.*

[11] This was Pierre Chouteau Jr., younger brother of Auguste Pierre, whose career is sketched in *Josiah Gregg's Commerce of the Prairies* (*The Lakeside Classics*, Chicago, 1926), 180–81. For his career see *Dict. Am. Biog.*

whom we both knew well, and the remark he made was, "Ah, if you had not deserved this, you would not have gotten it." Then, said he, "you are a Frenchman?" I replied in the affirmative. "You have some education," he continued; "why do you want to engage as a common hand?" I then told him that my desire was to see the Rocky mountains, that I was willing to undergo all the hardships of such a voyage, and that I wished to start from this place on horseback. He then referred me to Messrs. Sublette and Campbell, saying that, if I engaged with him, I should have to go as far as Fort Pierre,[12] and there start for the mountains with Mr. Fontenelle. Being anxious for an immediate ride, that proposition did not suit me. I then went to the office of Sublette and Co., which firm had bought out all Gen. Ashley's interests in the mountains, and were also making up an outfit to carry on an opposition to all the trading posts of the American Fur Co. on the Missouri; but I did not know this when I first applied to them. I found Mr. Campbell in his store, and on informing him of my intentions he appeared to have pretty much the same ideas as Mr. Sarpy. I soon discovered this

[12] Named for Pierre Chouteau Jr., and on the site of present-day Pierre, S. Dak.

and showed him my recommendation. Being very much of a gentleman, he had the politeness to invite me to his office, and there did all he could to make me abandon the idea of taking such a trip, giving me a full description of what I should be likely to undergo. But nothing could deter me; go I must, and under the promise that he should never hear me grumble, I signed an article of agreement for 18 months, for the sum $296 and such food as could be procured in the Indian country—that excluded bread, sugar, and coffee.

Now I was thus enlisted, ready for service; but Mr. Campbell was kind to me and always did his best to make my situation pleasant. So he employed me in St. Louis to assist in packing goods for the upper country, and in equipping the men who were getting ready to leave with the mules for Lexington, Mo., to await the arrival of the steamer which was to bring all their goods up to that point, and of the keel boat which was intended to be cordelled or towed as far as Fort Union with goods for the Indian trade. I was kept in the store until all the outfits had left St. Louis.

April 7th, 1833.—Now, my dear reader, my mule is saddled, bridled, and hitched at the store in Washington Avenue, St. Louis, ready to take me to Lexington, to join the party. If you wish to sacrifice all the comforts of civil life, come with me and share what I shall endure—but no! you can do better than that. For a small sum wherewith to purchase this book you can know it all without leaving your comfortable room. So good-by to civilization—not for eighteen months, but for forty years.

Myself and an individual by the name of Redman started in advance of Mr. Campbell, who was to join us at St. Charles. After we had been there two days he arrived with a young man named James Lee, and a little Snake Indian called Friday, who had been adopted by Mr. Fitzpatrick,[13] a trapper in the mountains and afterward an Indian agent—for which tribe I do not recollect. I

[13] Thomas Fitzpatrick was in his own time one of the most notable of the Rocky Mountain traders and trappers, ranking first in the trio of worthies whose other members were Kit Carson and Jim Bridger. Through the fortunes of chance and press-agenting these two men have become far better known to the present generation than is Fitzpatrick. In John Bidwell's *Echoes of the Past about California, The Lakeside Classics* volume for 1928, we remarked of Fitzpatrick that "his life story, if recorded, would make a volume of rare interest." Since then the volume in question has appeared, under the authorship of Le Roy R. Hafen and W. J. Ghent, *Broken Hand, the Life Story of Thomas Fitzpatrick, Chief of the Mountain Men* (Denver, 1931).

shall not be able to give exact dates, as I did not expect to ever write a book; but I will endeavor to come as near as possible. We were eight days on our journey from St. Charles to Lexington; we fared extremely well, Mr. Campbell having treated us like himself wherever we put up.

On the 18th [or 20th] of April we reached Lexington, where we found our party camped in tents, awaiting our arrival. There the sumptuous fares were all over. Mr. Campbell called me up and said, "Charles, I will now assign you to your mess. I have a mess of nine first-rate old voyageurs—French boys from Cahokia— you will be well off with them." I was not quite a stranger to them, having formed acquaintance with some of them before leaving St. Louis; and I am glad to say that they did all they could for me as long as I remained with them. None of those men had any education, and would frequently remark that if I took care of myself I could get into good business. Our fare during our stay at Lexington was not bad; we drew rations like soldiers, and having yet a little pocket money we could add to our provisions considerably. As to our bedding, it was not very soft, for we were not allowed to carry more than one pair of 3-pound blankets. A few days after our arrival mules were given to each of us—two to pack and one to ride. Mr. Campbell gave me his favorite mule Simon to ride; old Simon was not so kind that he would not buck me off his back when he took a notion to do so, but on the whole was a good fellow in comparison with many others. My two pack mules were very gentle, but would kick off their packs sometimes. My two loads consisted of beaver traps and a small top pack—a choice load, not likely to turn over like dry goods. As I was a green hand my mates assisted me a great deal, and I was always thankful to them for it.

Chapter 2

(1833)

ON the 12th of May we took our departure for the mountains, and at the same time the keel boat left Lexington Landing, manned by thirty men with the cordell on their shoulders, some of them for the distance of about 1800 miles. Our party consisted of 40 enlisted men; Robert Campbell, boss in charge; Louis Vasquez, an old mountain man; Mr. Johnesse, a clerk in charge of the men, whose place it was to remain in the rear to aid in readjusting the loads, which would get out of order, and to have an eye to the whole cavalcade. As guests, were Captain Stewart from England,[14] on a pleasure trip; old General

[14] Sir William Drummond Stuart (Steuart, Stewart) of Murthly Castle, Perthshire, Scotland. An informant of Coues who knew Sir William, remembered him in 1862–65 as then about seventy years of age, "very active still, though gouty and irascible." He was born in 1796 and died in 1871. He wrote (or afforded the incentive for) two books dealing with his American tour, both of which the Library of Congress classifies as fiction. One, *Altowan; or Incidents of Life and Ad-*

Harrison's son,[15] with the view to break him from drinking whiskey; and Mr. Edmund Christy, of St. Louis.

Now hard times commenced. At first the mules kicking off packs and running away was amusing for those who were all right, but mighty disagreeable for the poor fellows who were out of luck. I had my share of this, but it was not to be compared with the troubles of some of my comrades. This kind of kicking up lasted three or four days in full blast; it finally subsided, yet there would be a runaway almost every day. Our fare consisted of bacon and hard-tack—no sugar nor coffee—for three or four days, after which we each received a small piece of

venture in the Rocky Mountains (New York, 1846) purports to be edited by James Watson Webb the New York editor and politician, and to have been "written for the amusement of some young friends on Long Island." The other, rarer and more difficult to identify, is entitled *Edward Warren* . . . (London, 1854) and in the introduction is described as "a fictitious autobiography." Mr. W. F. Wagner, who gave the latter book to the Library of Congress, characterizes it as containing "nothing of historical interest."

[15] Dr. Benjamin Harrison, son of President William Henry Harrison. President Benjamin Harrison, to whom Coues appealed for information concerning his uncle, related that he had a "wild and adventurous disposition," and participated in the Texan War of Independence and "a good many other frontier scrapes."

sheep meat, as we had a drove to last us until we got into the buffalo. While the sheep lasted we had but that alone. I then commenced to think that what Mr. Campbell had remarked was on the march.[16] About a week after we had been under march the guard was established, and I was appointed an officer. It became the duty of the officer every third day to post his men around the camp, as soon as all the animals were brought in and picketed in the circle of the camp; those men were to remain quite still at their stations; the officer was to cry out "All's well" every 20 minutes, and the men to cry out the same, so as to find out whether they were asleep or awake. Should any one fail to reply, it was then the duty of the officer to go the rounds to find out the individual, and if caught asleep to take his gun to the boss' tent; then in the morning he would be informed of what he had to undergo, which was a $5 fine and three walks.[17] The men on guard were not permitted to move from their stations, as it was considered dangerous on account of Indians being known to creep up to camp and watch to shoot someone whom they

[16] That is, that Campbell's forecast was being realized.

[17] To march afoot for three days.

could discover strolling about; so the officer was more in danger than his men. The usual time of guard was 2½ hours. Having traveled all day, being obliged to remain quiet at one's post was very trying on the sleeping organs, and consequently there would be some poor fellow trudging along on foot almost every day. Our route, as well as I can remember, crossed the Little and Big Blue rivers and continued along the south side of the Platte. I complained, as my messmates did, of the sheep meat, but they consoled me as well as themselves by speaking of the fine feast we soon would have on the buffalo, which they said they would prefer to all the good messes that could be gotten up in the States. Three days after we had reached the Platte the hunters brought in one evening a load of meat; but the cry of "buffalo meat!" was heard long before they came in, and there was great rejoicement in camp. Sheep meat could be had very cheap that evening, and it was amusing to see the cooks hunting their kettles—some cursing them for being too small, as though it was the poor kettle's fault for its size; but it was not long before they found the kettles were large enough. Then came trouble—there was no wood to be found about camp, and all the fuel we could obtain was the stalks of some large dried weeds, the wild sunflower. Now and then some hungry fellow would bring in a small armful of that kind of fuel, and his first words would be, "Is the kettle boiling?" Upon being answered in the negative a long string of bad expressions would be heard, the mildest being, "Waugh! I believe that damned kettle won't never boil!" Thanks to the virtue of sunflower stalks, however, it boiled at last, and every countenance became pleasant at the thought of tasting that much-talked-of buffalo meat. When it was thought cooked by the old voyageurs, preparations were made to dish it out; but, as we had no pans, a clean place was looked for on the grass, and the contents of the kettle were poured out. All hands seated around the pile hauled out their long butcher knives, opened their little sacks of salt, and then began operations. But it was not long before bad expressions were again used in regard to the highly praised quality of buffalo meat. "I can't chew it"—"Tougher'n whalebone"—"If that's the stuff we've got to live on for eighteen months, God have mercy on us!" For my part I thought about the same, but said nothing; and after I had chewed as long as I could without being able to get it in swallowing condition, I would seize an opportunity to spit it into my hand, and throw it out unseen behind me. My comrades asked me how I liked buffalo meat; I replied I thought it might be some better than it was, and they said, "Never mind, Larpenteur; wait until we get among the fat cows —then you will see the difference." At this time of the year, in the early part of June, the cows are not fit to kill; for they have their young calves, and are very poor. For several days after this sheep meat would have kept up its price, and perhaps would have risen in value; but none was allowed to come into market, what little there was being reserved for the boss' mess. So we had to go it on buffalo alone; but, thank Providence! we soon got into fine fat cows, and fared well. My comrades had told me that we should now get a sickness called by them *le mal de vache*; it is a dysentery caused by eating too much fat meat alone, and some are known to have died of it. So it was not long after we fared so well on the fat of the land that very bad expressions were used in reference to living on meat alone.

I cannot say that anything of great importance took place during our journey to the rendezvous; but nowadays, when we have a great deal to say in the newspapers about traveling from Sioux City to Fort

Randall, I think that I may indulge in a few more remarks before I reach Green River. After crossing the South Fork of the Platte, the only curiosity of note is Chimney Rock; that part of the country is too well known at present for me to enter into any description of it. From this point to La Ramie's[18] fort nothing took place worth mentioning except the overthrow of our long friend Marsh. It happened that, in traveling through a country thickly settled with prickly pears, bad luck would have it that a small particle of one accidentally found itself under the tail of his riding mule. The poor animal, finding itself so badly pricked, kicked and bucked

[18] Comparatively little is definitely known about Jacques Laramie, here alluded to, but unlike Thomas Fitzpatrick, his posthumous fame has outgrown his real achievements. He may have been a relative of Louis Lorimier, a French trader of pre-Revolutionary Ohio, whose establishment was destroyed by George Rogers Clark, and who subsequently, encumbered by debt, fled to Spanish Louisiana, where he began a new career of influence and prosperity, being best-remembered, perhaps, as the commandant of the Cape Girardeau District. Jacques, our present subject, was active in the Rocky Mountain area from about 1816 until his death in 1820. He is supposed to have been slain by Indians, while exploring and trapping on the Laramie River. For an account of the forts, rivers, and mountains named for Laramie, see his sketch in *Dict. Am. Biog.*

at such a rate that our long friend was soon unsaddled, and thrown flat on his back in a large bunch of the prickly pears. Although he was over six feet in his stockings, the length of his limbs was not enough to reach out of the patch; and there he lay, begging for pity's sake of his comrades, as they passed by, to help him out of his prickly situation. But all he heard in reply to his entreaties was bursts of laughter throughout the company as they passed by, till he was relieved by Mr. Johnesse, who had charge of the rear. I could but pity the poor fellow, but, at the same time, his situation excited mirth. There he lay in a large bunch of prickly pears, stretched out as though he had been crucified. Poor Marsh! I shall remember him as long as I live.

On approaching La Ramie's River we discovered three large buffaloes lying dead close together. The party was ordered to stop and form in double line, while the hunters were gone to find out the cause of those buffaloes' deaths, surmising that they had been killed by Indians. They were gone but a little while before they returned, reporting that the animals had been killed by lightning during a storm we had the previous day; so our fears of Indians were removed, and the party resumed their march. We soon reached the [Laramie] river, where we were ordered to dismount and go to work making a boat out of the hides of the buffalo—quite a new kind of boat to me. But the boat was made, and the party with all the goods were crossed over by sunset. The next day, or the day after, according to custom Mr. Campbell sent Mr. Vasquez with two men to hunt up some trappers, in order to find out where the rendezvous would be, and we awaited their return at this place. They were gone eight days, which time we enjoyed in hunting and feasting on the best of buffalo meat. On the arrival of the trappers and hunters a big drunken spree took place. Our boss, who was a good one, and did not like to be backward in such things, I saw flat on his belly on the green grass, pouring out what he could not hold in. Early next morning everything was right again, and orders were given to catch up and start. Everything moved quite smoothly until we reached the Divide,[19] where my faithful old Simon—I may say the whole trinity—played out on me. About two hours before camping time the pack of one of my mules got so much out of order that I was obliged to stop to lash it

[19] The Continental Divide at the famous South Pass, near the head of Sweetwater River.

again. Mr. Simon, who was in the habit of waiting for me on occasions of that kind, changed his notion and took it into his head to follow the party without me; the well-packed one followed suit, and it was all I could do to prevent the third one from leaving before getting his pack on; but as soon as that was done the gentleman took to his heels, and all three got into camp about an hour before me. The want of Simon was the cause of my being obliged to wade a small creek—tributary to the Sweetwater—which was very cold, although it was the 2d of July. I was wet up to my waist, and it was my guard late that night. When I was awakened to go on guard my clothes were still wet, and on that morning, the 3d of July, water froze in our kettles nearly a quarter of an inch thick. I felt quite chilly and was sick for about eight days.

As near as I can remember we reached the rendezvous on Green River on the 8th of July. There were still some of Capt. Bonneville's men in a small stockade. He had come up the year previous [1832]. Thus ended our journey so far.

Chapter 3

(1833)

THE day after we reached the rendezvous Mr. Campbell, with ten men,
started to raise a beaver cache at a
place called by the French Trou à Pierre,
which means Peter's Hole.[20] As I was sick,
Mr. Campbell left me in camp, and placed
Mr. Fitzpatrick in charge during his absence, telling the latter to take good care of
me, and if the man Redman, whom he left
as clerk, did not answer, to try me. In a
short time a tent was rigged up into a kind
of saloon, and such drinking, yelling, and
shooting as went on I, of course, never had

[20] More commonly called Pierre's Hole, and subsequently known as Teton's Basin. It is a valley about
thirty miles long and several miles wide, lying between
the Teton and the Snake River ranges, and intersected
by the Wyoming-Idaho boundary. It was a famous
gathering place of the traders and the natives. A good
contemporary picture of the scene is given by John
Ball, in his letter of July 13, 1832 to his parents, printed
in *Miss. Valley Hist. Review*, V, 457–58.

heard before. Mr. Redman, among the rest, finally got so drunk that Mr. Fitzpatrick could do nothing with him, and there was not a sober man to be found in camp but myself. So Mr. Fitzpatrick asked me if I would try my hand at clerking. I remarked that I was willing to do my best, and at it I went. For several days nothing but whisky was sold, at $5 a pint. There were great quarrels and fights outside, but I must say the men were very civil to me. Mr. Fitzpatrick was delighted, and wondered to me why Mr. Campbell had not mentioned me for clerk in the first instance instead of that drunken Redman. After seven or eight days Mr. Campbell returned with ten packs of beaver. A few days afterward the rumor was circulated in camp that he was about to sell out their interest in the mountains to Fitzpatrick, Edmund Christy, Frap, and Gervais. In the meantime sprees abated, and the trappers commenced to buy their little outfits, consisting of blankets, scarlet shirts, tobacco, and some few trinkets to trade with the Snake Indians, during which transactions I officiated as clerk.

The rumors at last became verified; the sales were effected, but things went on as usual until Mr. Campbell sent for me one morning. On entering his tent I was presented with a good cup of coffee and a large-sized biscuit; this was a great treat, for I believe that it was the first coffee I had drunk since I left Lexington. Then he remarked, "Charles, I suppose you have heard that I sold out our interest in the mountains; but I have reserved all your mess, ten mules, and the cattle (we had four cows and two bulls, intended for the Yellowstone). I have 30 packs of beaver, which Fitz is to assist me with as far as the Big Horn River, where I intend to make skin boats and take my beaver down to the mouth of the Yellowstone. There I expect to meet Sublette, who is to take the packs on to St. Louis. You are one of the ten men whom I have reserved, but Fitz would like much to have you remain with him, and I leave you the choice, to stay with him or come with me." My reply was, "Mr. Campbell, I have engaged to you, you have treated me like a gentleman, and I wish to follow you wherever you go." Upon which he said, "Very well, very well," with a kind smile; "go to your mess." On returning, my messmates, expecting some news, asked me what was the result of my visit to the boss; and, on being informed, a great shout of joy was the answer. The beaver was all packed and pressed ready for the march; so the next day the order came to catch up the animals, receive our packs, and move camp. This was not our final departure; it was merely to get a fresh grazing ground for the mules and horses.

A day or so later we learned that a mad wolf had got into Mr. Fontenelle's camp about five miles from us, and had bitten some of his men and horses. My messmates, who were old hands, had heard of the like before, when men had gone mad. It was very warm, toward the latter end of July; we were in the habit of sleeping in the open air, and never took the trouble to put up the tent, except in bad weather; but when evening came the boys set up the tent. Some of the other messes asked, "What is that for?" The reply was, "Oh, mad wolf come—he bite me." When the time came to retire the pack saddles were brought up to barricade the entrance of our tent, the only one up in camp, excepting that of the boss. After all hands had retired nothing was heard in the camp except, now and then, the cry of "All's well," and some loud snoring, till the sudden cry of, "Oh, I'm bitten!" —then immediately another, and another. Three of our men were bitten that night, all of them in the face. One poor fellow, by the name of George Holmes, was badly bitten on the right ear and face. All hands got up with their guns in pursuit of the animal, but he made his escape. When daylight came men were mounted to go in search, but nothing could be seen of him. It was then thought that he had gone and was not likely to return, and no further precaution was taken than the night before. But it seems that Mr. Wolf, who was thought far away, had hidden near camp; for about midnight the cry of "mad wolf" was heard again. This time the animal was among the cattle and bit our largest bull, which went mad afterward on the Big Horn, where we made the boats. The wolf could have been shot, but orders were not to shoot in camp, for fear of accidentally killing some one, and so Mr. Wolf again escaped. But we learned afterward that he had been killed by some of Mr. Fontenelle's men.

As well as I can remember it was the first week in August when we were ordered to take final leave for the Horn.[21] Our party was then much reduced; the members of the new company remained on Green River with the intention, according to custom, to

[21] The original journal of Larpenteur gives the date as July 24, 1833. Chapter XXIII of Washington Irving's *Adventures of Captain Bonneville* gives additional information upon the events covered in our author's present chapter.

set out through the mountains so soon as trapping time commenced. Fitzpatrick came with us, with about 20 of his men; Harrison was with Fitz, intending to winter in the mountains. We turned back on the same route by which we had reached the rendezvous, to Sweetwater, from which we struck off for Wind River. Two days after leaving the Sweetwater we reached Wind River, near the mouth of a small stream called Pappah-ah-je, which place Dr. Harrison visited on account of the remarkable oil spring which puts into that stream. Some distance from the river we learned by one of the men, who had gone ahead to find a good encampment, that the Indians, the night previous, had shot a trapper asleep through the ear, that the ball had come out under his jaw, and that he had an arrow-point in his shoulder-blade. Three old trappers had left Green River some time before us, intending to meet us on Wind River. Dr. Harrison extracted the arrow-point and dressed the wound, which he pronounced not dangerous. We remained in camp two days. From this point until we got to the other side of the mountains, game became so scarce that we had to live for two days on such berries and roots as we could find. Two days before reaching the Horn one of our bulls commenced to show some symptoms of hydrophobia by bellowing at a great rate, and pawing the ground. This scared my poor friend Holmes, who was still in our party, but not destined to reach the Yellowstone. He was a young man from New York, well educated, and we became quite attached to each other on our long journey. The poor fellow now and then asked me if I thought he would go mad; although thinking within myself he would, being so badly bitten, I did all I could to make him believe otherwise. When he said to me, "Larpenteur, don't you hear the bull—he is going mad—I am getting scared," I do believe I felt worse than he did, and scarcely knew how to answer him. The bull died two days after we arrived at the Horn, and I learned, some time afterward, from Mr. Fontenelle, that Holmes had gone mad. For some days he could not bear to cross the small streams which they struck from time to time, so that they had to cover him over with a blanket to get him across; and at last they had to leave him with two men until his fit should be over. But the men soon left him and came to camp. Mr. Fontenelle immediately sent back after him; but when they arrived at the place, they found only his clothes, which he had torn off his back. He had run away quite naked, and never was found. This ended my poor friend Holmes.

It was about the 10th of August when we reached the Horn, which is the same as Wind River, only the latter loses its name after crossing the mountains. It is not navigable through the mountains, I am informed, even for a small canoe; and this is the reason why our boats had to be made on this side of the mountain. So, immediately after our arrival, a large party of hunters, with men and mules, started out, with the view of bringing in hides rather than meat; but, as luck would have it, Mr. Vasquez, clerk and old mountain man, killed one of the fattest buffalo I ever saw. Three days after this three boats were completed, and everything in readiness to leave. In the morning I was sent for by Mr. Campbell, who then gave me some instructions I was not expecting. "Now," said he, "Charles, I am going down by the river with my beaver. Mr. Vasquez will go down by land in charge of the party, with the mules and cattle. There will be but five of you. You are going to travel through the most dangerous part of the country. Mr. Vasquez will keep ahead of the party on the strict lookout, and should anything happen to him, I wish you to take charge of the party." My reply was, "Very well, sir," though such instructions, I must confess, made me feel a little nervous. But it did not last; I very soon became quite cheerful, and anxious to be under way. Mr. Campbell started that same day, and we all left early next morning. For the four first days we traveled slowly and quietly. We could not travel fast on account of the cattle, whose feet were badly worn out and tender. On the fifth morning, a little while after we left camp, we saw Mr. Vasquez coming back toward us, which made us suspect he had discovered something; we thought it might have been a band of buffalo. But when he came up to us he said that he had discovered Indians—three, on the other side of the river; but he was sure we had not been discovered by them, and moved that we should go near the river, to secure water and make some kind of a fort, for defense in case of attack. As he was in charge, and an old experienced man, we readily consented. So on we went to the river, but on arrival we found, to our great surprise, the opposite shore red with Indians, who commenced to yell enough to frighten Old Nick himself. No time to make a fort, or even to unsaddle, before they began to throw themselves into the river and make toward us. Mr. Vasquez ordered us to take position behind a large cluster of cottonwoods and cock our rifles, but not to shoot until he gave the order. So there we stood in readiness, like veterans; the first fright was over, and we were ready to make the Indians pay dearly for our hair. None of us understanding their language, we made sure they were Blackfeet, and fight we must. In less time than it takes me to write this, they were upon us. One tall scoundrel came up a little ahead of the rest with a white flag, making signs not to shoot. An old French mountaineer named Paulette Desjardins understood a few words of Crow, and as the Indian pronounced the name of his tribe, the old man said "They are Crows —there is no danger for our lives, but they are great thieves." Mr. Vasquez also knew as much about them as the old man did, and so we let them come up. Then the shaking of hands took place, and our hearts went back into the right place again. As we had a large supply of buffalo meat, we made a feast, which they appeared to relish very much, and then they expressed a desire to open trade; but we had no goods for that purpose.

We had not gone more than three miles when we discovered some ten Indians galloping toward us as fast as their horses could go; we stopped until they approached us, when we found that they were the chiefs and leading men of the camp. They looked splendid, dressed in the best of Indian costumes, and mounted on fat ponies. They all shook hands and made signs that they would look for a good place to camp, and for us to follow. Somewhat against our will we did so. It was not long before the desired spot was found, and the whole camp soon made its appearance, containing upward of 400 lodges. This was a great sight for me, who had never seen such a formidable Indian camp. The Crows, at that time, generally roamed together, and on this particular occasion they looked richer than any other Indians, for they had just made their trade at the fort, one day's march from where we were. The Crows did not drink then, and for many years remained sober; it was not until a few years ago, when they were driven out of their country by the Sioux, and became a part of the tribe on the Missouri, that they took to drinking with the Assiniboines. As they did not drink, their trade was all in substantial goods, which kept them always well dressed, and extremely rich in horses; so it was really a beautiful sight to see that tribe on the move.[22] As

[22] The details of the subsequent debauchery of this and other tribes by the liquor with which the traders plied them will abundantly appear in the further course of the narrative.

soon as the proper place was found for encamping, the chief made us a sign to unsaddle and to put all our plunder in a circle which he himself described; and on the arrival of the camp his lodge was immediately erected over it, so that all was safe.

We finally left the Crow camp and soon reached Fort Cass,[23] then in charge of Mr. Tulloch, who was a man possessed of good common sense, very reliable, and brave withal. He was called the Crane by all the Indians, on account of the extreme length and slenderness for which he was remarkable—almost a curiosity; he was extremely popular among the Crows, and well liked by the mountain men. When he left Fort Union to establish this new post, Mr. McKenzie[24] requested him to take all such articles as the Crows might fetch, so as to get them in the way of trade. His first returns consisted mostly of elk, deer, and all kinds of horns, which made great mirth at Fort Union; yet his trade had been profitable. It was started

[23] On the Yellowstone, two miles below the mouth of Big Horn River.

[24] Kenneth McKenzie, builder of Fort Union, and for several years director of activities of the American Fur Company on the Upper Missouri. He was the ablest representative the Company ever had in this region. His later life was passed at St. Louis. In Chap. 7, *post*, Larpenteur gives an account of his career.

again, and when we arrived there it was his second year. We learned that this was a very dangerous post; they had had some men killed by the Blackfeet, and were even afraid to go out to chop wood. This fort was situated about two miles below the mouth of the Horn.

Next day at ten o'clock we were again on the move, with a journey of about 250 miles before us, to reach the mouth of the Yellowstone. Nothing worthy of note took place during this part of our journey, which would have been extremely pleasant had it not been for anticipated danger from Indians. We had to erect a large pen for our animals every night, for fear of sudden attacks, and to stand frequent guard, as our party was small. But we lived on the fat of the land, as at that season game was in good order, and the Yellowstone Valley abounded with all kinds of game at that early period, and for many subsequent years. We were often frightened at large bands of elk, which, at a distance, bear the exact appearance of a mounted party of Indians, till, by the aid of a good spyglass, our fears were relieved. Our two cows added a great deal to our good living; as we had no coffee, milk was a great relish. We made but slow progress, on account of the cattle, whose feet became very tender, and finally got so bad that we were obliged to make shoes of raw buffalo hide.

We arrived safe and sound at the mouth of the Yellowstone on the 3d of September, and thus ended our long trip. We were soon discovered by our people, who were at the landing where our fort was to be erected, two miles below the mouth of the Yellowstone,[25] and were informed that Mr. William Sublette arrived there eight days before and Mr. Campbell three; but he had capsized in the Horn, lost two packs of beaver, and been near losing his life. Otherwise everything was right; they would have been glad to see us across, but it was too late in the evening to attempt this, as we had to swim. Now that I am obliged to pass a night on this side, if my reader will be so kind as to help me we will try to find out how long I have been in the saddle. As near as I can come, it is five months lacking four days. We

[25] This was Fort William, whose erection is described in the following chapter. The first fort was soon destroyed, but the name was long associated with the spot, being borne by a second fort. It was named in honor of William Sublette, leader of the opposition to the American Fur Company, whose rival fort, Union, was 2½ miles distant, about as far above the mouth of the Yellowstone as Fort William was below. Fort Union ultimately gave place to Fort Buford, which was established by the United States Army in 1866.

should have been much better pleased if we could have crossed over on our arrival; still we felt quite merry, and it was a long time before we could go to sleep.

In the evening, after we caught up our stock, one could hear great talk to the mules, calling them by name, telling them that they were near the end of their journey, and what they might expect in future; it was really amusing, and it was almost thought that the poor dumb beasts understood what was said to them. All hands were up early, mules and cattle turned out, and we waited impatiently to cross over. Between 10 and 11 a. m. Mr. Johnesse, who had come down by water with Mr. Campbell, and was still our foreman, appeared on the opposite shore to show us the place where we had to swim the stock across. The river at that season was low, and the channel so narrow that we could plainly hear all he said. When we got ready to drive the stock in, he hallooed to me, thinking I did not know how to swim, to take hold of the bull's tail. Not being an expert in the science, I took his advice and the bull's tail too, and, making use of my three loose limbs, I reached the opposite shore with ease. In a short time we were all safe on the north bank of the Missouri, upward of 2000 miles from St. Louis.

Chapter 4

(1833-34)

SOON after crossing the Missouri we were again in company with our former messmates, and some of our other acquaintances who had come down the Yellowstone by water; the meeting was indeed a cause for rejoicing. We were now altogether about 30 men, encamped in the willows on the river bank, about 300 yards from where Fort William was to be erected, and to be so called in honor of William Sublette. As we had no tents those willows sheltered us from the wind, and enabled us to make comfortable cabins. Next day operations commenced for building the fort; some men getting out pickets for the stockade, others sawing logs, etc. Seeing the necessity of having safer quarters, we went to work with all our might every day, and Sunday too; and by the 15th of November got into our comfortable quarters, after which the Sunday work was stopped. The day we moved in was a holiday, and in the evening a great feast was given us by Mr.

Fort William

Campbell—Mr. Sublette having left in the keel boat a few days after our arrival, taking with him about ten men. It consisted of half a pint of flour to each man, one cup of coffee, one of sugar, and one of molasses, to four men. Out of this a becoming feast was made, consisting of thick pancakes, the batter containing no other ingredient than pure Missouri water, greased with buffalo tallow; but as I had had nothing of the kind for upward of six months, I thought I had never tasted anything so good in my life, and swore I would have plenty of the like if I ever got back to the States.

After this our work was changed in some respects. I was appointed carter, as I was not a very good hand with an ax, and soon equipped with an old cart purchased from some of the half-breeds, who had come over early in the fall, and an American horse, which had been brought to this place by Paulette Desjardins, who had come with us as a freeman, but had sold his small outfit to Mr. Campbell and engaged in the capacity of cook. This horse was an old, overgrown, broken-winded beast, which would groan tremendously on starting his load, and keep it up for about a hundred yards afterward, at which I could not help laughing. Here I am, a regular carter of Fort William, dressed in cowskin pants, cowskin coat, buckskin shirt, wolfskin cap, red flannel undershirt, and a blue check shirt over that, stepping along behind my old horse and cart. This great suit was intended to last my time out, under faithful promise, made to myself, to leave the country as soon as my engagement should be up; for I began to find that I was in a bad box. There had been some trading previous to our entering the fort, but none of importance except one, which took place about two weeks after, as I will now relate.

The news came by an Indian that Gauché, the great chief of the Assiniboines and the terror of all the neighboring tribes, was coming in to trade with about 200 buffalo robes, beside many small peltries. As Mr. Campbell had not yet been able to turn any of the chiefs from the American Fur Company's Fort Union, Gauché was not expected to come to us. But as he was a queer kind of a grizzly-bear fellow, very odd in his way, Mr. Campbell thought he might try his luck with Gauché; so he sent his interpreter and me along to see what we could do—for I must remark that, although I was only a carter, I slept in the store and assisted in trade at night. This was the favorite time for the Indians, so that I frequently traded most of the night and went to my carting in the morning. When we reached the place where the Indians had stopped, as was the custom, to vermilion and dress themselves before entering Fort Union, where their reception was awaited with the American flag up and the cannon loaded, ready for the salute, the interpreter of the Big Fort, as Fort Union was called, had already arrived on the spot. Shaking hands with the old man, he said: "Well, I hope you will not fork to-day. The great chief of the big fort has sent me after you, and he is well prepared to receive you. I hope you will not make me ashamed by going with those one-winter-house traders." The old man was listening with half an intention; and, as we approached him, looked the interpreter straight in the face and said: "If your great chief had sent any other but you I would have gone to him, but I don't go with the biggest liar in the country." Then he made a sign to his people to get on the move, crying out now and then, "Co-han! Co-han!" which meant "Hurry up!" I found out afterward that this was a favorite expression of his. So, to the great astonishment of Mr. Campbell and all the others, we made our triumphant entrance into Fort William. We learned afterward that Mr. McKenzie was not at all surprised at the old fellow's caper, for he knew Gauché of old.

It was not until night that we all got ready to trade. It must be remembered that liquor, at that early day, was the principal and most profitable article of trade, although it was strictly prohibited by law, and all the boats on the Missouri were thoroughly searched on passing Fort Leavenworth. Notwithstanding this, Mr. Sublette had managed to pass through what he wanted for his trade all along the Missouri; but the American Fur Company, having at one time been detected and had their liquor confiscated, erected a distillery at Fort Union, and obtained their corn from the Gros Ventres and Mandans. I will say more, in future, about this distillery.[26]

The liquor trade started at dark, and soon the singing and yelling commenced. The Indians were all locked up in the fort, for fear that some might go to Fort Union, which was but 2½ miles distant. Imagine the noise—upward of 500 Indians, with their squaws, all drunk as they could be, locked up in the small space. The old devil Gauché had provided himself with a pint tin cup, which I know he did not let go during the whole spree, and every now and then he would rush into the store with his cup, and it was "Co-han"—telling me to fill it—and

[26] For this narrative, see *post*, 61–62.

"Co-han! hurry up about it, too!" This was a great night, but I wished that the old rascal and his band had gone to the big fort. At last daylight came and the spree abated; a great many had gone to sleep, and the goods trade did not commence until the afternoon; but old Co-han, with his cup, kept on the move pretty much of the time. It was not until midnight that the trade was entirely over, and early next morning they moved away, with the exception of the old man and a few of his staff of loafing beggars.

Mr. Campbell, who was anxious to secure Gauché for the winter, thought to make him a very impressive speech previous to his departure. So the old bear was invited into Mr. Campbell's room, and, after quite a lengthy speech, during which the old fellow made no reply, not even by a grunt, he merely said, "Are you a-going to give me some salt before I leave?" This being all the satisfaction Mr. Campbell received for his long speech, he could not refrain from laughing. The old devil got his salt, with some other small presents, and then departed without leaving any sign of his intention to return. Thus ended this trade.

Mr. Campbell happened to be out of luck this year, owing to the very warm fall of 1833, which kept the buffalo far north, and the winter trade of 1833–34 was a poor one; the Indians had no confidence in his remaining, so that the bulk of the trade went to the big American Company in spite of all we could do. Fortunately for us working hands, a small trade was done in the early part of the fall, or we should have fared much worse than we did—which was bad enough, as I will go on to explain. The jerked buffalo meat which had been traded from the Indians lasted but a little while, and after this our rations consisted of about a pint of pounded meat, which had been prepared and was brought in by the squaws. This is what pemmican is made of; it has to be mixed with grease to be eaten, but the tallow for this purpose we had to buy. This was sold at 50 cents per bladder, in which it was put up by the squaws, and which weighed from five to eight pounds. I had a partner, a German, and we could together purchase a bladder; but as to salt and pepper, which we had also to buy—salt $1 a pint, pepper $2—we were not in partnership; each had his small sack containing pepper and salt mixed, and used it as he thought proper. This was all we could get —no sugar, no coffee—nothing but cold water to wash the meat down. This was generally given to us for our breakfast, then lyed corn for dinner and supper. This was pretty good, but it went so hard on the salt and pepper that I began to think that I scarcely earned my salt. This kind of living lasted nearly all winter, with the exception of a deer or an elk which the hunters would now and then kill near the fort; but, true to my word, I entered no complaint.

I will here describe the construction of Fort William, which was after the usual formation of trading posts. It was first erected precisely on the spot where the Fort Buford sawmill now [about 1871] stands; but then it was about 200 yards farther from the river, the bank having caved in to that distance. It was 150 feet front and 130 deep. The stockade was of cottonwood logs, called pickets, 18 feet in length, hewn on three sides and planted three feet in the ground. The boss' house stood back, opposite the front door; it consisted of a double cabin, having two rooms of 18x20 feet, with a passage between them 12 feet wide. There was a store and warehouse 40 feet in length and 18 feet in width; two rooms for the men's quarters 16x18 feet, a carpenter's shop, blacksmith's shop, ice house, meat house, and two splendid bastions. The whole was completed by Christmas of 1833. The bastions were built more for amusement than for protection against hostile Indians; for, at that time, although they were constantly at war with other tribes, there was not the least danger for any white men except the free trappers, and we could go hunting in all directions with perfect safety. Large war parties frequently came to the fort, but behaved very well, taking their leave after getting a few loads of ammunition and some tobacco.

This post was not the only one which was out of luck, for all those along the Missouri proved a failure. Sublette, being apprised of this, sold out during the winter of 1833–34, to the American Fur Company—as I learned afterward, very much to the displeasure of Mr. McKenzie, who wished to break us down completely, as a warning to any one who might oppose such a formidable and well-conducted company.

It was not until about the 10th of June, 1834, that an express arrived, informing us of the sale, and that the steamer would be up some time between that date and the 1st of July. This news was of little importance to me, as I had made up my mind to leave, and thought that nothing could induce me to remain in the country. In those days there was but one steamer a year up river this far, and great was always the rejoicement on its arrival. This was the *Assiniboine;* the boat made her appearance on the 24th of June, having on board the gentlemen who were to take inventories of all the posts belonging to the American Fur Company, as old Mr. Astor had this year sold out to Pierre Chouteau and Co. A few days after the arrival of the steamer the transfer of goods and peltries took place. Of the latter there were very few—70 packs of robes, 10 in a pack, which made 700 robes; 16 packs of wolves, 30 to the pack; and some few red and gray foxes.

In the meantime preparations were made for departure, which was to be in a large Mackinaw boat. While these were going on my occupation was that of horse guard. The idea of returning to the States was indeed very pleasant; while lying on the grass the thought of relating to Baltimore friends my mountain stories would make me feel, as the Indian says, "Big man me." Best of all, I had the means to accomplish my journey; for, out of my wages of $296 I had saved over $200, thanks to not indulging too much in pancake parties. Coffee being $1 a pint, sugar $1, and flour 25 cents, many of my poor comrades came out in debt.

One fine day [July 2, 1834] I was sent for by Mr. Campbell—I could not imagine what for. I had not yet shed my winter garments, which had become by this time quite greasy; and had it not been for my blue check shirt, which happened to be clean at the time, I should have been taken for a very dirty man. Imagine my surprise, on entering Mr. Campbell's room, to find myself in the presence of Mr. McKenzie, who was at that time considered the king of the Missouri; and, from the style in which he was dressed, I thought really he was a king. Without any introduction he immediately asked me if I would engage to him. Having made my plans to go home and not knowing but what he wanted me for a common hand, my reply was a short "No, sir," after which I made for the door and returned to my duty. The same evening, after I had brought in the horses, Mr. Campbell sent for me again, and then said: "Charles, I omitted to inform you of the conversation I had yesterday about you with Mr. McKenzie. This was the cause of his coming to-day. He did not want to engage you as a common hand; he wanted you for a clerk, and I should advise you to see him. He is very much of a gentleman, and I think you will do well. You will act as you think proper—but this is my advice." Then I had to combat my made-up plans, and give up all idea of returning to Baltimore. This I thought I could never do. I did not sleep much that night.

Next morning, while I was not feeling disposed to see Mr. McKenzie, Mr. Campbell said, "Well, Charles, are you going to try your luck?" My reply induced him to think that I was not much in favor of that. Said he again, "Charles, try it—there will be no harm in that." Knowing him to be kind, and confident that he wished me well, I at last started. I had not gone more than halfway when I turned back a few steps; but I finally made up my mind to "try my luck" as Mr. Campbell had suggested. So I resumed my journey and soon entered Fort Union, where I met Mr. McKenzie in the yard, not quite so royally attired. He came to meet me, and offered me his hand. After the usual compliments had been exchanged I remarked that I had not been apprised of his intentions when he spoke of engaging me, and that, thinking he wished to hire me as a common hand, I had declined, having had enough of it; but that, having been since informed to the contrary, I had thought I would come to see him, and hoped there was no harm done, in case no bargain were made. To which he replied, "All right! All right! No, I did not wish to engage you as a common hand. I wanted you for a clerk. You will eat at my table, and fare the same as myself. Your work will be no other than that which is the duty of all clerks in this country. Now," he continued, "I will tell you how we engage clerks—that is, inexperienced ones. We engage them for three years, for which term we give them $500 and a complete suit of fine broadcloth; but as you have been already one year in the country I will engage you for two years." These terms did not suit me; my strong inclination to go home made me feel quite independent, and I preferred to miss the bargain. I replied I did not feel like engaging for so long a term; but that I would engage for one year, and then, if he were pleased with me, and I with him, we should have no difficulty in arranging for another year. Finally he consented to this and the bargain was struck for one year, for which he allowed me $250 and a complete suit of clothes.

Bargain made [July 3, 1834], I was almost sorry for it. I started back to Fort William, not after my wardrobe, which I could very well sacrifice, but to thank Mr. Campbell, and to bid adieu to my comrades. Mr. Campbell was extremely pleased to hear the result; he gave me a check for the amount due me, and after a long shake of the hand, with all his good wishes as well as

those of my old messmates and others, I left
Fort William. My load to Fort Union was
not very encumbering; my old saddle bags,
made of a yard of brown muslin, sewed at
both ends with a slit in the middle, containing two red flannel shirts, pretty well
worn, and one check shirt, and one old
white 3-point blanket,[27] were about all I had
brought to Fort Union;[28] my tin pan and
cup I left behind. I should have been
ashamed to be caught there in my skin suit,
which was also sacrificed to Fort William.
Now I am at Fort Union, in the service of
the great American Fur Company.

[27] The Hudson's Bay Company blankets were marked
in one corner with parallel bars, or "points," one for
each pound weight of blanket. A "three-point" blanket
was one which weighed three pounds.

[28] Fort Union was erected by Kenneth McKenzie
in the years 1829–33. It was for many years the
headquarters of the American Fur Company for the
Missouri River trade, and it finds mentions in many
journals and narratives of the period—in none more so
than the present one of Larpenteur.

Chapter 5

FORT UNION

I MUST remark here that my dress was a little improved. I happened to have a pair of gray cassinette pants which I had brought from the States, and had seldom worn; that and my clean blue check shirt and my old cap were the only dress I possessed on entering Fort Union. All the clerks were strangers to me, and when the bell rang for supper I saw them put on their coats, for, as I found out afterward, they were not allowed to go to table in shirt-sleeves. One of them, perceiving that I was coatless, was so kind as to lend me a coat, and so we started for supper. On entering the eating hall, I found a splendidly set table with a very white tablecloth, and two waiters, one a negro. Mr. McKenzie was sitting at the head of the table, extremely well dressed. The victuals consisted of fine fat buffalo meat, with plenty of good fresh butter, cream, and milk for those that chose; but I saw that only two biscuits were allowed to each one, as these were placed at each plate. I soon discovered, by the manner in which the clerks took their seats, that mine would come very near the end of the table, for it appeared to go by grade; but it was not many years until I reached next to head. I was hungry, and had such victuals been placed before me the day previous, while I was on horse guard, I should have played my part like a man. But among strangers I could not help being a little backward, and did not eat half to my satisfaction. As good luck would have it, some of the clerks used to take lunch before going to bed; so a large kettle of fat buffalo meat was put on to boil, and out of this I finished filling up. Then I went to bed with the expectation of curious dreams. What I dreamed I don't remember, neither do I now care. I awoke early, perhaps thinking in my sleep that I had my horses to turn out; but no, there were no horses for me to turn out. Mr. McKenzie, who played the nabob, went to bed late, and rose later, and as nothing could be served till he was ready, it was nine o'clock before we got to breakfast. But it came at last, and this morning I filled up fuller, with more ease.

Between ten and eleven, Mr. McKenzie sent his servant to tell me to call at the office. On entering he told me to sit down, and said, "Well, Larpenteur, we will assign you some little duty to try your hand upon, and if you prove faithful and attentive, as I hope and have all reason to believe you will, your salary will be increased next year, provided you wish to remain." My reply was that I hoped he would have no cause to complain. He then went to a place where the keys were hung, and handed me a bunch, saying, "Here are the keys of the fort gates, of the tool house and harness house, and of the bastions. Now it will be your duty to open the gates early in the morning, and lock them at night; to see that the tools and harness be kept in order, and all in their proper places; and you will also lend a hand, in case it should be required, about the stores." Such was my first employment at Fort Union.

Thus I went on quite easily for some time, and I thought my berth a very light one; but it was not long before I was promoted, and this made quite an addition to my former duties. Early in September, after all the hay had been hauled in, Fort William was to be rebuilt within 150 yards of Union. A clerk by the name of Moncrèvie, who was at the time a trader, and also in charge of the men, had this to attend to; but he was a little too fond of whisky, and much too fond of the squaws, to do this work or any other as it should be done.

One afternoon, after the rebuilding of the fort had commenced, Mr. Hamilton, who was in charge at the time, went to see how it was progressing. The men had half of one side of the fort up, but it was an awful piece of work. The pickets were set in crooked, some too high, some too low, and the sight made the old gentleman furious. "Where is that Moncrèvie, that he is not here to attend to the work?" he asked. Being told that Moncrèvie had gone to the fort, he started off quite mad and rushed into our room, his nose appearing to have grown bigger on a sudden—for such was the case whenever he got out of humor. "Mr. Moncrèvie," he exclaimed, "why are you not with your men? That is a nice piece of work they are doing there!" Moncrèvie, all confused, was hurrying out, when the old gentleman said, "No! no! you need not go," and then turned round to me, saying, "Mr. Larpenteur, go and oversee that work and see if you cannot do better than that Mr. Moncrèvie." So I started, and when I got to the men they began to laugh, saying they expected as much. I told them that I was ordered to boss the job, of which they appeared to be glad. Then I ordered them to take all the pickets down, which was soon done, after which I had the trench straightened and the bottom leveled. Next day about noon Mr. Hamilton came to examine the work, and said, with the pleasant countenance he could assume when he chose, "Oh! this looks something like work—not like what that good-for-nothing Moncrèvie has been doing." At that time I had only charge of the men allotted for the rebuilding of the fort; but that same evening Mr. Hamilton sent for me and said, "Larpenteur, I now wish you to take charge of all the men, for that Moncrèvie will not do." Thus came my first promotion. Notwithstanding this addition to my former duties I still thought my situation pleasant, although it was, at times, rather disagreeable to command the men, and not infrequently some fight would come off; but the most disagreeable part of it was to come. Early in the fall trade commenced, principally in jerked buffalo meat and tallow, both mostly traded for liquor. The liquor business, which was always done at night, sometimes kept me up all night turning out drunken Indians, often by dragging them out by arms and legs. Although the still house had been destroyed, the Company found means to smuggle plenty of liquor.

Before proceeding with my narrative I will detain the reader to explain how it happened that the distillery was given up. A certain gentleman from the Eastern States, by the name of Capt. Wheitte,[29] who had been on a tour to the Columbia, and returned by way of the Big Horn and the Yellowstone in 1833, reaching Fort Union about 10 days before we did, thought proper to have better means of going down the Missouri, and called on Mr. McKenzie to make the necessary preparations for this journey. Mr. McKenzie, who was a perfect gentleman, not suspecting the captain, who I cannot say was a spy, did all he could to make his stay pleasant, showed all the arrange-

[29] Nathaniel J. Wyeth, of Cambridge, Mass. He had formed a design to engage in the colonization of the Oregon country, and in pursuance of it had led a party of "hale young men" across the continent in 1832. Some of the party abandoned the enterprise at Pierre's Hole (one of those who persevered was John Ball, whose letter is cited, *ante*, 27) and one of these, a cousin of Wyeth, published a narrative of the expedition which is reprinted in R. G. Thwaites, *Early Western Travels* series, Vol. XXI (Cleveland, 1905). Nathaniel Wyeth's first expedition was largely a failure, but he conceived an enthusiasm for the Oregon country which led him to plan and lead a second one in 1834. It was while retiring from the first that he visited Fort Union, as here related. This journey has been narrated by Irving in his *The Rocky Mountains*, II, Chap. 16.

ments of the fort, explained how trade was carried on, what immense profit was derived, and also showed him the distillery. Capt. Wheitte appeared to be delighted to see this fine establishment, and probably would not have done what he did, had he not found, when everything was in readiness for his departure and he came to settle his bill, that the charges were exorbitant. He said nothing, settled, and started; but made it his business, as soon as he arrived, to report Mr. McKenzie. A dispatch was sent up that winter for the distillery to be destroyed. This was the last distillery in the Indian country.

All went on as smoothly as could be expected through our many drinking scrapes with Indians and obstreperous Canadians. The time to re-engage came, and pretty soon my case was carried to the office. Mr. McKenzie said, "Well, Larpenteur, what do you think? Will you hire for another year?" My reply was, "I believe so, sir." "Well," said he, "if you wish to remain, I will allow you $350 for this year." "All right," was my answer. And now for another year in the American Fur Company.

My first year was not yet up, but all engagements had to be made before the arrival of the steamer, and the shipping of the returns; so that, in case any men declined to re-engage, they could be sent off by one or another conveyance. All the clerks were re-engaged except Moncrèvie, who happened to be discharged. Nothing took place worth mentioning until the fall,[30] after the return of some of the free trappers. There was a half-breed family named Deschamps, consisting of ten persons, among whom were the old man and three grown sons, who were in the habit of trapping, and were the very worst of subjects; and another half-breed family, headed by Jack Rem. He had two sons-in-law, and a son 19 years of age, all of whom started on their trapping expeditions together, and returned together. It was customary, on their return from a hunt, to have a spree; and as they had been lucky the hunt was big, and so was the spree. They soon began a fight in which Jack Rem's son had his brains knocked out with the butt of a gun by one of the numerous and wicked Deschamps family. Mr. Lafferrier, who was at the time the trader and storekeeper, became alarmed, for they began to threaten his life, and attempted to get liquor of him without paying for it. Mr.

[30] That is, of 1834. The author's original journal records the killing of young Rem under date of Oct. 19, 1834.

Hamilton, who was still in charge, did not know what to do to stop them, but at last advised Mr. Lafferrier to put laudanum in the whiskey. This advice was followed; they soon fell down and lay stretched out on the ground in every direction, so sound asleep that Mr. Hamilton became alarmed, thinking the dose had been so strong that they would never wake up again. I happened not to be there at the time, having that afternoon gone down to the garden, which was about three-quarters of a mile distant from the fort. Mr. Hamilton came there as fast as he could, half scared to death, to tell me the story. I could not help laughing at the idea, and we immediately returned to the fort. On my arrival I saw this amiable family scattered along the river bank, still fast asleep; but at dark they awakened and went home to Fort William, where all those families were kept, as were also some of the Company's men who had squaws, and the horse guard with the horses. Thus this spree ended. Nothing remarkable took place until May of the following spring [1835]. It was customary, when buffalo got too far from the fort, for hunters to camp out, and from time to time send in loads of fresh meat. On such occasions all their families also went into camp to make dried meat for their own use, and also for a kind of recreation. Such a camp was called by the half-breeds of the north, who spoke broken French, mixed with many Cree words, "nick-ah-wah"; and to go into it was "aller en nick-ah-wah." It happened that, in this camp, there was a beautiful half-breed by the name of Baptiste Gardepie. The Deschamps family, who were there also, got jealous of him and, it was reported, had attempted to take his life. I will now relate an affray which took place at the fort, while they were in camp.

In the spring, after the trade was over, some stragglers always remained in camp at the fort, in spite of all we could do to get them off; for they were great nuisances, and it was dangerous for them to camp at the fort on account of hostile Indians. Early in May an express arrived from Fort Clark[31] by which we were apprised that there would soon be a large war-party of Gros Ventres and Mandans at Fort Union. The chief wished to inform us of this and to warn our

[31] Fort Clark was built in 1831 to serve as the station of the American Fur Company at the Mandan town where Lewis and Clark had wintered in 1804-05. It was one of the most important posts of the Company, ranking after Fort Union and Fort Pierre. Its location was about fifty-five miles above Bismarck, N. Dak., and about eight miles below the mouth of Big Knife River.

young men not to sleep in any of the Indian lodges; for, should there be any at the fort when the war-party came, they would shoot into the lodges, but would not like to kill any of the whites. So the young men were notified, and for my part I did all I could to induce Mr. Hamilton to let the Indians sleep in the Indian house, but he would not listen to me. There were only two lodges of Indians, and almost every night, unknown to the old gentleman, I let them into the fort. But, fearing to be caught at this and thus displease my boss, some nights I made them stay outside. It happened to be one of these nights that the war party of Gros Ventres arrived about twelve o'clock and fired into the two lodges. We heard the shots plainly, and immediately the cry of "Open the door!"—for there had been three white men in the lodges at the time. On our entering them to ascertain what damage had been done we found one squaw dead, shot plumb through the heart; one shot through both thighs; one through the calf of her leg, smashing the shin bone; an old woman shot through the wrist; a little boy 12 years of age shot through the bowels; and one of the white men with two balls through the left thigh, a little above the knee, cutting the artery. He died the same morning at ten

o'clock; the squaw shot through the thighs
died two days afterward, and the little boy
the next day—sad indeed was this affair!
Mr. Hamilton repented not letting them into
the fort, but it was too late—the damage
had been done. But the old Englishman was
soon to see what could not be called fun,
and be badly put to his trumps.

About a week later a party of Assiniboines,
who had gone to war on the Gros Ventres
and Mandans, arrived at Fort Union; and
about ten o'clock at night a rap was heard
at the door. As I was still doorkeeper, I
went to see who was there. On asking who
they were, they replied that they were a war
party of 20 men, on their return from the
Gros Ventres. At this time all the wounded
and well Indians were inside the fort, and
we were but few whites, as most of our men
were in camp. Not thinking it prudent to
let the Indians in, for fear of a row, I apprised Mr. Hamilton of the arrival; but he
told me to let them in if there were but 20
men. I suggested to him to send them to
Fort William, where there was no one at the
time, the families having all gone to camp;
but, as usual, he would not listen to me, and
in I let them. Soon afterward more knocking
at the door was heard, and the Indians in
the fort said it was the balance of their party,

consisting of 70 men. I went again to Mr. Hamilton, who said, "Well, we may as well let the balance in, for it may make matters worse to send them to the other fort." A little while after their entrance something unpleasant was evidently going to happen, and from what I could understand it became necessary to adopt means for our safety. So I informed Mr. Hamilton of what was going on, upon which the old gentleman, who had a sound old English head, told me to bring eight or ten muskets out of the bastion and put them on the men's table in the dining room; also to put one of the smallest cannon in the passage of the main quarters. This was to be done with all care possible, that the Indians should know nothing of it until the proper time came; for if they saw us make such preparations, they might nip his plan in the bud. Very soon we were ready; the window blinds of the dining room were opened, and there could be seen by the three candles the bright muskets, plenty of cartridges scattered over the table, and four men ready for action. The piece of artillery was rolled back and forward in the passage, making a tremendous noise, and two men mounted guard with muskets and fixed bayonets. Such preparations the Indians had never seen or heard of before, and they became, in their turn, more frightened than we had been. They had been very lively on the move and very insulting at times, but they soon lay down and went to sleep, or pretended to, so that all became suddenly quiet. Still, we did not feel quite safe; we thought that perhaps they were shamming and that they might try what they could do before morning. This was about midnight. To my great surprise, just at the peep of day, I was called up; that was easily done, for I was wide awake, with all my clothes on. The partisan said that the Indians wished to go out, and asked me to open the door for them; and in less than ten minutes not one of the party was left in the fort. One may imagine how relieved all hands were, when informed of this, for most of them had almost made up their minds that this would be their last night. As it was yet early, I told them to go and take a nap. I then went to Mr. Hamilton's room, and, after I had informed him of this, he said, "Well, Mr. Larpenteur, what do you think of my stratagem?" To which I replied that I felt confident it had been the means of saving our lives. "Yes, yes," said he; "now go to the cellar, fill this bottle with that good Madeira; we will have a glass, and then you will have time to take a little rest before breakfast, for I presume you have not slept much." I obeyed his orders, took a drink of Madeira, and went to bed. Thus ended the fright.

As I have had frequent occasion to mention Mr. "Hamilton," I will introduce him to the reader. His real name was Archibald Palmer.[32] He was an English nobleman who, from some cause or other unknown to many, had been obliged to leave England and come to America, apparently without any means. How Mr. McKenzie became acquainted with him I am not able to say. Mr. Hamilton was a man of uncommon education, conversant with many subjects, and quite capable of keeping books. As Mr. McKenzie required a bookkeeper at Fort Union, he made arrangements with Mr. Hamilton to come here. What salary he received I never learned. Mr. Hamilton—as I shall continue

---

[32] Our knowledge of this individual is chiefly that which Larpenteur here sets down. Dr. Matthews supplied Coues with an interesting characterization of Palmer, who was "an object of wonder and gossip" to the inhabitants of the Upper Missouri. Among other marvels reported by the voyageurs, he was reputed to take a bath and put on a clean shirt "every day." He had a hearty dislike for the natives, illustrated by a story that he once threw into the fire a beautiful silk handkerchief because an Indian had picked it up to examine. He later served as cashier for the American Fur Company at St. Louis, where he died.

to call him, for his real name was not known until after he left Fort Union and his English difficulties were over, when he resumed his proper name—was a man of fifty, who had habitually lived high, in consequence of which he had the gout. This brought him to the two extremes of being either very pleasant or very crabbed, but, upon the whole, kept him crabbed; so he was not liked, though much respected. He remained a few years at Union, and died in St. Louis as cashier of the American Fur Company. I must say I got along remarkably well with him and was very sorry to learn of his death. Now I will return to my stories, of which I have many in store.

Chapter 6

(1835–36)

A WEEK or ten days after the above-mentioned fright, the hunters were ordered to return; the camp was broken up, and all the half-breed families went into their former quarters in Fort William, as well as some of the company's men who had families, and were to take care of the horses. When they had all arrived and were reorganized, a conspiracy was gotten up, unknown to me, to kill old man Deschamps and his eldest son, François. The conspirators were Baptiste Gardepie, the two sons-in-law of Jack Rem, and Mr. Lafferrier—the latter a great hypocrite. This was in July, 1835. As Deschamps used to come to our room almost every morning after breakfast, the killing was to take place there. For this murderous work a rifle barrel was placed in the chimney corner, and Lafferrier put his dirk under his pillow, for Gardepie, who was to commence the job. François Deschamps, the son, was about 27 or 28 years old—a fine stout young man; he

72

was then interpreter for Fort Union, and ate at the table with the boss and the clerks. Soon after breakfast the father and son came into our room, where the conspirators were already assembled. It was a fine July morning[33] and I, knowing nothing of this, had taken a walk alone down by the garden which was already progressing well, about three-quarters of a mile from the fort. After some little conversation, which naturally took place before coming to the point, Gardepie got up and addressed the old man, saying, "Deschamps, I want to know now whether you will make peace or war with me; you have frequently attempted my life, and I find it necessary to ask you this question— now, what is your answer?" To which old Deschamps replied, "I will never make peace with you as long as there is a drop of blood in my veins." Some blood was quickly out of his veins, for Gardepie immediately seized the rifle barrel and struck a fatal blow on the old man's head. Then he turned round to the son, and, with another blow, knocked him down. But this wound not being a mortal one, François made out to creep under one of the beds, where he begged for his life until the conspirators took pity on him.

[33] July 23, 1835, according to the author's original journal.

Gardepie was induced to desist from killing him; but, not thinking that the father had been mortally struck, he reached for the dirk and ripped the old man's bowels out—which operation was not necessary.[34] All this was done in a very short time. Returning from the garden and approaching our quarters I observed that the curtains were down, which was an unusual thing, and when I came to open the door I found it locked on the inside. At my request it was immediately opened to admit me, but directly closed again. The door being shut and curtains down, I could not at first discover what had taken place, but soon saw a sheet spread on the floor and

[34] Terrible as the fate of Deschamps was, the account which Larpenteur has recorded leaves little room for sympathy over him. In the affair at Seven Oaks in 1816, where Governor Robert Semple and his followers were slain, it was Deschamps who slew the governor after he had been wounded by another. Informants of Larpenteur related that after the battle he also put to death several more of the wounded. "Some of those poor creatures would request of him a little time to pray, which he would allow, in saying, 'Make haste, you d—d son of a —': and when he thought the prayer was long enough he would shoot them down and rob them of what they possessed." Since coming to the Missouri, the family had been involved in numerous misdeeds, including robbery, adultery, and murder. In extenuation it may be said that deeds of violence were all too common to the society in which they lived.

knew there was a corpse under it. On looking about, I saw young François Deschamps sitting at a table with his head held down in his hands, which were still all bloody. No one else was in the room but Gardepie, who said, "I have settled with the old man, and I would have done the same with this coward here, had he not begged so hard for his life." I made no reply, though, of course, I pitied the poor fellow, who was so near the corpse of his father, and uncertain as yet of his own life. It was a sad sight. Mr. Lafferrier, who, as I have already remarked, was a great hypocrite and had thus acquired his popularity among the Indians and half-breeds, had gone to the fort with the pipe of peace, to try to bring about a reconciliation between those two families; and in this he finally succeeded. The old man was buried the same day, and to all appearances everything went on as usual.

It was thought that this peace would last, as Jack Rem's family was considered revenged by the death of the old man, and had thus been made nearly equal in strength to that of the Deschamps. What afterward induced us to think the peace would be kept was that Gardepie went on a beaver hunt with the three young Deschamps and never offered to molest them. Michel Gravel and

Little Frenchman were the names of Jack Rem's two sons-in-law who went the following fall [1835] on their hunt on Milk River, which abounded with beaver, and, like all beaver trappers, fell in with a war party of Blackfeet, by whom they were both killed. This accident reduced Jack's family considerably and enabled the Deschamps to show their wicked dispositions again. But before describing a big battle which took place the following summer [1836], I will relate a little story to show you how cunningly and quickly Indians can work destruction, and also give the character of Gauché, Robert Campbell's chief, whom I have already called Co-han (Hurry Up). Gauché was his French name, which means Left Hand. But by his tribe he was called Meenah-yau-henno, meaning the One who Holds the Knife—with which they said he could cut a rock in two, owing to his strong medicine. As I have already remarked, Hurry Up was feared by all the surrounding tribes, and was called by the whites the Wild Bonaparte. The old fellow had been so successful in his warfare that he found no difficulty in raising the number of warriors he wanted. At this time he had raised a party of 250 to 300, to make war on the Blackfeet, who were very rich in horses. Being considered so great a medicine man and warrior, he had no trouble with his young men, and could order the rush as he thought proper. On this their success always depends, for Indians seldom stand a long battle, and when they do it does not amount to much. About the middle of March the old man came within one day's march of Fort McKenzie, where he fell on the trail of a camp of Blackfeet, containing about 30 lodges, on the way to their fort to make their last spring trade. The old fellow could tell by the looks of things in their camping-place that they were rich in trade-goods and in horses, and that a big drunk would be sure to take place; for the Blackfeet are great drunkards. After the chief had well examined everything about the camping grounds he went to work at his medicine. He then told his people that he had seen a great deal of blood on the enemy's side, but very little on theirs, and that most, if not all of them, would return on horseback with many scalps, if they would obey his commands. The old fellow was not mistaken. They soon approached the Blackfoot camp, which was near the fort, making ready for a big spree. It was Gauché's intention to rush on the camp when they should be at the height of the spree, too drunk to defend themselves. When it was near daylight

the order was given for the rush, and so well
was it executed that in a very short time
few were left alive in camp, and all the
horses were captured with ease — as we
learned, upward of 300 head. So great and
glorious was the old man's campaign; and
then it was "Co-han! hurry up! let us go
home and dance the scalp dance"—for many
were the scalps they had taken of men,
women, and children. We will let them go
and I will return to the little story I promised to relate.

There was an old Assiniboine who had remained after our last trade, with the intention, as he said, to go down to Fort Clark
in the steamer, although no peace as yet
had been made between the Assiniboines and
the Gros Ventres. In the meantime a war
party of about 150 Blackfeet, all on horseback, came to Fort Union in search of the
Assiniboines, to be revenged on the camp of
old Co-han; this was about the 1st of June,
and at that season men were always scarce
in the fort, as most of them were required
to take down the returns. So we would not
allow more than 20 Indians at a time in
the fort. The partisan and other important
men in the Blackfoot party commenced by
making a great deal of the old man, smoking
with him, and telling him that they were in

search of the Assiniboines with the intention
of making peace with them, and that they
would be very glad if he would go with them.
They also said they had some fine horses
which were intended for the Assiniboines,
in case they would make peace, and if he
would go with them they would make him
a present of a nice pony. They did all they
could to persuade him to go, and we did all
we could to put him out of the notion.
Finally the time came for them to start, and
not finding the old fellow quite decided, they
sent in a beautiful pony, saddled and bridled,
telling him it should be his if he would come
along. The old man was tempted, mounted
the pony, and started. By this time most
of the party had left, and were seated on the
hills back of the fort, awaiting the rest, and
expecting that the old Assiniboine would be
along with them; there were also 12 or 15
young men mounted on ponies, ready apparently to serve as an escort for the old man.
As soon as I had turned him out—for I was
still the doorkeeper—I made haste to run
up on the bastion to see what would happen.
The escort had not gone over 200 yards from
the fort before they fired a volley into the
old man, who fell dead off his pony, and in
less than no time was scalped. After they
had all reached the hills they made us signs

that there was no danger for us, and disappeared. I then took a party of six or seven men, wrapped the old man in his robe, and stuck him up in a large elm tree to dry, as this was their own custom.

Now, reader, make ready for the battle, as it will soon come off. In the latter part of June,[35] shortly after the last-mentioned affray took place, the company's steamboat arrived. After her departure, it was customary to have a big drunk throughout. At this time there were between 60 and 70 men at the fort. The half-breeds who were in Fort William with some of our own men also got gloriously drunk. About midnight old Mother Deschamps said to her children, "Now, my sons, if you are men, you will revenge the death of your father." This struck them favorably, and being in liquor they immediately killed old Jack Rem, swore they would also kill all the half-breeds whom they considered his friends, and even threatened the whites in the fort. This took place about midnight, when the spree in Fort Union had subsided and all hands had gone to sleep. I was awakened by loud raps and voices at the door, which latter I could distinguish to be those of females, crying,

[35] The gory affray which our author now describes occurred June 28–29, 1836.

"Open the door! quick—they are fighting—
they have killed my father." They were the
widow of Michel Gravel and her mother, the
wife of Jack Rem. I had not shut the door
before eight or ten of our men came running
in great fury, swearing vengeance against the
Deschamps family, all of whom they would
destroy, big and small. They raised all
hands, and in a body went to Mr. McKenzie,
of whom they demanded arms and ammunition in angry tones, declaring they were
determined to put an end to the Deschamps
family. This demand was made in such
terms that Mr. McKenzie could not well refuse, fearing the consequences, and not being
himself much averse to their intention. Having been furnished with a cannon, muskets,
and ammunition, they went to work. But,
in the first place, all the horses and all the
company's effects were removed from the
fort, and before the fight commenced the
Deschamps were required to turn out their
squaws, who were Assiniboine women, whom
we did not want to kill for fear of the tribe.
Thinking the fight would not take place as
long as they kept in the squaws, they refused
to turn them out. After allowing them what
time we thought necessary to make up their
minds on this subject, the order to fire was
given. As we had a cannon we supposed

they would not go into the bastions, and as we found their shots were only fired out of their own dwellings we aimed altogether at these houses. When they found we were determined to put our threats into execution they turned out their squaws, who told us that we had already killed one man, but that it would be difficult for us to destroy them all, as they had dug holes under the floors, where our balls could not reach them. Yet we kept constantly firing into the houses, until at last the old lady herself came out with the pipe of peace, begging for her life and that of her children; but she was shot through the heart in stepping out of the fort. As she was holding her pipe straight in front of her when she was hit, she fell precisely on top of it, at which the boys exclaimed in great mirth, "There's an end to the mother of the devils." In the meantime our firing was kept up; but few shots were heard from them, and at last some of our party ventured into the fort, thinking they were all killed; but that was a mistake. They commenced firing again, and our side made a double-quick retreat; but one of them was shot through the neck as he was stooping through the small door of the fort. It was by this time getting rather late in the day, and it was feared that the fight might continue until night, under cover of which they could make their escape, which would prove serious to the Company in future; and as the bloody work had been begun, it was obliged to be accomplished. In order to do so it was thought proper to set the fort on fire, with the view of burning them in it; but for fear that some might escape through the fire, the hunter of the fort and several other good horsemen were mounted on the best horses to run them down like buffalo, should they make such an attempt. These precautions having been taken, a fire was started; as the fort was dry it soon began to blaze, and in a little while the houses were consumed. We saw one man run out of them and take refuge in the east bastion, into which the cannon was fired several times, but the ball went through without other damage than making its hole. Meanwhile the fire stopped, having burned only one side of the fort and the houses; so the bastion stood with this individual inside it, and was dangerous to approach. One of our men [Vivié], wanting to display his bravery, went near it to get a good shot through the cracks; but this cost him his life. A shot through the heart made him jump up about six feet in the air and fall dead on the spot, on which a loud yell was heard from the man in the bastion. The firing on our side was renewed faster than ever, until it was found that no shot was fired out of the bastion, when some of the boldest of our party determined to see if the individual inside it was dead or alive. On entering the bastion they discovered him backed up in one corner; they immediately fired and he fell dead. This was François Deschamps, the last survivor, as all the rest had been burned or shot in the houses. After he was brought out we found that he had a broken wrist and was out of ammunition. Had he not been thus disabled and defenseless he would probably have killed several of us and made his escape. The men thought he might go, like the balance, into flames; so they threw him into the fire with one of his brothers, and both were burned to ashes. A hole was dug, into which the old woman was put without any ceremony. Thus the battle ended, about sunset, in the death of eight of the family. The youngest son, about ten years of age, after being wounded, was suffered to come out; but he died the next day. Such was the end of this troublesome family, after which peace and comfort were enjoyed.

Now, as I have remarked, all was quieted. Outfits were made up and started for the Blackfeet and Crows, and we were left with

none but the men allotted for Fort Union,
numbering about 30, all told. These were
assigned to their several duties, including
the horse guard, for which a Mexican, a
Dutchman, and a Canadian named Tibeau
were appointed. The Mexican was not fit
for anything else; the Dutchman was very
green in one sense, and very white in another, as will be seen presently. All went on
peaceably until about the middle of September [1836], when the Mexican thought he
would take a ride back to Mexico on the
best horse in the band, and picked out the
green Dutchman to assist him in the execution of his plans. But it seems that they
both were tolerably green. On one fine day
they proposed to Tibeau to go to their dinner
first, saying that they would not be long,
and that he could go afterward and stay in
the fort as long as he pleased. The proposition was accepted by Tibeau, and off started
the two gentlemen, who, sure enough, were
not gone long; and immediately on their return Tibeau went to his dinner. At this early
time the guard was kept up more with a
view to prevent the horses from straying
away than for fear of their being stolen by
hostile Indians. This induced Tibeau to delay; but, fearing that he might be hurried
out of the fort by the proper authorities,

which he had reason to believe would be done rather roughly, he at last started back. On his return to the guard he could see neither of the two men; but, thinking that they might have gone a little way, made nothing of it and began to look around. Still seeing nothing of them, he commenced to hallo; but no answer was heard. Then he began to surmise that things were not all right, the men having been so willing to remain, and thought he would examine the band of horses. He soon discovered that the two best American horses were missing. Yet, as all the men were in the habit of strolling in search of antelope, and sometimes for pleasure, he waited a while, thinking they would soon make their appearance; but no one came, and he finally went to report the matter. Men were immediately sent in search of the thieves. Thinking that the Mexican would attempt to cross the river above, the men were first ordered up, but returned at night, having seen no tracks. Instead of going up, as it was thought they had, the Mexican and his man had concealed themselves in the point below the fort, it being his plan to steal the ferryboat at night and cross over. That night they came within three-quarters of a mile below the fort, where the Mexican left the Dutchman with the horses, while he went after the ferryboat. But when he came to the fort, it seems that he got scared at the barking of the dogs and could find no opportunity to get the boat off. When day was about breaking, he concluded to abandon that project and returned to the Dutchman, whom he found sound asleep and the horses gone. By this time it was daylight, and fearing to be discovered if they should attempt to look for the horses, they thought it advisable for each one to do as he thought proper. The Dutchman decided to give himself up to the mercy of the authorities; the Mexican concluded to try his luck at large for a while. When the door of the fort was opened one of the men, who happened to go out first, saw two horses near the hills, and came to me saying, "There are two horses which look very much like the stolen ones." I immediately sent after them, and to be sure they were the very two—Mr. McKenzie's favorite horse and the next best, a fine iron-gray. The question then was, What had become of the men? Some thought one thing, and some another, but none guessed right. Soon after breakfast Mr. Dutchman appeared, all in a tremble, and commenced to make up a story which had neither head nor tail. Not even giving him time to finish it, Mr. McKenzie requested me to take his gun from him, and put him in irons in the blacksmith shop. This was done immediately. He knew not what had become of the Mexican. Four or five days after this the Mexican came to deliver himself up, saying, "Mr. McKenzie, I have done wrong; here I am, do with me what you choose; but please don't send me to the States." Without replying to him Mr. McKenzie requested me to have him ironed and placed in confinement with the Dutchman, to await trial. Four days afterward they were tried, convicted, and sentenced to receive thirty-nine lashes. So they were tied to the flagstaff to take their punishment. The Dutchman was flogged first. When stripped to the waist his skin looked fair and tender, and was actually so; for at every blow the blood flew at such a rate that his sentence was reduced one-half. But the Mexican's hide was brown and tough; he hardly groaned, and received the full number of lashes. Both were soon taken to the States by James Beckwith,[36] the great

[36] James P. Beckwourth was a notable hunter and trader the details of whose adventurous career were recorded by T. D. Bonner in a book entitled *Life and Adventures of James P. Beckwourth, Mountaineer, Scout, and Pioneer, and Chief of the Crow Nation of Indians.* Beckwourth's tales are so remarkable that he has

mulatto brave among the Crows, whose life
was published some time afterward. Thus
ended this scrape.

commonly been set down as an irresponsible braggart
and liar, but so competent an authority as William E.
Connelley, Secretary of the Kansas State Historical
Society, regarded the book as entitled to rank as a serious historical narration. It was first published in 1856.

Chapter 7

(1836–38)

HAVING frequently mentioned Mr. McKenzie as a member of the American Fur Company, I will give him a more ample introduction to the reader. Kenneth McKenzie was born in Scotland of very respectable parents, and was some near connection of the great explorer, Sir Alexander McKenzie.[37] He engaged to the North West at the time that Company was formed to oppose the Hudson's Bay Company. It was the custom to engage clerks for the term of three years; but after they had served seven, they had the privilege of entering the Company as partners. Those young men had to be of good standing and bear good characters. The North West could not compete with the strong Hudson's Bay Company and were finally obliged to abandon the country.[38]

[37] For whom, see *Alexander Mackenzie's Voyage to the Pacific Ocean in 1793*, *The Lakeside Classics* volume for 1931.

[38] The North West Company, from its headquarters at Montreal long conducted an exceedingly vigorous competition with the Hudson's Bay Company for the

Mr. McKenzie, who had taken some liking to the trade and thought there was money in it, struck off for the upper waters of the Mississippi, in the regions where the American Fur Company was carrying on trade, in small furs particularly, to a great extent. Whether he had any means at the time I am unable to say, and also in what capacity he entered the American Fur Company; but he probably came in as a member, and they soon placed unbounded confidence in him. Having served the North West, he had become acquainted with the manner in which trade was carried on in the north, and also with the tribes in that region. He soon persuaded the American Fur Company to extend their trade on the Upper Missouri, for he knew that the Hudson's Bay Company did not and could not trade buffalo robes, which would not pay for transportation over their portages, and that their trade was entirely confined to fine furs. This idea in regard to extending trade was correct, but the distance was tremendous, as those going up had to be towed in keel boats

trade of the interior of the continent. Ruinous to both rivals, the contest ended with their amalgamation in 1821, under the name of the older company. It is incorrect, however, to say that the Northwesters "abandoned" the country.

a distance of 2,000 miles. But, as I have remarked, the persuasion of Mr. McKenzie, and the unbounded confidence they had in him, overcame all difficulties. About the year 1827 an outfit was made up and started for the mouth of the Yellowstone, Mr. McKenzie in charge. They did not reach that far the first year, but established a wintering post [1827–28] at the mouth of White River, halfway between Forts Union and Berthold—say 150 miles below the Yellowstone. After the post was finished Mr. McKenzie started for the States, and Mr. Honoré Picotte remained in charge. The returns were found encouraging, and the following year [1829] he went on to the mouth of the Yellowstone, where the chief of the band of the Rocks had desired him to build, and which was a beautiful site, abounding in the best of timber, above, below, and opposite the fort, and with all kinds of game. Mr. McKenzie made this his residence and very soon messengers were dispatched north, inviting all Assiniboines, Crees, and Chippewas to the Missouri. When they learned that Mr. McKenzie was there it was not long before large numbers of these Indians came over, together with many half-breed families. Next year [1830] he determined to extend the trade, both up the Missouri for the

Blackfeet and up the Yellowstone for the Crows. As to the Crows there was no difficulty, but the Blackfeet, who were deadly enemies to the Americans, he could not well manage against their will, nor did he think it advisable to start up an outfit before learning how they were disposed. It happened at the time that there was then at the fort an old trapper named Berger, who had been in his young days in the employ of the Hudson's Bay Company, at the Fort of the Prairie, when Mr. John Rowand was in charge; and this having been a post for the Blackfeet, he had acquired the language and could speak it fluently. So Mr. McKenzie proposed to send Berger to the Blackfeet, to try to bring down a party with whom he would endeavor to make a treaty before sending up an outfit. Berger consented; but as this undertaking was extremely dangerous, Mr. McKenzie would not take it upon himself to order any of the men on the expedition. Not less than 12 men would do; but there was no difficulty in raising the required number of volunteers, who were soon ready for the march. The forlorn hope, as they were called, started with the American flag unfurled, hardly expecting to return. But Mr. McKenzie was in good hopes, for they were young Canadians, who knew not a word of English, and the Blackfeet were accustomed to them, as they were also employed by the Hudson's Bay Company. He anticipated no danger, except that of being surprised by a war party while encamped, which was also Berger's fear. Having searched for the Blackfeet for about four weeks, the men were at last so fortunate as to discover a large camp, without being discovered themselves; and the time had come to try their pluck. "Blackfeet in sight—that awful tribe, of whom we have heard so many terrible stories—what is going to be our fate?" was the talk. Some moves were made to abandon the idea of entering the camp, and to skedaddle if possible; but old man Berger was grit, and succeeded in getting his men along. He knew the Indian customs as well as their language; the men put great confidence in him, and determined to follow, saying, "Now for the butcher shop!" Berger took the lead with the flag bearer by his side, and his little frightened party close in the rear. Soon after they had got on their march they were discovered, and in less time after that a large party of mounted Indians were making for them at full speed. Berger, having caused his little party to stop, advanced with the flag bearer. The Indians, perceiving this maneuver, and not knowing what to make of it, paused for a while. Berger advanced, and when at a hearing distance cried out his name; at which they rushed up to shake hands, and the party which had kept their position were ordered to come up. How their pulses quickened and their hearts thumped is not hard to imagine, for fear had not entirely left them, and they did not know what fate was reserved for them in the Blackfoot camp. They would have preferred to turn back, but it was too cowardly as well as too late, and on they had to go. On entering camp there was great yelling and shouting in all directions; but after this had subsided they were lodged, feasts commenced, and all was done in such a friendly manner that the boys began to feel reassured. When Berger had made his intentions known, a party of 40 Indians consented to accompany him to the Yellowstone. None of them had ever been there, and some showed a little reluctance; at which Berger, in order to induce them to come, represented the distance to be somewhat shorter than it really was. The party was soon ready, and they all set off. Then came trouble and renewed fear in camp, for the Indians soon commenced to complain of the distance, thinking a trap had been laid by the whites to destroy them, and it was with great difficulty that Berger could make them agree to proceed. Things began to look rather dark, but at last they consented to go on a few days more. One night, when they had come within one day's march of the fort, as Berger knew very well, the Indians swore they would go no further—that he had lied to them, and they would have revenge. Berger was put to his trumps; but, being sure of reaching the fort next day, made them a speech, saying, "I tell you you will be in the fort to-morrow, smoking the pipe of peace with the great chief who sent me. Here I am with my party and horses; if I don't bring you to the fort to-morrow, you are welcome to my scalp and all the horses." This struck them with a great deal of force, and they consented to go on another day. Next morning an early start was made to give ample time to finish the journey, and about three in the afternoon they arrived on a ridge, in full view of the fort, where they sat down to smoke and vermilion themselves. Soon they saw the large flag hoisted, heard the cannon firing, and a little while after that the forlorn hope, with all the Blackfeet, entered Fort Union. In course of time a treaty was made, and next spring [1831] an outfit was started under Mr. James Kipp, with instructions to build at the mouth of Marias River, which was the first trading post established for the Blackfeet, and called Fort McKenzie.[39] Fort Cass was built next spring [1832]; and after those two forts were established, the Upper Missouri Department was formed, of which Mr. McKenzie was the agent. Berger received $800 per annum as interpreter for the Blackfeet.

Having done my best to post the reader on these matters [of 1827–33], I resume my personal narrative. Yet a few words more in reference to the energy of Mr. McKenzie, who once remarked to me, in a conversation on Indian trade, that his intention had been at that time to extend the trade into the Rocky Mountains; and that, not feeling disposed to do so without a charter, he made application to the government; but that ours

[39] James Kipp was a native of Canada who entered upon the fur trade in early manhood, and about 1818 came to the Upper Missouri, being stationed at Fort Mandan (later the site of Fort Clark) as agent of the Columbia Fur Company. He later joined the American Fur Company, for whom he commanded Fort Clark for several years. The fort which he established among the Blackfeet in 1831 was called Fort Piegan. It should not be confused with the more famous Fort McKenzie which was established in 1832 (Fort Piegan having been burned, meanwhile) about seven miles up the river from the site of Kipp's fort. Prince Maximilian of Wied spent two months here as a guest in the summer of 1833, and his well-known book of *Travels* contains much information about the place and the period.

being a free government, no charter could be allowed him, and thus the project was abandoned.

After the flogging of our gentlemen nothing special took place until a certain free trapper named Augustin Bourbonnais came down the Missouri in a canoe. As it was yet early, about the 1st of November [1836], his idea was to keep on to Fort Clark and winter there. But as he found many of his friends at Union, he changed his plans and made up his mind to spend the winter at this place. He had been lucky on his hunt, and had about a pack of beaver, worth something like $500, which made him feel rich and quite able to pass a pleasant winter. Bourbonnais was only about 20 years of age, a very handsome fellow, and one thing in his favor was his long yellow hair, so much admired by the female sex of this country. This they call pah-ha-zee-zee, and one who is so adorned is sure to please them. A few days before his arrival Mr. McKenzie, who was nearly 50 years old, and perhaps thought it was too cold to sleep alone in winter, had taken to himself a pretty young bedfellow. Mr. Bourbonnais had not been long in the fort before he went shopping, and very soon was seen strolling about the fort in a fine suit of clothes, as large as life, with his long pah-ha-zee-zee hanging down over his shoulders; if he had looked well in his buckskins, he surely looked charming then. Cupid, I suppose, commenced to shoot his arrows so fast that they struck Bourbonnais, unfortunately for himself, as they also had Mr. McKenzie; and as such arrows generally wound to the heart, Mr. McKenzie determined to go on the war path. Being somewhat advanced in age, he found he could not carry on the war with arrows; so he armed himself with a good-sized cudgel and watched his opportunity. It happened one evening that Mr. Bourbonnais, encouraged by favorable returns of affection, went so far as to enter the apartments reserved for Mr. McKenzie. The latter, hearing some noises which he thought he ought not to have heard, rushed in upon the lovers and made such a display of his sprig of a shillelah that Mr. Bourbonnais incontinently found his way not only out of the house but also out of the fort, with Mr. McKenzie after him. It was amusing to see the genteel Mr. Bourbonnais, in his fine suit of broadcloth, with the tail of his surtout stretched horizontally to its full extent; but, unfortunately for the poor fellow, he would not let the affair end in that way, and swore vengeance on Mr. McKenzie. Of course, having been driven out of the fort with a club, he did not think it proper or consistent with his dignity to attempt to enter again; so he took board and lodging in an Indian tent, many of which were pitched near the fort, and all his effects were delivered to him. Then it was reported that Mr. McKenzie would be killed; for, "kill him I must," Bourbonnais had said; but, thinking that his angry passion would soon subside, we made or thought little of the threat. Yet, sure enough, he was seen next morning dressed again in buckskin, with his rifle on his shoulder and pistol in his belt, defying Mr. McKenzie to come out of the fort and swearing that he would kill him if he had to remain on the watch for him all winter. Still thinking that such performances would not last long, Mr. McKenzie preferred to remain a day or so in the fort, rather than have any further disturbance. But Bourbonnais kept up his guard longer than Mr. McKenzie felt like remaining a prisoner in his besieged fort; in consequence of which a council of all the clerks was called with the view of raising the siege either by persuasion or by force, and so it was agreed that Bourbonnais' life was to be taken in case he could not be induced to desist. As a measure of precaution a written instrument was immediately prepared and presented to the men of the fort, to sign if they thought proper, and they were particularly informed that the main object was to scare Bourbonnais away—as in reality it was. Next morning one of his friends was sent to him on the part of Mr. McKenzie, to notify him of what had taken place, and to advise him to leave; but that availed not, for he continued his hostile demonstrations. Having given him ample time to change his mind, and seeing that he did not budge, a mulatto named John Brazo—a man of strong nerves and a brave fellow, who had on several occasions been employed to flog men at the flagstaff—was sent for and asked if he thought he had nerve enough to shoot Bourbonnais, in case he should be desired to do so. To which he replied, "Yes, sir—plenty!" "Well, will you do it?" "Yes, sir; I am ready at any time." John was then ordered to take his rifle into one of the bastions, and shoot when he got a chance. John, as good as his word, took his position. I recollect that it was early one Sunday morning, a little before sunrise, when Brazo came to my room, saying, "Mr. Larpenteur, I have shot Bourbonnais." As none of the men were up, I went to apprise Mr. McKenzie of it, who said, "Has Brazo killed him?" Bourbonnais had fallen, but it was not yet known whether he had been killed or only wounded, and I was told to take three or four men to see about it. Mr. E. T. Denig, the bookkeeper, who understood some little surgery, went with us. When we reached the spot we found Bourbonnais only wounded and that not mortally, the ball having struck him above the right breast, and gone out through the right shoulder. He was then brought into the men's quarters, where his wounds were dressed by Mr. Denig, but it was not until the following spring that he was able to leave the fort. He remarked that when he was shot he was on his way to his canoe, at the mouth of the Yellowstone, with the intention of going down to Fort Clark. He left early in the spring and what became of him I never heard; as he was quite pale and not entirely cured when he left, it was thought he might die.

Now, gentle reader, that story is told, and next comes one concerning myself, which has nothing to do with Cupid's arrows, but something to say of those made and shot by Indians. That same spring, on the 1st of March [1837], an express arrived with the information that an individual named Millieu was coming with a small outfit to trade with a band of Canoe Assiniboines who generally remained in the neighborhood of White River, and requesting Mr. McKenzie to send

a party from Fort Union to oppose him. I
was pitched upon to go, and next day started
down with a small outfit on three one-mule
sleds. These Canoes were considered at that
time the worst band of Assiniboines—great
thieves and troublesome to the traders; they
seldom came to the fort and left it without
committing depredations, and it had happened that they stole several head of horses
the previous fall. As liquor was the surest
means to recover stolen horses, I was provided with the article for that purpose, as
well as for another. But as luck would have
it, I was prevented from reaching the Indian
camp on this trip, for at our first camp,
which was at the Big Muddy River, 24 miles
below Union, a young Assiniboine appeared
with a letter from Mr. McKenzie, requesting me to turn back, as Millieu had been
killed by the Sioux and there would be no
opposition; besides which, the Indians had
threatened to cut the ears off my mules,
and would be likely to rob me. Early next
morning we were on our way back to Fort
Union, which we reached in good time that
day.

Having been quietly reinstated in my former functions, I thought no more of taking
a tramp until another express brought the
information that the Opposition had come

up river and were already with the band of Canoes; and that Mr. D. D. Mitchell,[40] the person in charge of Fort Clark, had sent a half-breed named Pierre Garreau after them, but requested Mr. McKenzie in the meantime to send some few goods, such as Garreau did not have. I was called on again, and started next day with three dog-sleds and some liquor, to recover the stolen horses if possible. The third day I arrived in camp, which was then called the Tobacco Garden;[41] it was 100 miles by water from Union. Soon after my arrival I sent for the chiefs, and told them that the chief of the big fort had requested me to assemble them to assist me in recovering the stolen horses, and that I would make them a present of a little liquor. I then gave them each a pint of whiskey. Two of the horses were soon brought to me, for which I gave the Indians a small keg

[40] It was Mitchell who in 1832 built Fort McKenzie, as recited in the preceding note. He was one of the most capable agents of the Company. In 1841 he became Superintendent of Indian Affairs for the Western Department, with headquarters at St. Louis. Here he died in 1861.

[41] Tobacco Garden Creek is a small stream which enters the Missouri from the South about forty miles below the mouth of the Yellowstone. The name is an erroneous translation of the Indian name, which meant "place where the reeds grow."

containing one gallon. For fear that those horses might be retaken, I mounted two good men upon them, and ordered them to put for the fort. There was an Indian by the name of Pet-cah-shah, which is their word for Tortoise, who was known as the greatest scamp of this band; he was the son of their biggest chief, and the identical genius who had stolen the horses. The liquor trade meanwhile commenced. Mr. Tortoise got very drunk, and rushed into my lodge, saying, "You are the meanest white man I ever saw—you traded a lodge from me too cheap last fall—you would not give me the knife I asked you for." He went on enumerating his grievances and exclaimed, "I will kill you to-night!" We knew he was not a bit too good to do it, and soon heard him yelling in an awful manner. Suddenly he rushed into the lodge with his bow and arrows, and had it not been for a young Indian—a friend of mine—who had time to draw his knife and cut the bow string, very likely I should not now be writing. After this performance he came up to me holding a handful of arrows with which he punched me in the breast, saying, "You dog of a white man, I will kill you yet!" He rushed out again and was soon seen with a short Indian gun cocked, but it was taken out of his hands by main force and the priming removed. Then he went to the fire, from which he took out some large smoldering chunks of wood and commenced to rub his dirty head with them, making the live coals fly in all parts of the lodge, as though he intended to set it afire. I don't believe Old Nick himself could have cut a worse figure in his infernal regions. But he was plainly getting too drunk for this sort of thing to last; after cutting a few more capers he rushed out again, and this was the last we saw of him that night.

Soon after that another and still uglier-looking devil of an Indian made his appearance, rushing about in the same manner. This was Hooting Owl, upward of six feet tall, blind in one eye, naked but for his breech-clout, painted in a most hideous manner, and with a long scalper in his hand. Standing immediately before us, he commenced to talk at a great rate, and was apparently very angry; but what he meant by his remarks I could not understand, as I was not well acquainted with the language. But from his postures and gestures I made sure we were gone up this time. To strengthen me in this belief he began to tear up the ground with his long knife, like a furious bull; then, without saying another word, rushed out of the lodge. I asked Garreau

what this meant, to which he replied that
the Indian was all right; he had only been
saying that he had just heard how we had
been treated by the Tortoise, and that he
intended to cut up the first Indian who
should trouble us again, just as he had cut
up the ground. This was good news, and I
thought that if I were to adopt a bird as an
emblem, I would take the hooting owl in
preference to the eagle. I had already made
away with the liquor on the sly, as the Indians would not let me do so publicly; the
noise subsided and finally ceased, and thus
the frolic ended.

Next morning some chiefs and big men
came to express their regret that I had been
so badly treated, and everything went on
quite smoothly; but Mr. Pet-cah-shah never
showed himself again. My orders being not
to remain more than three days, and not
knowing the way back from this camp to
the Big Muddy, but wishing to make the
fort the same day—a distance of 40 miles—
I hired an Indian as guide. When I told him
that I intended to reach the fort that day
he remarked that I could not do it; that we
would have to travel at night, which was
impossible, on account of the prickly pears.
Seeing him determined to turn back when
we had come in sight of Big Muddy, and

knowing the road myself from that river to the fort, I agreed to let him go. I sat down, took out my pocket book, and drew him an order for what he was to receive for his trouble, as Garreau could neither read nor write. Although I was not much of a draughtsman he understood the picture very well when I was through with the drawing, which indicated a looking-glass, a number of hawk-bells, a knife, a pallet of vermilion, and a piece of scarlet cloth in the shape of a breech-clout—though this last I had to explain to him. After he had got this and smoked his pipe we separated, and about eleven o'clock at night I entered Fort Union with my feet nearly frozen. As this was the end of March, and it had thawed all day, the river bottom was all water; but at sundown the wind changed to the northwest, the water commenced to freeze, and when I got to the fort my moccasins were so hard frozen that I had to let them thaw before I could get them off. Had there been an hour longer to travel, my feet would surely have been frozen.

Thus ended my first introduction to an Indian camp. Hoping that I should never have another occasion, I went to bed and slept soundly; but it will be seen in the sequel that I was frustrated in my hopes, if my reader will have the patience to read this book through. As I have to go on with my stories in rotation, it will be some time before I again take him to trade whiskey in an Indian camp.

After my return from the Canoe camp nothing worthy of remark took place until the arrival of the steamer, late in June [1837]. The mirth usual on such occasions was not of long duration, for immediately on the landing of the boat we learned that smallpox was on board. Mr. J. Halsey, the gentleman who was to take charge this summer, had the disease, of which several of the hands had died; but it had subsided, and this was the only case on board. Our only apprehensions were that the disease might spread among the Indians, for Mr. Halsey had been vaccinated, and soon recovered. Prompt measures were adopted to prevent an epidemic. As we had no vaccine matter we decided to inoculate with the smallpox itself; and after the systems of those who were to be inoculated had been prepared according to Dr. Thomas' medical book, the operation was performed upon about 30 Indian squaws and a few white men. This was done with the view to have it all over and everything cleaned up before any Indians should come in, on their fall trade, which commenced early in September.[42] The small-pox matter should have been taken from a very healthy person; but, unfortunately, Mr. Halsey was not sound, and the operation proved fatal to most of our patients. About 15 days afterward there was such a stench in the fort that it could be smelt at the distance of 300 yards. It was awful—the scene in the fort, where some went crazy, and others were half eaten up by maggots before they died; yet, singular to say, not a single bad expression was ever uttered by a sick Indian. Many died, and those who recovered were so much disfigured that one could scarcely recognize them. While the epidemic was at its height a party of about 40 Indians came in, not exactly on a trade, but more on a begging visit, under the celebrated old chief Co-han; and the word was, "Hurry up! Open the door!" which had been locked for many days, to keep the crazy folks in.

[42] A good account of the smallpox epidemic of 1837 on the Upper Missouri, which Larpenteur here describes in part, is given by H. M. Chittenden in *The American Fur Trade of the Far West* (New York, 1902), II, 619 ff. It is also described by John James Audubon, the famous naturalist in *Audubon and his Journals* (Maria R. Audubon, ed.), II, 42–47. Unlike the natives around Fort Union, those at Fort Clark endeavored to retaliate upon the whites, whom they blamed for their disaster.

Nothing else would do—we must open the door; but on showing him a little boy who had not recovered, and whose face was still one solid scab, by holding him above the pickets, the Indians finally concluded to leave. Not long afterward we learned that more than one-half of the party had died— some said all of them. In the course of time the fort became clear of the smallpox, but the danger of infection continued. Fort William was still standing, and the remaining houses, which were no longer inhabited, were used as hospitals for Indians, with no other attendants than some old squaws. It became the duty of John Brazo to take out the dead and dump them into the bushes, and some mornings, on asking him "How many?" he would say, "Only three, sir; but, according to appearances in the hospital, I think I shall have a full load to-morrow or next day." This seemed to be fun for Brazo, but was not for others, particularly myself, as I happened to be the trader, who was liable to be shot at any time; but, singular to say, not even a threat was made, though the tribe was reduced more than one-half by next spring [1838]. Trade continued very nearly up to the average; on being asked how it happened that there were so many robes brought in, the Indians would say laughingly that they expected to die soon, and wanted to have a frolic till the end came. The winter [of 1837–38] was spent in great suspense and fear, but, fortunately, nothing serious occurred except some few shots fired at me through the wicket during the night liquor trade; and as this had frequently happened before, it was not attributed to revenge for the smallpox.

Chapter 8

ROUND TRIP TO THE STATES

IT happened that this was an open winter; the ice broke up early in March, and the river was clear on the 22d of that month, at which date I left for Baltimore in a small canoe, with Mr. Robert Christy of St. Louis. He had come up in the fall to winter at Fort Union for his health, and becoming anxious to return, had made up his mind to leave, in spite of all the dangers represented to him. On my part, I had not seen my parents for ten years, and as this early start would give me ample time to visit them, until our party should be ready to return in the fall, nothing could persuade me out of the notion. Mr. D. D. Mitchell, a member of the Company, and very much of a gentleman, got me to engage for another year, previous to my departure, allowing my wages to run on during my absence; so this trip was considered as a furlough.

Matters being thus well fixed Mr. Christy and I left, with two men to row our canoe.

The day was calm and beautiful; and we

made good speed. I was young, and full of mirth at the idea of returning to my parents, whom I intended to take by surprise, and many other fine plans I had formed made me so happy that I forgot the danger of Indians. Suddenly a party of them, who had concealed themselves along the river banks, rose up with their bows and arrows, ready to shoot. We were not more than 20 yards from them, and their work of destruction would have been quickly done had it not been for one among them whom we saw running to and fro with his bow in his hand, striking right and left. He finally succeeded in preventing the threatened attack; and, as one can imagine, the progress of our little craft was speedily increased. We were told, on our return, by Mr. Chardon,[43] a member of the Company in charge of Fort Clark,

[43] Francis Chardon was at this time in charge of Fort Clark. His extensive manuscript journal, preserved in the Library of Congress, was published by the South Dakota Department of History in 1932, under the editorship of Mrs. Annie H. Abel. Chardon was a well-known trader on the Upper Missouri for twenty years prior to his death in 1848. Prior to coming there he is said to have traded for years among the Osage of the Lower Missouri. While in charge of Fort McKenzie he was a principal actor in the perfidious massacre which Larpenteur describes *post*, 187–89.

that we had no idea how near we came to losing our lives on that occasion. Those Indians were a party of 80 Rees [Arikaras], who had gone to war on the Assiniboines; and had it not been for their partisan's great influence over them we surely would have all been killed. The Rees had had the smallpox severely, and were therefore badly disposed toward the whites. This was fright No. 1, after which I remember well the first words spoken by Mr. Christy: "Larpenteur, I think we had better stayed at Union." But it was already too late to repent; we were under way and could not turn back.

At ten o'clock of the second day after this, when we were near Heart[44] River, on the south side of the Missouri, we discovered six Indians, who had gone hunting while the ice was still strong; but it had broken up before their return, and now they had no means of crossing the river. Thinking this a good opportunity to save themselves the trouble of making their own boat, they made signs to us to come for them. These Indians belonged to the band of Canoe Assiniboines, who had had the smallpox badly, and whom I had known to accept pay for being ferried

[44] An error of the author; the party was still above Fort Clark; while Heart River enters the Missouri near Bismarck, a considerable distance below Fort Clark.

over the river, instead of paying us for the privilege; so of course I declined the job. As soon as they saw our craft steered away from them, they threw off their robes, and, with nothing on but their leggings and breech-clouts, ran to head us off. This they were near doing, as we had to go close to the shore to avoid the waves caused by the strong current washing against sand bars. As we approached they seated themselves, steadied their guns with the ramrods to take good aim, and let fly at us. But by this time we had got a little ahead of them, rowing all the time with all our might, though we could see the flashes from the muzzles of their guns and hear the bullets strike the water. Mr. Christy, who was steering, dodged like a duck passing under a bridge, to avoid the balls which whistled about his ears. We soon got out of their reach, but this danger was not the worst that appeared. The Indian camp was only a little way off, and, having heard the firing, they were all on the alert, thinking we were enemies. They soon found out the cause of the firing, and ran down to the next bend with the intention of giving us another volley. They fired at us again, but, fortunately for us, the river was wide, the current free from waves, and we could keep our distance from the shore.

Bullets fell on the water like hail, some even beyond us, and three of them lodged in our canoe. These we afterward extracted with our knives. At length, finding ourselves out of danger, and also out of breath after having paddled with all our might through two attacks, those who had pipes began to smoke, and jocose remarks were made in regard to our scare. Some said, "This is fright No. 2; I wonder what No. 3 is going to be? It cannot fail to happen, as we have already had two in so short a distance, and the third time we must surely go up!" I began to feel like agreeing with Christy, that we had better have remained at Union.

After the pipes were emptied, the paddles were again plied, and our little wounded craft slid down stream gently. We kept on in a pleasant manner until next day, at about eleven o'clock, when we discovered a large number of Indians on the south side of the river, running back and forth and gathering on a small hill quite near the bank. Their maneuvers appearing hostile to us, we knew not what to do, and began to fear we were surely gone up this time. It was thought best to land on the opposite shore, to decide upon what course to adopt, and it was left optional with each one to take it by land or water. Not feeling like footing

it, I went in for the boat; and after a little
further parley, seeing me determined to do
so, they all agreed to follow my example.
So I placed a good supply of tobacco on the
bow of the canoe, in full sight, to produce
a good effect, if possible, and on we started.
When they saw us coming they increased in
number and our fears rose in proportion; but
keep on we must. When our fears were at
the highest pitch we perceived an individual
with pants and a red flannel shirt on, looking very much like a white man. To our
surprise and joy, we found that it was old
Mr. Charbonneau,[45] who had been 40 years
among the Missouri Indians. He used to
say that when he first came on the river it
was so small that he could straddle it. Imagine our joy to find ourselves befriended
instead of butchered, as we had thought we

[45] This was Toussaint Charbonneau, who is best
known to fame as the interpreter for Lewis and Clark,
and as husband and owner of his slave-wife Sacajawea,
heroine of the Lewis and Clark expedition. Charbonneau had numerous wives; the last one was acquired
Oct. 27, 1838, when he was reputed to be eighty years
of age, and the new bride fourteen. The young men
at Fort Clark gave the bridegroom a splendid "Chiva-
ree," beating pans and firing off guns, which so alarmed
the Indians at the fort that they ran away. For this,
and other interesting information concerning Charbonneau, see Grace R. Hebard's *Sacajawea* (Glendale,
Calif., 1933), Chap. II.

were surely going to be. The tobacco was presented to such Indians as the old gentleman advised, and we resumed our paddles.

Charbonneau told us that we were then something like 70 miles from Fort Clark, but thought that we would be detained by the ice, as frequently happened, this being about the most northern point on the Missouri. Gladdened again, fright No. 3 being over, and fairly under way, we traveled well the balance of that day. The next day we found but little current, and had to paddle hard to make much headway. We went on thus until about three in the afternoon, when we found the river nearly blocked by large dykes, which had formed across it and caused the slowness of the current; but we forced our way through a narrow channel, and kept on by hard paddling. By the time we were about 10 miles from Fort Clark the dyke broke loose and the ice came down upon us with such a rush, and tossing our canoe like an old log at such a rate, that we thought ourselves in greater danger of our lives than we had been from the Indians; but at last it brought our canoe of its accord to shore about a mile above the fort, where we were obliged to remain two days till the ice subsided. Mr. F. A. Chardon, who was then in charge, and a very singular kind of a man, entertained us in the best manner. Mr. Christy had a two-gallon keg of good whiskey, of which Mr. Chardon was so fond that he helped himself about every fifteen minutes, saying he had "a great many worms in his throat"—to the sorrow of Mr. Christy, who found his keg so nearly empty that he concluded to make Mr. Chardon a present of what was left. We remained there two days; on the third we took leave of Mr. Chardon who, not knowing he was to fall heir to the balance of the whiskey, and not having as yet destroyed all the worms in his throat, would have been glad for us to remain another day, and insisted very strongly that we should do so. I cannot say whether it was because the whiskey had been put on board before Mr. Christy made up his mind about it, that Mr. Chardon accompanied us to the boat, or whether he did so through politeness; but he felt very happy at the presentation, and hastened back to the fort in double-quick time.

All right and off again; and I am glad to say that, with the exception of high winds, which at times kept us, for three days together, camped in the willows, nothing took place worth mentioning till we reached the Vermilion Post. Mr. Dickson, who shortly afterward committed suicide, was in charge, and showed us great kindness during the night we stayed with him. After relating to him our narrow escapes, he remarked that we were now out of danger, being among a different kind of Indians. This information sounded pleasant.

After a good breakfast next morning we left the kind Mr. Dickson, who, it appeared, did not quite know his Indians; for we had not made more than 20 miles when a volley of rifle-shots was fired at us by a deer-hunting party of Omahas. Fortunately we happened to be in a wide part of the river. The attack was so sudden that we had no time for fright before it was over; but, after this, we came to the conclusion that we could not consider ourselves safe until we reached the States. In constant dread of Indians, we kept paddling on our way, trusting to good luck to get out of the Indian country; it was a long way to travel, as there was no settlement at that time on the Missouri above Independence, Mo. Our provisions were getting low, and altogether we were not in very good humor. On reaching the mouth of the Platte we perceived a steamer; and as but one steamer a year came that far up, we made sure it was the Company's boat. Our hearts were glad, expecting to hear all the news and procure a supply of eatables. We were soon on board the *Antelope*—that being her name. Mr. McKenzie, who was on his way to Fort Union, was much surprised to see me. Said he, "My God! Larpenteur, what's the matter? Why have you come down so early in the season?" After learning the circumstances and being assured that all was right above, he became reconciled, and told me that he had been to my father's, in Baltimore, and had left them all well; "but go on," said he, "they will be very glad to see you." After a little more talk, we continued down river, well supplied with provisions and in a very good humor, though we had still a long distance to paddle. A few days after leaving the steamer we reached a small town called Camden, where we met a boat bound for Fort Leavenworth, and made arrangements for our passage to St. Louis on her return, which we awaited at this little town. Having no further use for our little craft, we made a present of it to our two men, and next day we were comfortably lodged on board the steamer, whose name I have forgotten, as well as that of the captain. Great was the change, after paddling our own canoe for a month through all kinds of dangers, to find ourselves seated at table and gliding down stream at the rate of 20 miles an hour. At that rate it was not many days before we reached St. Louis.

I left next day for Baltimore by stage to Louisville, thence to Cincinnati, thence to Brownsville; then stage again to Baltimore. But at that time the stage stopped at Frederickstown[46]—I believe 40 miles from Baltimore—where we took cars which were propelled by horse power, not having as yet any engine.

As it is mostly my object to relate what happened in the Indian country, I will merely state here that I had great pleasure in seeing my relatives again, after the absence of 10 years; and as nothing was spared to make my stay agreeable, I enjoyed myself very much. Leaving the reader to imagine the surprise of my unexpected return, I will soon take him with me on the way back to Fort Union. But, before starting up the Missouri, I will give a little incident of my return to St. Louis. This took place in a small town in the Alleghany Mountains called McConnellstown, and will show how one may get praised without deserving it, as happened to be my case. Mr. Denig, the bookkeeper of Fort Union, whose parents resided in this town, had given me a letter of introduction to his father, the doctor, and

[46] Apparently, Frederick, Md.

also a letter of his own to his parents, both
of which I delivered with pleasure, as the
place was on the stage route. There was
great rejoicing on my arrival at Dr. Denig's.
The old gentleman was about fifty and the
old lady not far from it; both were good,
respectable people, who paid all the attention to me that could be expected. I remained three days, during which a report
was circulated that there was, at the Doctor's, a certain gentleman who was said to
be a crack shot. So a target was prepared
for a shooting match. Although I did not
consider myself a marksman, and, in reality,
was not, I accepted the challenge. There
was no betting—it was merely to try me as a
sharpshooter. Their best marksman was
picked out—one that could knock out a
squirrel's eye on the top of the highest tree
in the mountains at every pop. Accompanied by the two sons of Dr. Denig, and
two hired men, we started for the appointed
place, where a large crowd of all sorts of
people was awaiting my arrival, with targets
all ready for action. The conditions were
best three out of five shots at thirty paces,
unless the center was driven. My opponent was a stout, fine-looking Pennsylvania
Dutchman named Keizer. It was my first
shot, and I made a close one; he shot nearly

a tie; but out of the five I happened to have the best three. The target was taken down and handed to me, and another immediately put up. It was my first shot again, close to the black on the right side; Keizer shot next, on the left, somewhat nearer than mine. Then came my second shot, when I re-marked, by way of braggadocio, being far from expecting to make good my boast, "Now, gentlemen, this is what I like! When there is a shot on each side of the black, it serves as a guide to me, and I generally drive the center." As much to my own surprise as to that of all the rest, it was driven—so well that this could not have been more precisely done by hand. Imagine the looks in that crowd, disappointed to see their crack man so badly beaten! But Keizer said it was owing to his having chased his sheep that day, which made him so nervous that he could not shoot. I put both targets in my pocketbook, and brought them to Mr. Denig at Union. Old Dr. Denig was well pleased, and said, "Were I in your place, now that your name is up, I would not shoot any more." Neither did I.

Next day I left McConnellstown, and nothing took place worth mentioning on the journey to St. Louis until our departure thence for Fort Union. I should have said before that I left Baltimore on the 13th of September, 1838. Mr. D. D. Mitchell, who had come down in the steamer, and was about to return to Union, was our chief; besides whom, Clerk Jacques Bruguière, myself, and two men composed the party. We traveled on pleasantly until we reached Ponca Creek, when most of our men were taken with fever and ague at such a rate that, instead of eating down they were all throwing up. This kept us two or three days longer than we should have stayed at the creek. The day we left to strike for White Earth River[47] I was taken with such an awful shake that, when on horseback, I could keep my seat only by holding on with all my might to my rifle across my saddle; and I cut such a figure that it excited the mirth of the party, who laughed at me all through their pretended sympathy. After the shake came the fever, and then thirst—but no water—I thought I should die for want of water. I had two such shakes before we arrived at Fort Pierre, where we remained two days. Mr. Halsey gave me some good medicine, and after a couple of light shakes I recovered entirely. Then came the tre-

[47] Apparently White River, S. Dak., which enters the Missouri opposite Chamberlain. Ponca Creek was between this stream and the Niobrara.

mendous appetite. I was really ashamed of myself at meal time. But Mr. Mitchell was very liberal in helping us to well-filled plates, and when he saw that I had made away with the contents of mine, would say, "Back up your cart, Larpenteur, for another load." Only those who have traveled the prairie know what a voracious appetite is acquired on such tramps. Having had the ague, which is always followed by an increase of the regular prairie appetite, we became ravenous, and soon made away with our provisions. Three days before our arrival at Fort Clark, at the Mandans, we were out of everything except sugar and coffee; for, singular to say, even at that early period buffalo had become scarce.

Thus far I had proved myself to be about the best hunter in the company, having killed some few antelopes, badgers, and prairie-dogs, as we had been all this time in the open prairies. When we were approaching Fort Clark, and had reached the points of timber of the Missouri, I proposed to Mr. Mitchell to try my luck in search of deer, as our rations had given out and we had but one cup of coffee left. He readily consented, saying, "Take Brazo along; he is somewhat of a hunter." Having been told where he would camp, I and my man started together;

but we soon separated, each choosing his own direction through the wooded point. I soon perceived a fine large buck. I knew that my old horse would stand fire—you might shoot off the whole of the United States artillery around him without making him move—standing still was his forte. I rose in my stirrups and pulled the trigger; but away went the buck, not without leaving a lock of his hair, which I saw fly. Being sure that I had made a good shot, I got off my steady old horse and commenced the search. In the meantime Brazo, who had heard the shot, came up and asked what I had fired at. I replied, "A large buck, which I am sure I wounded." So he joined me in the search; but, as I could find no blood, I soon proposed to abandon the trail. Brazo then remarked, "No, Mr. Larpenteur, I have seen blood; let us look a little while longer." Encouraged by this we resumed our search, and in less than ten minutes we saw the fine buck, stretched dead, having been shot through the heart. In a little while he was cut up and put on my horse, and we were on our way to camp. Brazo, not liking the idea of coming into camp without any game, struck out to try his luck again. I did not expect to get any more game on the way to camp; but luckily came full on a band of five deer, which stood about 80 paces from me. I drew a bead on one of them, which fell at the crack of the gun. No need looking for this one, as it was shot through the neck. Poor Brazo, who had got but a little way off, came up to ask what I had killed. I told him "A fine fat doe." "Well, you are in luck!" said he. Having cut up the meat and loaded it on Brazo's horse, we struck for camp, which we reached just at dark. I leave the reader to imagine the exclamations of joy made at the sight of so much fine meat; but the question arose, "Who killed all that?" I said I had killed both deer. Then it was "Hurrah for Larpenteur! Come, boys, get up your kettles!" While the kettles were boiling French voyageur songs resounded, and all felt quite set up except poor Brazo, who seemed to be down in the dumps.

The third day we entered Fort Clark early and found Mr. Chardon in charge, who received us with hoisted flag and several rounds from his small piece of artillery. There we took supplies to last us to Union, and the following morning resumed our journey, Mr. Mitchell being our boss and guide. It was now October and the mornings were getting quite cold, with heavy white frosts. The second morning after we left Fort Clark my old horse tumbled into a miry little creek, and, not being able to extricate himself, came down broadside before I could jump out of the saddle. When they saw me so well drenched they could not refrain from indulging in mirth at my misfortune. Our guide, not being very well scienced, struck too far south, in consequence of which we were three nights without wood and had to burn buffalo chips; but, as good luck would have it, we were favored with clear, dry weather and could make good fires. But our animals fared badly, as the route we took brought us into alkali country; some we had to leave, and others died at the fort.

On the fifth day after we left Fort Clark we struck White River, too far up; but we got into some scrawly timber, which was mighty good after having nothing but buffalo chips to burn for three nights. Brazo, who was in the habit of coming into camp last, said he had heard dogs barking, and also thought he had heard squaws talking, and added, "There's Indians close by." This news put a stop to our pleasant feelings and a guard was set. Apprehending attack early in the morning, sleep was light that night; but we happened to be mistaken in our apprehensions. Daylight came all right, breakfast was gotten up, and still no Indians; so we commenced to think Brazo had been mistaken. But we had not left camp more than an hour when some one cried out, "Indians!" Before any preparations could be made, a whole host was upon us; but we soon found that they were some Assiniboines who had camped a little above where we did last night; it was only on account of our late arrival that they had not discovered us. They told us it would take us two more days to get to Fort Union, for our horses were poor and we could not travel fast. Some of the leading men proposed to go along with us, which was agreed upon; for the sake of a little whiskey they would have gone any distance. But some of the rabble followed, whose looks we did not like, and whom we would have been glad to see turn back; for they looked very much like those who made it a habit to borrow, and forget to return, a white man's horse. As they excited great suspicion, the guard was doubled; but, in spite of all our precautions, they managed to get off with two horses, one of which belonged to an individual by the name of Antoine Frenier, a half-breed whom Mr. Mitchell had engaged at Fort Clark as interpreter for Fort Union. When he found that his favorite horse had been borrowed and was not likely to be returned, he began to give the Assiniboines such a blessing, with the aid of the Virgin Mary, whom he invoked to assist him in strengthening his remarks, that I defy any Catholic priest to make a better one. The Indians, who had learned by this time that he was to be the interpreter, were convinced, by this blessing, that he understood their language. In spite of all this we were under way by sunrise, with glad hearts after all, thinking that we had but once more to sleep outside, excepting the old interpreter, who now and then addressed a prayer to the Holy Virgin for the benefit of the Assiniboines, and to the great mirth of the company, sometimes in French and sometimes in Assiniboine, but always mixed with a little Cree, as he was a half-breed from the North. It seemed impossible for him to recover from the loss of his nag sufficiently to abstain from his devotions.

Our last camp was on the Big Muddy. Although we hoped that we had gotten rid of the horse thieves, it was thought proper to keep up a strong guard, which consisted of one-half of the party for each half of the night; but as it was very dark, the Assiniboines made out to take two of our best horses, one of which was Mr. Mitchell's. The chiefs said that they knew who had stolen the horses, and told us not to be uneasy, for we should get the animals back again. They proved as good as their word; our two horses were returned shortly afterward, though the interpreter's was never recovered. Thus, half consoled, we again got under way, and did not stop until we entered Fort Union, which we did about 4 p. m., with a salute of many shots from the artillery, and the large flag flying. This was on the 12th of October [1838];[48] and my reader can guess who felt good after a six-weeks' ride through the wild prairies.

[48] The journey from Baltimore to Fort Union could not have been made in a month's time; either this date, or the one given for the departure from Baltimore (Sept. 13) is incorrect. The "six-weeks' ride through the wild prairies" seems to indicate that the trip from St. Louis to Fort Union alone consumed six weeks.

Chapter 9

(1838–42)

THANKS to kind Providence, here I am again in good old Fort Union, at a splendid table, with that great prairie appetite to do it justice. The day after my arrival I was reinstated in the liquor shop, and as it was the height of the meat trade I had enough to do, night and day. Excepting plenty of buffalo, deer, and rabbit hunting, nothing took place worth mentioning until Christmas [1838]. On this anniversary a great dinner is generally made, but that was never the case here, as it was always taken out in drinkables instead of eatables; and I, who did not drink, had to do without my dinner. At the height of the spree the tailor and one of the carpenters had a fight in the shop, while others took theirs outside, and toward evening I was informed that Marseillais, our hunter, had been killed and thrown into the fireplace. We immediately ran in, and sure enough, there he was, badly burned and senseless, but not dead yet. We were not at first sure

134

whether this was the mere effect of liquor, or had happened from fighting; but we learned that a fight had taken place, and on examination we found that he had been stabbed in several places with a small dirk. Knowing that the tailor had such a weapon, we suspected him and demanded it. He was at that time standing behind his table; I saw him jerk the dirk out of his pocket and throw it under the table. I immediately picked it up; it was bloody, and from its size we judged it to be the weapon with which the wounds had been inflicted. Having learned that the carpenter had also been in the fight, they both were placed in irons and confined to await their trial. As such Christmas frolics could not be brought to a head much under three days, the trial took place on the fourth day, when a regular court was held. Everything being ready, the criminals were sent for, the witnesses were well examined, and after a short session the jury returned a verdict, "Guilty of murder." The judge then pronounced sentence on the convicted murderers, which was that they be hanged by the neck, until they were "dead, dead, dead!" But, not considering it entirely safe to have this sentence executed, he changed it to thirty-nine lashes apiece. John Brazo was appointed executioner.

Always ready for such sport, he immediately went in quest of his large ox-whip, and, not making any difference between men and oxen, he applied it at such a rate that Mr. Mitchell, the judge, had now and then to say, "Moderate, John, moderate"; for had John been suffered to keep on, it is very likely that the first sentence would have been executed.

After this everything went on perfectly smooth. A very large trade was made, and everybody was satisfied; and in time preparations were made to take down the returns. On the 3d of June [1839] I was sent to St. Louis in charge of eight Mackinaw boats, each containing 250 packs of buffalo robes, besides many small furs. The trip was very pleasant, with the exception of being nearly shot by Assiniboines at the same place where we had been attacked the previous spring. The disagreeable features of these trips are caused, mainly, by the crews getting whiskey and becoming unruly; but I managed to get along admirably well, and succeeded in landing all my boats safe in the port of St. Louis. These were the last landed there, as no companies would insure below St. Joseph, on account of the drunkenness of the men, which had caused the loss of many boats.

For what reason I have never been able to find out, though I always attributed it to that old tyrant, Mr. Laidlaw, the Company would not then hire me again; so I remained that winter [of 1839–40] in St. Louis. It happened during this time that Mr. McKenzie, Mr. Mitchell, and old Mr. Chabané[49] got at difference with the American Fur Co., in consequence of which they raised a large outfit to oppose it; but by some means the misunderstanding was made up.

In the meantime I had been re-engaged, and arrangements were made for my return to Fort Union. On the 31st of March [1840] I was on the steamer *Trapper*, and after a long, tedious trip we reached Union on the 27th of June. My being a sober man was not much to my advantage, keeping me constantly in the liquor trade, and out of the charge of posts which some of my fellow-

[49] John P. Cabanné (variously spelled) was one of the early partners in the American Fur Company, whose high-handed course in destroying an opposition trader, Narcisse Leclerc, at the Council Bluffs in 1832 provoked a storm of public opposition to the Company, and led to Cabanné's retirement from it. The affair is narrated in H. M. Chittenden's *History of Early Steamboat Navigation on the Missouri River* (New York, 1903), I, 24–27. Cabanné was a native of France. His home for many years was at St. Louis, where he died June 27, 1841, aged sixty-eight years.

clerks took charge of, while I did all the work, and was really in charge when they got dead drunk. Mr. Laidlaw the Father, Mr. Denig the Son, and Mr. Jacques Bruguière the Holy Ghost, formed the Trinity at Union last [?] winter, and a trio of greater drunkards could not have been got together. The consequence was that the large meat trade was lost. Indians would trade robes with Mr. Laidlaw in the office, steal them back, and trade them again with Mr. Bruguière at the regular shop. The reason why Mr. Laidlaw opened trade in the office was, he said, that Bruguière got too drunk to hold out; but Laidlaw was the greater drunkard of the two.

About the latter part of May, 1842, Mr. Alexander Culbertson, who was in charge of Union, sent me up to Fort Van Buren, at the mouth of Rosebud River, on the Yellowstone, with a party of 10 men, to bring down the returns. He also instructed me to build another post at Adams Prairie, about 20 miles above, where he expected me to remain in charge, as he was not sure that Mr. Murray, who was then in charge of Van Buren, would be re-engaged. Next day we left Union, and a pleasant trip we had. Our guide, a young man by the name of Lee, who was a first-rate hunter, made us live on buffalo tongues and marrow bones. A few days after my arrival at Van Buren the boats were off with the returns, and I remained in charge of my first post.

Nothing of importance occurred during the time I remained at this place except one little incident, which I think deserves a place in this narrative. Two or three weeks after the boat left, a certain Mexican, who had been employed at Fort Union, made his appearance with his squaw nearly naked, and said to me, "Mr. Larpenteur, I will tell you the truth. I killed a squaw at the meat camp. I did not intend to kill her; but she made me mad. I took a stick, struck her on the back of the head, and she fell dead. I then ran off, fearing some of her connections, who were in camp. That is the whole truth, captain"—as he called me. "Now I am very poor," he continued, "and my India" —as he called his squaw—"is going to have a child. Will you please let me go into your fort? I will do anything you want me to do." Having but four men with me, all told, and seeing the Mexican so pitiable, I allowed him to come in. Mexicans being only fit to herd horses, I employed him on horse-guard. Had his India not been with him and so near confinement, I would not have given him that employment. For a while he did very well, being attentive to his duties, and all were pleased with him. One fine afternoon he came to me, saying, "My horses are all doing well. I have got them in a good safe place. Will you be so kind as to let me go with my India in search of some *pomme blanche?*" which is the French name for Indian turnips. As he had done so well and his India was so near her time, I consented, and off he started, assuring me that he would not be gone more than a couple of hours. But that time passed, and neither the Mexican nor his India appeared; and some of the men said they should not wonder if he had made his escape. This being the general impression, they examined a little old box in which he kept his duds and found it empty. I immediately sent after the horses, which we supposed he had mounted, but found them all right. Next morning, knowing the situation of his squaw, and thinking that he might be lurking around for a chance to steal horses, I sent my hunter and an old Crow in search of the Mexican, under promise of $10 reward if they should find him. About 3 p. m. I saw them returning; the old Indian having the squaw behind him on his horse, with the child in her arms, and the Mexican trotting behind with nothing on but his shirt—thus all ready to be tied up to the flagstaff. This was immediately done, and he would have received a good dose, had not he begged so hard and looked so pitiable that he was let go unpunished. They had found him about 10 miles below the fort on the banks of the Yellowstone, where he had made a raft to cross over; but the raft, not being well constructed, came apart when in the middle of the river, and he lost all his duds except his shirt in saving his squaw, who, he said, had her child immediately on landing, the fright having hurried the birth. I pitied the squaw, but the Mexican I determined to ship off. So the next morning I gave him a skin boat, a little dried buffalo meat, a knife, a steel for striking fire, and a fish-hook and line, with which I told him to clear out and never make his appearance at this place again.

Not long after this occurrence Mr. Auguste Chouteau arrived with the outfit for the Crows, also bringing back the Mexican and his lady. On reprimanding him for so doing, he told me that he could not well help it, considering the situation in which he had found them. It had happened that the Mexican, on his way down river, saw a buffalo mired near the bank; and, having no meat, thought this would be a good opportunity to lay in a supply. Judge of his surprise when Mr. Bruin, who was lying in wait behind the buffalo, made a grab at the man, tearing him so badly that, when he was met by Mr. Chouteau, he was scarcely expected to live. Thus ends the story of the Mexican, except that, some time afterward, he was killed by the relations of the squaw he had murdered at Union.

Among the news that Mr. Chouteau brought up was that of Alexander Harvey's killing Isidoro, the Spaniard. As I shall have frequent occasion to mention Harvey, I will here give some idea of his character. He was a native of St. Louis, who served some time learning the saddle trade with Thornton Grimsley. As he happened to be one of those men that never can be convinced, and with whom it was no use to argue unless one wished to get into a fight, he remained but a short time at his trade. Though not yet of age he engaged with a fur-trapping company for the Rocky Mountains. Having found his way to the mouth of the Yellowstone about the time that Fort McKenzie was built, he engaged with the American Fur Company for that post. There he remained for a number of years [to fall of 1839]; but became so wicked and troublesome, and was so much feared by all hands at the fort, that reports were made to Mr. Chouteau in St. Louis, who sent him his discharge by the fall express, which did not reach Fort McKenzie until about Christmas. He was undoubtedly the boldest man that was ever on the Missouri—I mean in the Indian country; a man about six feet tall, weighing 160 or 170 pounds, and inclined to do right when sober. On hearing of his discharge, and being requested to report in person at St. Louis—which was simply to get him out of the country—he remarked, "I will not let Mr. Chouteau wait long on me. I shall start in the morning; all I want for my journey is my rifle, and my dog to carry bedding." Sure enough, in spite of all remonstrances regarding the hardships to which he would expose himself on such a long journey alone at that season of the year, he set out, good as his word.

Early in March he reached St. Louis, to the great astonishment of Mr. Chouteau, who, after hearing Harvey's story, and learning what a journey he had performed, could not but re-engage him to return to Fort McKenzie. He returned at the same time that I reached Union, in the steamer *Trapper* [June 27, 1840]. On the way up he now and then remarked to me, "Larpenteur, I have several settlements to make with those gentlemen who caused me last winter's tramp; I never forget or forgive; it may not be for ten years, but they all will have to catch it." Being as good as his word, at Fort Clark he pounded awfully one of the men who had reported him, saying, "That's No. 1." On his arrival at Fort Union, where many had come down with the returns, intending to go back with the outfit to Fort McKenzie, and never thinking of coming in contact with Harvey, they were much surprised when he made his appearance among about 60 men, in search of reporters; and at every glimpse he could get of one of them it was a knockdown, followed by a good pounding. Whiskey had nothing to do with this; he was perfectly sober, only fulfilling his promises. This will show what sort of a man Harvey was; but there is more to tell, and now we return to the Spaniard's story.

It was in 1841, when the Spaniard and Harvey happened to go down together with the returns, which were then taken in Mackinaw boats to St. Louis. Both intended to return in the steamer, which they expected to meet below Fort Pierre. The report was generally believed, though I placed no reliance on it, that a plot had been laid on the way up to Union, by some members of the American Fur Company, for the

Spaniard to kill Harvey. Both had long been stationed at Fort McKenzie, but had never agreed, being jealous of each other and great enemies. The next day after the departure of the steamer—a day given to the men to look about and arrange their little effects—the Spaniard took occasion to commence hostilities, and was soon parading with his rifle, saying that he would kill Harvey. For the first time in his life Harvey was persuaded to remain in the house, supposing it was only liquor that caused the Spaniard to make those threats; so the day passed, and Harvey was still alive. The second day, all the clerks were called up to get the equipments ready for Fort McKenzie. Mr. Culbertson, who was in charge of Union, came into the warehouse; not seeing the Spaniard with the other clerks, he asked where the man was, and, being told, sent for him. But Isidoro, instead of going to the warehouse, went into the retail store and remained behind the counter. Mr. Culbertson and Harvey both being in the store, Harvey began by asking the Spaniard what he meant by his behavior the day before. "You are too big a coward to come out and fight me like a man; you want to shoot me behind my back!" So saying, he left the store and dared the Spaniard to come out; but the latter never moved. When Harvey found that his enemy would not come out, he went back in the store and said, "You won't fight me like a man, so take that!" and shot him through the head. After this he went to the middle of the fort, saying, "I, Alexander Harvey, have killed the Spaniard. If there are any of his friends who want to take it up, let them come on"; but no one dared to do so, and this was the last of the Spaniard.

Now we will set fire to Fort Van Buren, according to instructions, and proceed to erect Fort Alexander, which I named in honor of Mr. Alexander Culbertson.

Having burned Fort Van Buren, I left with 20 laboring men for Adams Prairie, 20 miles above by land, about 40 by water. With the exception of having my horses stolen by Assiniboines on two occasions, and going on a bear hunt with Indians, which latter incident I will narrate, nothing took place at Van Buren worth mentioning. The theft of the horses put me to a great deal of trouble, and was a great drawback in the building of the new fort. One fine evening, early in September [1842], a certain Crow returned from searching for his horses, saying that a Mr. Grizzly was breakfasting on one of them, and that, as one man was not enough to make the bear let go his prey, he came for assistance. A bear being considered by Indians a more dangerous enemy than a man, a good force was raised, and I, wishing to see the fun, volunteered to go with them. We soon came to the spot, where we saw Bruin lying fast asleep behind the remains of his breakfast. Knowing that Indians considered it braver to strike an enemy after he had been shot down, than to shoot him down, I was prepared to be very brave. When we were within 30 steps, one of the Indians made a little noise, at which the bear awoke and rose up to see who were the intruders. A volley was fired; the bear dropped dead behind his breastworks, and we all counted coups upon his carcass with our ramrods, I among the first.

Soon after that Mr. Chouteau returned from St. Louis to Fort Union, having gone down with Father De Smet,[50] who was on

[50] Father Pierre Jean De Smet, the notable missionary to the Indians of the Great Plains and Rocky Mountain areas, whose career is sketched in John Bidwell's *Echoes of the Past about California, The Lakeside Classics* volume for 1928, p. 24. De Smet was in the company of California emigrants to which Bidwell belonged, and the latter conceived a great admiration for him, describing him as "a genial gentleman, of fine presence, and one of the saintliest men I have ever known." A recent brief account of his career is in *Dict. Am. Biog.*

his way from the Columbia to the States.
His most important news was that a strong
Opposition had arrived; the firm was Fox,
Livingston and Co. of New York. They had
come up in a steamer, with a large outfit,
and were building a Mackinaw boat for the
Crows' trade of the Yellowstone; so that we
should have opposition here. This news I
did not relish; for opposition is necessarily a
great nuisance.

In the meantime the work on Fort Alexander was progressing finely; my men were
good hands, determined to put up a well-
built little fort, which was very near com-
pletion by the 15th of November [1842]. I
was already in my quarters, very comfortably located, thinking that I was going to
pass a pleasant winter with my family. Like
all other traders I had taken a better half,[51]
who had made me the father of my first
child on the 9th of last August. But all these
fine expectations were ended by the unexpected arrival of Mr. Murray, who had been
engaged to take charge of Fort Alexander,
with letters from Mr. Culbertson requesting
me to return immediately to Fort Union,

[51] This was Larpenteur's second Indian wife, the first
having died in the smallpox epidemic, Aug. 4, 1837.
The story of the tragic death of the second is narrated
post, 259–61.

where I was wanted mighty bad in the liquor department. This was not the first time I had found out that being a sober man was no advantage to me.

I left next day with one man and two horses—one to ride and one to pack. As it was cold, and snow on the ground, I had to leave my better half behind. One of our horses soon gave out, and our trip of eight days was a tough one.

I should remark here that, about two weeks before I left Fort Alexander, a gentleman by the name of Frederick Groscloud arrived in charge of a Mackinaw boat, with a fine equipment. He had been formerly in the employ of Mr. Tulloch, and understood the Crow language, but was not considered a person of much force of character.

Chapter 10

(1843–44)

WINTERING AT WOODY
MOUNTAIN

ABOUT the 1st of December, 1842, I made my entrance again in Fort Union. It was at night; a large trading party were at the highest pitch of drunkenness; boss and clerks not far behind them in this respect. But I did not find it strange or surprising. Mr. Culbertson, on seeing me, remarked, "Well, Larpenteur, I am mighty glad to see you. We are having a hot time, and I'm tired of it. I suppose you are tired, too, and want to go to sleep." I supposed that he, having drunk so much, did not think about eating, for I had not got that invitation as yet, so I replied, "I'm not so tired as I am hungry." "Well," said he, "there's plenty to eat." I ran to the kitchen, and the cook got me up a rousing supper. I ate too much, and next morning found myself foundered; but I had received orders to resume the grog department, and, notwithstanding my stiffness, went on to set things in order. They needed it very much.

Wintering at Woody Mountain

In the course of time I was informed of the cause of this appointment. A certain individual by the name of Ebbitt had, a year previous, brought up a small equipment and made his way as far as the Sioux district. He had a small Mackinaw with 12 men, which was considered by the American Fur Company too slight an affair to oppose; in consequence of which he made a very profitable return of 500 packs of robes. Elated with his success he went to New York with his returns, and there formed an acquaintance with the great firm of Fox, Livingston and Co., telling them how cheaply he had traded, and also remarking that the American Fur Company so abused the Indians and clerks that everything was working against them—in fact, if a large company, such as would inspire confidence among whites and Indians, should be organized, the American Fur Company would soon leave the country. This story took well; such a company was formed, and started in charge of a gentleman by the name of Kelsey, one of the members of the new firm. Mr. Kelsey had not ascended the Missouri very far before he began to regret what he had done, which was that he had put $20,000 into the concern. The farther he came up river the more he regretted it; and when he arrived at the mouth of the Yellowstone and saw Fort Union in its full splendor, he could not refrain from remarking to Mr. Culbertson, "Had I known how the American Fur Company were situated, I would have kept clear of investing in this opposition"; and concluded by saying, "I hope you will not be too hard on us." The old gentleman went off, leaving a man named Cotton in charge. Mr. Kelsey, who, according to agreement, was to remain in the Indian country and make his headquarters among the Sioux, chose a point 20 miles below Fort Pierre, opposite a beautiful island. Upon this there were four men living in a small cabin, which he considered his. He ordered them several times to leave; but they paid no attention to him, and remained in possession. One morning the old gentleman armed himself and determined to make the men leave. On entering the cabin he fired at one of them, who was in the act of taking a kettle off the fire, and who fell dead in the fire. Another one, who ran out, was also shot, and fell dead over the fence. By that time a third man, who was trying to escape in double-quick time, was shot through the shoulder, of which wound he came near losing his life. During the following night the old gentleman made his escape. I was informed that he went to Mexico. This was the last of Mr. Kelsey.

Mr. Cotton, the person left in charge at Fort William, which he now called Fort Mortimer, had not yet got dry—he was still green cotton, full of Mr. Ebbitt's stories about the general discontentment of Indians and whites. He soon commenced to try his hand on one of the most important chiefs of the tribe, Crazy Bear, who, like many others, on learning that a big Opposition had arrived, came in with his band to pay them a visit. Mr. Cotton invited him into his room, made him a great speech, dressed him up in a splendid military suit, such as had never been brought into the country before, and then laid a two-gallon keg of whiskey at his feet. Crazy Bear's band was at Union, waiting for his return; but, instead of going directly to them, he went into Mr. Culbertson's private room, not very drunk, took a seat, and remained some time without saying a word. Mr. Culbertson, surprised to see him so splendidly dressed, and thinking that he had lost his chief, was also silent. Finally Crazy Bear broke the ice by saying, "I suppose you think I have left our big house. No; I am not a child. I went below to see the chief, who treated me well. I did not ask him for anything. I did not refuse his presents. But these cannot make me abandon this house, where are buried the remains of our fathers, whose tracks are yet fresh in all the paths leading to this place. No, I will not abandon this house!" After which he rose from his seat and took off his fine fur hat and feathers, which he threw on the floor with all his might; then unbuckled his beautiful sword, with which he did the same; and kept on till he had stripped himself of all his fine clothes, without speaking a word. When this performance was over he said to Mr. Culbertson, who stood in great astonishment, "Take away all these things and give me such as you see fit, and don't think I am a child who can be seduced with trinkets." This Crazy Bear, who was not at all crazy, proved afterward to be the greatest chief of the Assiniboines.

Mr. Cotton, on hearing of this, was so surprised he could scarcely believe it; but when Mr. Culbertson showed him the suit which had been badly torn, he was convinced, and began to think that Mr. Ebbitt's stories had been somewhat exaggerated. That was the way the green cotton commenced to dry. Still, his trade was pushed to the extreme. He had plenty of goods and was very liberal with them. Both sides then began to send out men to the Indian camps; but as all the most important camps were soon supplied, I began to think that I might escape that disagreeable trade. Being always an unlucky man, I was still disappointed in this.

One evening toward the last of January [1844], while I was thinking of anything but that which was forthcoming, Mr. Culbertson sent for me to come to his room. It was extremely cold and a great deal of snow was on the ground. This, I believe, was the reason he did not broach the subject at once, but finally said, "Larpenteur, I want you to go to Woody Mountain,[52] to a camp of Crees and Chippewas, who have plenty of robes, and have sent for traders from both companies. The Assiniboines have also sent for traders at the meat-pen, which is on the same road that you are going. I want you and Mr. Denig to go into the store, get up your equipment to-night, and start in the morning." Such were my orders, at short notice, after thinking I was going to remain at the fort. I had to make a trip of at least

[52] Woody Mountain is in present-day Saskatchewan, a few miles north of the international boundary. It is "a long, irregular mass of drift," making a series of elevations running East and West, mainly between 106° and 107° W. Longitude.

100 miles, northward into the British possessions, and this was not calculated to make me feel very good. But Mr. Denig and I went to work, and at midnight the equipments were ready. Next morning with one sled apiece, two mules and one driver to each sled, we started on our journey, accompanied by several Indians, among whom was one called Wounded Leg, chief of the band of the Rocks, whose camp was at the sand hills, about 60 miles on our road from the fort to Woody Mountain.

At our first camp my interpreter, a half-breed named Andrew, was taken sick; he complained of headache, and in the morning he was so ill that I had to let him go back to the fort. I understood some little Cree, and, as many of them spoke Assiniboine, I thought I could do without him. Next day we reached Wounded Leg's camp, and took a night's lodging with him. My friend Denig had been for the past few days in such a state that it was impossible for him to freeze—he was too full of alcohol. He had not walked one step; this disgusted the chief, who proved an enemy afterward. The morning was so stormy that we would not have left camp had we not learned that the Opposition had gone by with dogsleds. Not wishing to be outdone by them, I awoke

Mr. Denig, who was still under the influence of liquor, and told him that we must be off—that the Opposition had gone by, and that if they could travel I did not see why we should not. When the chief saw that I was determined to leave, he remarked that it would be well for us to go; that a certain Indian was expected from the fort with a large keg of whiskey, and that it would not be well for us to remain in camp while they were drunk; for, as he knew, we had to leave Mr. Denig behind. The mules were soon harnessed up, and into the hard storm we started, with but one Indian, who was my guide. It was an awful day; we could see no distance in any direction, floundered in deep snowdrifts, and knew not where to go for timber. But our guide was a good one, who brought us to a small cluster of scrubby elms. The snow had drifted so deep that we could find no dry wood and had to go to bed without a fire. We made ourselves as comfortable as we could by digging holes in the snow for shelter. We were then only a little distance from the meat-pen, where Mr. Denig was to stop, and reached it early next day. Mr. Denig wanted me to remain with him over night, but as he had to make a liquor trade, and I did not wish to be serenaded, I declined his kind offer. Having packed the contents of my sled on my two mules, and left the sled, which I found to be a nuisance, I proceeded on my journey to Woody Mountain. After this snowstorm the wind changed to a strong, extremely cold northwester. There were only three of us—myself; my guide, a young Chippewa; and my driver, a young Canadian named Piché, which means pitcher. As my poor Pitcher contained more water than whiskey, I was much afraid he would freeze and crack; but he was made of good metal, that could stand heat or cold. Early this evening we came to a good camping place, with plenty of dry firewood; but it was so intensely cold, and we had to dig so deep in the snow to make a fireplace, that it was with the greatest difficulty we could start a fire. But we succeeded at last in making a comfortable camp—the best one we had had since we left the fort. A little while after this we were sitting at a good supper of dried buffalo meat, a few hard-tacks we had saved, and a strong cup of coffee. After supper arrangements were made for sleeping, as a bedroom had yet to be cleared out, in a deep snowdrift, where my friend Pitcher was to be my bedfellow. We proceeded to excavate, and soon had ourselves buried alive in the snow. I believe this was the coldest night I ever felt. The guide got up first, to make a fire, to the delight of Pitcher and myself. A breakfast much like our supper was soon ready, the mules were packed, and we were off again. We had not traveled more than an hour when the wind rose, and the snow began to drift, so blinding us that we could scarcely see. We had over 10 miles to travel to timber; but, fortunately, we were on the main road, which the Indians had made so hard, in going from one camp to another, that the drifting snow could not lodge on it; so the tracks remained visible, which enabled us to reach camp in good time. At sunset the wind fell, and we had an easy time in making preparations for our last night out. There being no road between this place and the Indian camp, which was 20 miles off, over level prairie, and wishing to reach the camp in good time, we made an early start next morning.

The day was clear, cold, and calm. In my small outfit I had about five gallons of alcohol, in two kegs of three and two gallons, neatly packed in the bales of goods. I thought this quantity would be too much to bring in camp at once and concluded to cache one of the kegs on the road, for I knew it would be impossible to keep it concealed in the Indian lodge. In order to do this my guide must be dispatched ahead, for I did not think he could be trusted. So, when we got within about five miles of the camp, I remarked to him that I wished him to go on into camp and tell Broken Arm, the chief of the Crees, that I wished him to prepare me a large lodge and make ready for a big spree to-night. To this proposition the guide readily consented, and, having pointed out the direction of the camp, he left on a dog-trot. As soon as he was out of sight and we had reached a place that my friend Pitcher would be sure to find again, we cached the smaller keg in a snowbank and resumed our journey.

We had made but a few miles when we came in sight of Indians; but, as we could see no lodges, we presumed they were Indians returning from a hunt. We soon discovered men, women, and children; still no camp, and the prairie looking level as far as the eye could reach. We could not imagine what this meant, and were not relieved of our uneasiness till some of the bucks came running up and told us that there was the camp, pointing to a deep valley. Having gone about half a mile we came to a precipice, on the north of which the Indians were camped, near the bottom. It was an awful place; I could not imagine how they could stand such a place without freezing, for the sun did not reach them more than two hours out of the twenty-four. "Now," said I, to my friend Pitcher, "we are north of north here." "Yes, sir," said he, "and we'll freeze. I can't see what made them d——d Indians camp here." For the first time my good Pitcher was overflowing with bad humor, and indeed I did not blame him, for the prospect of staying in such a hole was anything but encouraging. But there was no alternative; we had to enter the lodge—a large double one—which we found already prepared for our reception. After our mules were unpacked and our baggage was arranged, a kettle of boiled buffalo tongues was brought in; a strong cup of coffee was made from our own stores, and we took supper alongside a good fire, after which symptoms of good humor returned.

Being now ready for operations, I sent for water, telling the Indians it was to make fire-water, and it was not long in forthcoming; the news circulated through the camp, and before I was prepared to trade the lodge was full of Indians, loaded with robes, ready for the spree. The liquor trade commenced with a rush, and it was not long before the whole camp was in a fearful uproar; but they were good Indians, and there was no more trouble than is usual on such occasions.

This was the first time that I ever felt snowblind; during the spree, which lasted the whole night, I complained considerably of sore eyes, attributing it to the smoky lodge. They told me the lodge did not smoke, except at the place where it ought to, and said I must be getting snowblind. This I found to be the case, and, though I was soon over it, it was bad enough to be extremely painful. By morning I had traded 150 fine robes, about all there were dressed in the camp, and during the day I traded 30 more for goods. I then feared no opposition, as their robes were nearly all traded—that is, the dressed ones. We had plenty of leisure after that, but tremendously cold weather. It frequently happens in that part of the country, that, after a clear, calm morning, a cloud rises in the northwest about ten o'clock, and in a very short time a tremendous snowdrift comes on, which lasts all day; but the weather generally becomes calm at sunset, turning very clear and cold. Such weather we were blessed with most of the time we remained there, which was about six weeks. Imagine the pleasant time we spent in camp under that steep hill, where I am certain the sun did not shine more than 24 hours altogether during those six weeks.

Wintering at Woody Mountain

The third day after we arrived I sent my Pitcher to see how the mules were getting along; the Indians had them in their charge, but I wanted to know their actual condition from a surer source during such intensely cold weather. The Pitcher was so benumbed that he was unable to tell the news on his return until he had warmed his mouth, which appeared so stiff with cold that he could not move his jaws; but I could see in his countenance that something was wrong. Being anxious to learn what the matter was, and giving him scarcely time to thaw out, I said, "Well, Pitcher, how are the mules?" "Ha! the mules both froze dead—one standing up, the other down. My good fat white mule standing up—thought she alive, but she standing stiff dead." By this time his jaws had got limber, and he made them move at a great rate, with some mighty rude expressions in regard to the place where we were. When well warmed up he began to crack a smile again, and all went well until a couple of days afterward, when I found him so much out of humor one morning that I thought surely my poor Pitcher must be broken, or at least badly cracked. When breakfast was served by the wife of Mr. Broken Arm, the great chief of the Crees, who had been to Washington,

Pitcher would not partake. "What is the matter, Pitcher," said I, "are you sick? Why not have some of this good fat buffalo meat?" "Not much the matter," he replied; "I will tell after a while"—fearing perhaps that the story he had to tell would not agree with my digestive organs. Some time after that, when the things were removed, dishes washed up, and the cook had gone out, my Pitcher poured out his story. "Mr. Larpenteur," he said, "if you please, after this I will do our cooking." "Why so," said I. "Why, sir, because that enfant de garce—that old squaw is too dirty. Sacré! She scrape the cloths of that baby of hers with her knife, give it a wipe, cut up the meat with it, and throw into the kettle. This morning I see same old crust on the knife—that what the matter—too much for me." After this explanation I was no longer surprised at poor Pitcher's looking so broken; and if my digestive powers had not been strong, as they have always proven to be, I am afraid my own breakfast would have returned the way it went; but with me, whenever the meat-trap was once shut down it was not easily opened again, and things had to take their natural course.

Shortly after the death of our two mules, I traded a pony of an Indian, and Pitcher would now and then go to see how the animal stood this latitude. Then the time came when I thought the Indians might have robes enough dressed to raise a frolic; so one morning I sent for the keg of alcohol I had cached on the road. Not wishing the Indians to know what we were about, on their asking where my man was going, I told them he was going to look after my pony. He delayed longer than they thought necessary, and they remarked it; but finally he appeared in the lodge with the keg on his back—that being the kind of a pony he had gone to take care of. I was soon prepared for operations, and another glorious drunk took place; but the robe trade was light, only 50 in number. This ended the business, there being no liquor and hardly any robes left in camp.

I then sent the Indian to Fort Union with a letter for Mr. Culbertson, requesting from him the means to bring back the robes I had traded. Notwithstanding continued severely cold weather, ten days afterward a party of eight men and 20 horses arrived in camp, in charge of the hunter of the fort, Antoine Le Brun. Those men had suffered so much with the cold that it was almost impossible to recognize them—noses, cheeks, and eyes all scabby from frost-bite, and so dark from exposure that they looked more like Indians than white men. Mr. Culbertson's letter was anything but satisfactory, its contents being about as follows: "Larpenteur, I send you 20 horses, thinking them sufficient to bring in your trade; if not, try to get some good Indians to help you; tell them I will pay them well. From what I can learn some Indians, who are moving north on your route, have said they will steal all your horses; therefore I advise you to take a different route."

Now, what to do? The snow was drifted so deep in all the hollows that I could not possibly take any road but the old beaten one. To go any other way would be at the risk of freezing to death—or at least of losing all my animals in the snow; I preferred to take the chances of being robbed and perhaps beaten on the old road.

Next morning by ten o'clock we were under way, with all my trade. I had some few goods remaining, which I carefully concealed between the packs of robes, so that they could not be seen by the Indians whom we expected to meet; and I kept a few trinkets in sight, to make some small presents, should it be necessary. With much difficulty we made out to extricate ourselves from the awful abyss into which we had plunged when we came to this camp. The morning was clear, but extremely cold, and as we reached the level prairie we perceived the usual cloud, indicating a snowdrift. Not long afterward it came on, so bad that we had great trouble to keep our horses in the track. As the old saying is, "There is no bad wind but what will bring some good." This wind was one of them. We should have reached our camping place in good time, had it not been for this heavy snowdrift. A little before dark, when we came to camp, we were surprised by the barking of Indian dogs, which appeared to be not far off. The country was here very broken, and wooded with small oaks. We concluded that this was the camp of the very Indians who intended to rob us. Owing to the heavy snowdrift, which had lasted all day, they had not discovered us, and we arrived unknown to them. Finding ourselves undiscovered, I told the men to make no noise, build no fires, and early in the morning to go for the horses, as I wanted to be off by the peep of day. Some were reluctant to obey orders, but consented to do so on my telling them they did not know what might happen. Sleeping without any fire, in such cold weather, was certainly a hardship, but I thought it necessary for our safety. Supper

was made on a little dried buffalo meat—
about all we had. After a long, sleepless
night, at break of day the horses were all
brought up to pack, and at clear day we
were under march. On the first hill we ascended we perceived an Indian with his
hand on his mouth, which is a sign of surprise. He called out, "Ho! ho! have you
traveled all night?" I answered, "No, we
camped at the spring." "Why," said he,
"did you not come to our camp? You would
have been well off with us—we have meat,
sugar, and coffee." I told him that if I
had known the camp was so near, I certainly would have gone there. All this time
my men were filing by, and as each one
passed me I told him to hurry up; that I
would remain behind with my packhorse,
and get out of the scrape the best I could.
The news soon reached the Indian camp,
and in a little while I was surrounded. Their
main object was to trade horses, and they
wanted me to stop my men. I told them
the men would not stop; they were cold,
and had gone too far off. "Well," said they,
"we have got a few robes we would like to
trade." I found from their actions, after my
poor excuse for declining the horse trade,
that they were not so badly disposed as
Mr. Culbertson had represented them to be;

yet, if they had got the chance at night, I believe they would have relieved me of some of the horses, if not the whole band. They brought a few robes, which I traded; and not wishing my men to get too far off, I made the Indians a present of what little stuff I had left. When they found I was so generous they let me go in peace, with my good Pitcher, whom I had kept by me.

With much relieved hearts we started double-quick, and soon overtook the party. We found them delighted at our good success, and glad they had followed my advice, saying, "If we had been discovered, we should not have one horse left, and God knows what would become of us." One said, "Did you see that big painted rascal, how he look? Bet you he'd have mounted one of them"; and, after several such expressions, it was agreed among them that I was a first-rate leader.

The day became pleasant, we traveled well, and came to camp at the meat-pen, where we fell in with two Indian lodges. One of these was that of He Who Fears his War Club, a respectable and brave man, who I knew could be relied on. After we had gotten everything righted in camp, the old fellow told me to come to his lodge, that he had something to tell me. As we had little to eat in camp I was in hopes that I would get a supper out of him, and perhaps something for my men to eat; but I was disappointed in that, for he was as bad off as we were. On entering he bade me sit down; and having smoked a few whiffs, he asked me if I had heard the latest news from the fort. I told him I had learned none since the news brought to me by my men. "Well," said he, "something very bad has taken place since, and, if I were in your place, I would not go to Wounded Leg's camp; for he has had a quarrel with Long Knife (meaning Mr. Denig) and your chief (meaning Mr. Culbertson). They took him by the arms and legs and threw him out of the fort, and he has sworn vengeance against the whites. It will not be good for you to go to his camp, or even in sight of it, for I tell you he is very mad."

This news struck me pretty hard. I had got out of one scrape, but was already in another; this was something else for me to cipher on that night, and if my stomach was empty my head was full. On my return to camp I was asked what the old fellow had said; the men suspected that all was not quite right, so I told them the whole story. "Now we are in a pretty fix again," said one. "Yes," said another, "they get drunk with the Indians and fight, but don't think much of us poor fellows on the prairie," and all such expressions. One said, "Don't go that way"; and another replied, "You d——d old fool, what other way can we go in this deep snow?" Finding them disconcerted, I said, "Don't be uneasy, boys; I'll figure out a plan to get through."

Meanwhile two strapping big bucks made their appearance in camp, and, of course, they were supposed to be horse thieves; but their story was that they were going to the fort, expecting to join a war party. Notwithstanding this, a guard was placed over them and I took care that they should have a good bed in camp, where they could be easily watched. Early in the morning all hands were roused up; our thieves were all right, but one of the old chief's little boys, about fourteen, had got up still earlier and mounted one of our best horses. He was seen in the act, but could not be overtaken. His father, a good man, was very sorry, and said that the horse would not be lost to the Company. The theft, at this time, was of great importance, as all our horses were getting very poor and weak.

From this place to Wounded Leg's camp was a good level road, about 25 miles, which we expected to make early. Now that all was ready for the move, the boys expressed a desire to know what plan I had to get them through safe. I said to them, "This is my plan: I am going on this road right straight to Wounded Leg's lodge. I know him well; he is a good friend of mine, and I am sure I can fetch him all right. When we come in sight of the camp I will go ahead alone. You can come on slowly; if anything happens to me, do the best you can for yourselves; but if things are all right, I will make you signs to come in." They were apparently satisfied, placing confidence in me and so we started; but, moving at too fast a gait, we were obliged to leave two horses, which had given out. This made three loads which had been divided on the others; it was very hard on them, and we commenced to think we should be forced to leave some of our robes on the way also.

About three in the afternoon the dreaded camp was in sight. I caused all hands to halt, and told them, "Now, boys, I am going to the camp. When you get within 400 or 500 yards of it, stop. If you see Indians coming, not out of a walk, remain until they reach you; but if they come rushing, make up your minds that Larpenteur is gone up, and defend yourselves the best you can." Off I started. When I came into camp I inquired for Wounded Leg's lodge, which was immediately shown to me. On entering I found his old woman alone. She felt somewhat surprised, but looked cheerful, and we shook hands. She had always been a good friend of mine, and I thought myself pretty safe as far as she was concerned. I asked her where her old man was. She said he had gone to the lodge of such a one. I then requested her to send for him, which she did, and a few minutes afterward he made his appearance. His countenance was not calculated to inspire confidence. Having shaken hands, he sat down and prepared to smoke, as is customary before conversing. I had to hold my tongue, but my eyes were wide open, watching the face of my enemy while he was making ready for the smoke. To my great satisfaction I thought I could perceive a change in my favor. The pipe being ready a few whiffs were exchanged, and time to break silence came. Upon which I commenced, saying, "Comrade, I have heard some very bad talk about you. I was told not to come to your lodge, or to your camp; that you intended to harm me and my men. Knowing you to be a good friend of mine, I would not mind that talk, and you see I have come straight to your lodge." His first remark was, "Who told you all this?" On my naming the individual, he said, "He told you the truth. I did say all that. I was very angry at the way in which I had been treated at the big house. But I have thought the matter over, and given up the idea of putting my threat into execution; though I am not pleased yet." I soon found that I was in a pretty fair way of success; yet something farther on my part was to be said. So, knowing the Indian character, and, for one thing, that praise of their children goes a long way with them, I commenced thus: "Now, my comrade, you know that the difficulty you had with those men at the big house was when you were all in liquor. You know very well that you are liked by the whites. You are a chief; you have a son—your only child— you love him. He is a fine boy. Although but a boy, you know that the chief of the big house has already armed him like a chief. Would you do anything to deprive your only child, as well as yourself, of chiefhood? No! certainly not. I know you too well for that." At this speech I heard the old woman groan; and, during the pause which ensued, I observed that I had them both about melted down into my affections. The idea of his boy's being so much liked and respected by the whites took the old man's fancy, and a pleasanter or more cheerful chap could scarcely have been raked up.

"Now," said I, "this is not all. I want my men to come in camp and stay with you to-night, and I want you to go to the fort with me. I assure you they will be glad to see you, and I will see that you are well paid for your trouble." Turning to the old lady, I added, "I will send you a nice cotillion."[53] "How!" said she, which meant "Thank you!" Then Wounded Leg said, "That is all right, but you must not come into this camp; it would not be good for you. We are starving, our dogs also; they would eat up your saddles and the cords of your packs. You had better go to camp in the cherry bushes," which he then showed me about a mile off.

Taking his advice, I started back to the boys, and when near them made signs for them to come on. Meeting me and learning the result of my mission, they could not help laughing at the way I had "buttered the old fool," as they said. We steered our course for the cherry bushes, which we reached at sunset. The wind had changed to the north; it became again very cold, and to save our lives we could not get a fire out of those green bushes. There was not a stick

[53] A piece of cloth for a dress.

of dry wood to be found, and a tremendous hard night we had. Sleep was out of the question, and it was too cold to stand a good guard; the result was that the two bucks, who had followed us thus far, disappeared with two of our best horses, one of which we called Father De Smet, because he had been brought from the Flatheads on that missionary's return from the Columbia. We were then nearly 50 miles from the fort, which distance would have taken us two days; but now, being short of horses, it would take us double that time. I found an Indian, whom I knew to be a good traveler, and asked him if he could go to the fort by sunset; he said he could, for he had already done it. I dispatched him with a letter to Mr. Culbertson to send me more horses, and also some dried meat, as we were starving. Dividing the loads as best we could, we got under way again, making but slow progress, with Wounded Leg, several other men, and some squaws in company. We again camped, as we all hoped for the last time; but where was supper to come from? We had not a thing to eat and were mighty hungry. I thought of trying rawhide cords, of which we had a few bundles left. I got a squaw to cut them up fine and boil them; besides which, as a great favor, I got an Indian dog killed and boiled. That I knew would be good; and as I could not obtain more than one dog, the cords, if the cooking proved successful, would help to fill up. I am sorry to say that I was defeated there, for the longer they boiled the harder they got, and they could not be brought into condition to swallow. So there was only the dog for supper. I had sent it to a squaw to cook for us, and when she gave it to us some of the boys cried, "Mad dog! mad dog!" Sure enough, he did look like a mad dog; for there was his head sticking partly out of the kettle, with a fine set of ivories, growling as it were, and the scum was frothing about his teeth. After the mirth had abated, and no one offered to dish out the "mad dog," I appointed Pitcher master of ceremonies, thinking a pitcher could pour out soup and hold some of it too. He commenced with great dignity, but some of the boys refused to partake, saying they would rather be excused, and could stand it until they got to the fort. This made the portions so much the larger for the balance of us; the biggest part of the thigh fell to my share, which I soon demolished, and I must say it sat very well on my stomach. But some of the boys began to say the "mad dog" was trying to run out the same way he went in; and some noises heard outside might have been taken to signify that the animal was escaping.

It was no trouble to get all hands up next morning, but some of our worn-out horses had to be whipped up. When once loaded and warmed up by means of the whip, they could only be made to keep on their feet by the same cruel means, which we were obliged to use pretty lively all the morning. Between the hours of eleven and twelve o'clock we perceived the re-enforcement from the fort, at which a great cry of joy was heard throughout the company. The loads were soon rearranged; each man took a piece of dried buffalo meat in his hands to eat on the way; the march was resumed, all eating and whipping, as there was no time to spare to reach the fort that day. Owing to those double exertions, by sunset we were on the ridge, in sight of Union and of its fine large American flag. This had been hoisted on our return from an expedition which had caused much uneasiness, from the many reports which had made it doubtful whether we could ever get back. We were also in sight of the Opposition, and I afterward heard that Mr. Cotton, on seeing us, said, "Well, Larpenteur was not badly robbed— see what a fine lot of robes he has!" In ten minutes after reaching the ridge we were safe in the fort.

Chief Wounded Leg, like the rest of us, met with a cordial welcome; and as a large trading party had just arrived, a keg of liquor was presented him, to drink with his friends. Among them was a certain Indian named The Hand, the greatest rascal in the tribe, it was believed, who had retaken two horses from some Assiniboines who had stolen them from the fort, and he had come to return them, in company with us. In some drunken spree he had killed an individual whose relations were in the trading party above mentioned. Fearing that he might be killed, I remarked to Mr. Culbertson that it would not be advisable to let him go out and drink with the other Indians— better let him have a little liquor in the fort, and if he got too troublesome we could tie him. This plan was adopted; and as I was much fatigued, I retired, telling Mr. Culbertson to awaken me in case they could not manage him without me. He got so drunk they could do nothing with him, and insisted on leaving; so the door was opened and the gentleman turned out. Early in the morning, I was again on duty. The doors were still shut; but, being tired of hearing a constant knocking, I went to see who was there. By the sound of the voice I knew who he was, and that he was all right; so I opened the small door. "Here," said the Indian, "I killed a dog last night. Take him in and shut the door." This dog was Mr. Hand, whose corpse had been wrapped up in his robe and bundled on a dog-travaille. So much for him, and we were not sorry, as he was a devil.

Shortly afterward we learned that another individual had killed his own father. I shall have occasion to mention him again. Some time before our return I learned that my interpreter had died about eight days after he reached the fort, complaining of headache. The vulgar said he died of the hollow horn; and others, of the hollow head. My good friend Pitcher, I was informed long afterward, struck for Virginia City, where I hope he became a pitcher full of gold.

Chapter 11

(1844-45)

CARNIVAL OF CRIME

JIM BRIDGER,[54] being a great trapper, and having been told that there were many beaver on Milk River, thought of trying his luck in that direction. He left the mountains with a picked party of 30 men, all good trappers and Indian fighters. Nothing unusual transpired at Fort Union until about the month of November [1844] when Bridger and his men made their appearance, having come from Milk River with

[54] James Bridger was a native of Virginia, who while still a young boy was taken by his parents to St. Louis. In 1822, when but eighteen years old, he joined General Ashley's expedition to the Upper Missouri, and in doing so entered upon the career as trapper, trader, and frontiersman which was to make him famous. In 1843 he established Fort Bridger on the Oregon Trail in southwestern Wyoming, and until driven away by the Mormons in 1853, this was the center of his many activities. He was the first known white discoverer of Great Salt Lake (in 1824); over thirty years later he guided thither the army sent by the government to reduce the Mormons to its authority. He died in 1881. His career has been advertised in published biographies and on the silver screen.

the intention of passing the winter with us. Mr. Laidlaw, who was in charge at the time, offered him all assistance he could afford, to make his winter quarters pleasant and comfortable, and so Bridger pitched his camp about half a mile from the fort. But he had been deceived by exaggerated reports of the quantity of beaver that could be had on Milk River, and his hunt had been a very poor one. The main substance of Bridger's conversation was his brave men, his fast horses, and his fights with Blackfeet, till we were induced to believe that, with such a party to defend us, there would be no danger for us in case of an attack by Sioux. At that time such affairs became quite frequent, and the Sioux generally came in large parties. Bridger soon had an opportunity to display the bravery of his men, whom he had cracked up so highly. A few days before Christmas [1844] a large war party made a raid on the band of horses belonging to the fort, running off six of them, and wounding one of the guard in the leg with buckshot. The alarm was immediately given, and the braves were mounted to pursue the Sioux. Bridger's clerk, who had been left in camp, came running into the fort out of breath, scared to death. "Get up all the men you can! The Sioux are in camp—they are butchering us!"

Carnival of Crime

Mr. Denig and I, with a few men, all we could get, took our guns, and ran with all our might to render what assistance we could. Finding that this was a case in which we had to be cautious, we went along under the steep bank of the river till we thought ourselves about opposite the camp, where we stopped to listen for the cries of the reported butchering. Hearing nothing, we cautiously raised our heads over the bank, to see some of the performance. Neither seeing nor hearing anything, we came to the conclusion the murderous work had been done, and determined to go to the camp, expecting to find people cut to pieces and scalped. To our great surprise we saw nothing—not a sign that any Indians had been near the camp. Now assured that Bridger's brave clerk had lied, we returned to the fort laughing at his fright.

During our absence on this dangerous sortie, Mr. Laidlaw was left alone—that is, without a clerk. I had, in my hurry, taken the key of the store with me, and pressing demands were made for ammunition. Mr. Laidlaw, who was a fiery, quick-tempered old Scotchman, smashed in the window of the retail store. Seeing this, on our entrance, we could not imagine what could have been the matter. No word had been received from

Bridger's army, but we expected them to
return with the recaptured horses and with
scalps flying. But soon, to our great disappointment, came the report that a man
had been killed; that a mare belonging to Mr.
Ellingsworth, the Opposition bookkeeper,
had been shot through the hip, and that the
Indians were daring the whites to fight. The
Opposition, who had seen Bridger's men turn
out to fight, had concluded to join them.
Mr. Ellingsworth had bought this fine American mare of Mr. Laidlaw, who had brought
her here in the fall. An old half-breed Creek
was also well mounted, and they both very
soon came up with Bridger's party, who had
halted at the foot of the hills. When Ellingsworth and the old man approached they saw
the cause of the halt; the Sioux were on a
hill, making signs for them to come on and
fight. By this time their party had been re-
enforced, and Bridger's men, not accustomed
to deal with such a large force, declined the
invitation. The old half-breed, who was
clear grit, put the whip to his horse, telling
the balance to come on; but only Ellingsworth followed. The Sioux, who understood
this kind of warfare, and expected the whites
to accept the challenge, had left concealed
in a ravine a small body of their party, ready
to let fly in case the enemy attempted to

come on. As the old Indian went by at full speed with Ellingsworth, the Indians fired a volley, which dropped the former dead off his horse, and wounded Ellingsworth's mare in the hip; but did not come so near killing her that Ellingsworth could not make his escape. The Indians, seeing this, commenced to yell, and renewed their defiance. But the brave party concluded to turn back, somewhat ashamed of themselves. Bridger was extremely mortified, and said he could not account for the cowardice of his men on this occasion. At the funeral of Gardepie—that being the name of the old man—these words were pronounced: "This burial is caused by the cowardice of Bridger's party." This expression, it was thought, would result in a fight with the Opposition; but the discontentment disappeared without any disturbance. In the meantime the Sioux went away, having killed one man, wounded another's mare, and taken six head of horses. Bridger became very much dissatisfied with his men, who dispersed in all directions, and he returned to the mountains.

Before I come to the story of the Blackfoot massacre, which is not yet known, I will explain the manner in which trade was carried on this winter [1844–45]. Owing to the local laws which were put in force, we were not allowed to go into Indian camps to trade; the trade had to be done either at the fort, or at an outpost allowed by the agent. So we had to drum up Indians to get them into the fort, and be on the lookout for trading parties coming in. Being well supplied with horses, which we kept constantly in the fort, we had a great advantage over our opponents, who were deficient in that respect. As soon as our pickets, whom we always kept out, in every direction, made the signs agreed upon, we immediately mounted; and, according to signs understood by us, the required number of horses followed. With our pockets full of tobacco and vermilion, we galloped as fast as we could, in order to get ahead of the Opposition, and induce the Indians to consent to come to our fort. But frequently, whether yes or whether no, their robes were put on our horses, and taken to the fort. When the party was large, and some trouble was expected in bringing in the chiefs, a sled was brought out, having a small keg of liquor placed on it, to treat the gentlemen; and a band of music, bearing the flag, was also in attendance. The instruments consisted of a clarionette, a drum, a violin, and a triangle, besides the jingling bells on the sled, and it was almost impossible for Indians to refuse such an invitation. They laughed with delight at the display, and the Opposition could not "come it over them," as the saying is. Mr. Cotton found himself about as badly used up this winter as he had been last; he learned that he stood a poor show in opposing the American Fur Company, and that it would take Mr. Ebbitt, or any other man, a long time to get a footing in the country.

This winter [1844-45?] we learned that Mr. F. A. Chardon had had a fight with the Blood Indians, a band of Blackfeet bearing that name; but no particulars were known until the arrival of the returns, which generally came down the latter part of April or the first part of May. At that time I was well informed on the subject by Mr. Des Hôtel, one of the clerks, in whom full confidence could be placed.

Mr. Chardon, who, as has been stated, was the man who [in 1843] built the Blackfoot post at the mouth of Judith River, generally called Fort Chardon, happened to have a man killed by that band of Blood Indians last winter.[55] This man was a negro

---

[55] Although the affair here described is sufficiently celebrated it seems difficult to fix with certainty its date. Coues fixes upon the winter of 1842-43 as the date of the massacre. The present Editor has elsewhere given the date as 1844; the evidence available does not justify disputing Coues' chronology.

by the name of Reese. Mr. Chardon, it appears, set great store by that negro and swore vengeance on the band. He communicated his designs to Alexander Harvey, who, wishing no better fun, agreed to take an important part. They also got old man Berger to join them. The plot was, when the band came to trade, to invite three of the head men into the fort, where Harvey was to have the cannon in the bastion which commanded the front door loaded with balls; when the Indians should be gathered thickly at the door, waiting for the trade to commence, at a given signal the three head men were to be massacred in the fort, and Harvey was to kill as many others as he could at one discharge; on which they expected the surviving Indians to run away, abandoning all their robes and horses, of which the three whites were to become the owners, share and share alike. But it did not happen quite to their satisfaction; for, through some means, the wicked plot was made known in time for the chiefs to run out of the office and escape by jumping over the pickets. Mr. Chardon was quick enough to shoot, and broke the thigh of the principal chief. Harvey touched off the cannon, but, as the Indians had commenced to scatter, he killed but three and wounded two. The rest quickly made their escape, leaving all their plunder; but saved nearly all their horses, most of which were at some distance from the fort. After firing the shot, Harvey came out of the bastion and finished the wounded Indians with his large dagy. I was told he then licked the blood off the dagy and afterward made the squaws of the fort dance the scalp dance around the scalps, which he had raised himself.

I will conclude this chapter with one more of Harvey's awful deeds. It happened that, while he was at old Fort McKenzie, some Indians, who had a spite against the fort, took it into their heads to kill some of the cattle. One day a party of five chased away some of the milch cows, one of which they shot when they had gone a short distance from the fort. On learning this, Harvey and some others got on their horses and went in pursuit. Harvey, who always kept a No. 1 horse, soon overtook the Indian who had shot the cow, and when he got within a few steps fired and broke his thigh; the Indian fell off his horse, and there he lay. Harvey came up to him, got off his horse, and took his seat near the wounded Indian, saying, "Now, comrade, I have got you. You must die. But, before you die, you must smoke a pipe with me." Having lighted his pipe and made the poor Indian smoke, he then said, "I am going to kill you, but I will give you a little time to take a good look at your country." The Indian begged for his life, saying, "Comrade, it is true I was a fool. I killed your cow; but now that you have broken my thigh, this ought to make us even —spare my life!" "No," said Harvey; "look well, for the last time, at all those nice hills— at all those paths which lead to the fort, where you came with your parents to trade, playing with your sweethearts—look at that, will you, for the last time." So saying, with his gun pointed at the head of his victim, he pulled the trigger and the Indian was no more.

Chapter 12

(1845–46)

POPLAR RIVER CAMP

THE steamer made her appearance at the usual time, in June [1845], Mr. Honoré Picotte in charge. As it was customary for all the partners to meet in St. Louis in summer, I was left in charge of Fort Union until one of them returned in the fall. I asked Mr. Picotte what kind of men he had brought up; to which he replied, "First-rate men." "Will they not be apt to desert?" "No," said he, "not one." My fear of their desertion was based on their probably being unwilling to go to the Blackfoot post, on account of the massacre of last [?] winter. The steamer left the same day, in the evening. During the night I was made the father of a fine son. In the morning the artillery was playing, and, in consequence of this, something extra must be done. All hands had a holiday, with the promise of a big ball at night. Scrubbing, washing, and cooking went on all day, and at night the ball opened; it went off peaceably, which was rarely the case in this place. All hands retired in good time, and had a good night's sleep. Mr. Auguste Chouteau, who was clerk and had charge of the men, came to my room early in the morning, saying, "Mr. Larpenteur, twelve men left last night." Although I expected some desertions, I did not think any would occur until the men were notified to go to the Blackfeet; but they had been persuaded by some of the Opposition who came to the ball, and being afraid they would have to go, they thought best to disappear while they could get employment elsewhere. I had still many men left, went on preparing the outfit, and in a few days all was ready for their departure. James Lee had been sent for by Mr. Chardon, who had heard he was a bully and a bravo. Lee was to go up to the Blackfoot post, and it afterward appeared that he intended to chastise Harvey. During the outfitting we learned enough to induce us to believe that a plot had been made to pound Harvey on their arrival, but not to murder him. Mr. Chardon was then at Fort Clark, his old station. Mr. Culbertson was in charge of the Blackfoot outfit, with the understanding that he was to burn down Fort Chardon, and build farther up the Missouri.

I finally succeeded in getting the outfit all right, but with a frightened set of men. As they pushed off a large number of the Opposition men were on the shore, crying out to them, "You are going to the butcher-shop —good-by forever!" But the boys, who felt the effects of a good jigger to which they had just been treated, scoffed at this, and went off finely. After this I had the Crow outfit to start off; but there were plenty of men left for this, and for my own use at the fort. Early next morning Mr. Chouteau came to me again, saying, "Seven more men gone last night." This was rather a striker, but on counting the number left, I found that I could send up the Crow outfit, and went to work at the equipment. The following morning, however, three more had deserted, and others kept leaving, one by one, until I had to abandon the Crow outfit. Desertions continued until I was left with but four men all told. This number being too few to keep the fort in safety until the return of the gentlemen in the fall, I immediately dispatched Owen McKenzie, the son of Kenneth McKenzie, with letters to Fort Pierre, to be forwarded thence to St. Louis. Much were they astonished when the dispatch arrived. Men were immediately engaged and sent up by Mr. Denig, who had gone on a visit to his friends this summer. Having so few men with me, the Opposition men became very troublesome; so much so that I had to lock the door on them.

Shortly after the return of McKenzie from Fort Pierre, a party of Sioux came to war on the Assiniboines, and had taken all the horses belonging to the Opposition when the alarm was given. We ascended the bastion to see the performance, but it was all over, and the Sioux made bold enough to sit on the hill, quietly smoking their pipes, in full view of both forts. McKenzie, who was very young, active, and brave, said to me, "Mr. Larpenteur, this is too bad; let us go and exchange shots, and see if we cannot get back some of those old plugs." As I agreed to this, we ran down at once, mounted the two swiftest horses in the fort, and off we went. Bullets were soon flying about us, but we succeeded in recapturing four head of horses, which we generously gave back to the Opposition, and our names went high up among the bucks and squaws who were singing and dancing around the fort.

After this times passed off somewhat more smoothly. Mr. Denig, who had been started up with a new supply of men, arrived early in October [1845], and things became quite lively again. Soon after his return, when we were sitting on the porch one evening, we saw Harvey walking up to the house with

his rifle across his arm. At a little distance
he stopped to ask, "Am I among friends or
enemies here?" Being told that we did not
think he was in any danger here, he entered
and commenced his story with, "Boys, I
came very near being killed." Being asked
by whom, he replied, "By Malcolm Clark,[56]
Jim Lee, and old man Berger; but the d——d
cowards could not do it." Then he pulled
off his hat, showing the mark of Clark's
tomahawk, with which his head had been
broken; and his hand was injured where Lee
had struck him with a pistol. Being then

[56] Malcolm Clark was the son of Captain Nathan
Clark of the Fifth U. S. Infantry, who served many
years in the western country, at Fort Snelling, Fort
Winnebago, and other posts. Malcolm Clark attended
West Point for a time. His career there was terminated
by expulsion after a quarrel in which he whipped an
adversary with a rawhide. He later went to Texas
where he served in the struggle for Texan independence,
and subsequently to the Upper Missouri, where he
engaged in the fur trade, married a squaw, and established a ranch where he lived a semi-patriarchal life.
He was passionate and impulsive, and although his
talented relatives have defended his name, much re-
quires explanation. In 1864 he killed Owen McKenzie,
as described by our author, *post*, 298, and in 1869 he
was himself murdered by Indians of whom he is said
to have been the benefactor. Sketches of his career
by his sister, and by his daughter are in Montana Hist.
Soc., *Contributions*, I, 90–98, and II, 255–68.

asked the particulars, he said that, on learning of the arrival of the boat, he got on his horse to meet it and learn the news, as is customary on such occasions. Having gone about 20 miles below the fort, he saw the boat, and beckoned them to land. As he had been left in charge of the fort, they could not well refuse to do so. As the boat landed he gave his horse in care of the man whom he had taken with him, and suspecting nothing, but glad to see the men, he jumped on board and entered the cabin where the three gentlemen were sitting. He offered his hand to Clark, who said, "I don't shake hands with such a d——d rascal as you," on which a blow of his tomahawk followed, and then a blow with the butt of a rifle from Berger. In spite of all this he would have succeeded in throwing Clark into the river, had it not been for Lee, who struck him such a severe blow on the hand with a pistol that he had to let go his hold and make his escape. "I then got on my horse," he continued, "and when I arrived at the fort I told the men my story. They were much displeased, and as they did not like Clark, and had already learned Lee's character, they consented to protect me. I told them that I intended to hold the fort and not let a d——d one in."

To this the men agreed, and preparations were made for defense. When the boat arrived no one was allowed to enter, not even Mr. Culbertson. But after hard pleadings Mr. Culbertson, who had always proved a friend to Harvey, made him agree to give up the fort, on condition that Mr. Culbertson should give him a draft for all his wages, and a good recommendation. On receiving those papers, Harvey left in a small canoe with one man.

He remained but a couple of days at Union, and, on leaving, said, "Never mind! you will see old Harvey bobbing about here again; they think they have got me out of the country; but they are damnably mistaken. I'll come across Clark again."

Fort Pierre was then the headquarters of the trading posts on the Missouri; all drafts and papers had to be examined and signed there. The company owed Harvey $5000, and he had to get his draft there for the whole amount. Mr. Picotte appeared somewhat slow and did not come to time until Harvey threatened to pound him, when the draft was made out.

It happened that, when Harvey arrived at Fort Pierre, the most important clerks of the post were dissatisfied with their treatment, and had made up a company in opposition to the American Fur Company. The members of this new organization were Harvey himself, Charles Primeau, Joseph Picotte (nephew of Honoré Picotte), and Bonise, the bookkeeper of Fort Pierre, under the firm name of Harvey, Primeau and Co. Under those agreements, which were not known at the time, Harvey immediately left for St. Louis. There he apprised Colonel Robert Campbell of the arrangements, and in the spring [1846] the company started operations, with a large outfit, sufficient to establish themselves at all the posts of the American Fur Company. Harvey came up to the mouth of the Yellowstone in the steamer, and went on to Benton in a Mackinaw with his outfit.

A short time after Harvey left us Mr. Kenneth McKenzie arrived to take charge of Fort Union. He had left the country six or seven years previously, but had reserved a share in the Company, on condition that in case of opposition he would return, should it be deemed necessary by the members of the Company, and on that understanding he now returned. This was about the commencement of the meat trade [of 1845]; on his arrival my charge ended, and I was reinstated in the liquor shop. Mr. McKenzie was pleased with my administration; he found everything to his satisfaction, and said I had done well, though I ought not to have left the fort, at a time when I had so few men, to fight Indians.

The American Fur Company, having always had more influence in this country than the Indian department, thought they would abolish the local law, and carry on trade on the old principle, which was camp trading. So when the robe trade commenced, traders were dispersed in all directions. But Mr. McKenzie, like Mr. Culbertson, kept me at the fort until the last. Finally my turn came, and I was sent with a good outfit into a large camp on Poplar River, about 60 miles by land above Union. As a matter of course I took plenty of liquor. I had four men and ten horses—more than I wanted—but the intention was for me to send them back loaded with meat for the fort. A certain Indian by the name of Iron-eyed Dog was known as the greatest rascal and ugliest Indian in the camp; his brother had been killed while camped at the fort by a war party of Sioux, who surprised them in the night. This brother was a chief, called the One who Guards the Whites—a very good Indian for us to have. He was shot in the back, the ball passing through his breast. The Indians, knowing that the whites thought much of him, and believing their medicine might cure him, brought him to the fort from camp, which was not more than 300 yards off. That happened about midnight. Shortly after he was brought in his brother, the Iron-eyed Dog, came knocking at the door to be let in; but as many others had knocked, we paid no attention to him. This made him extremely angry, and he swore he would kill me on the first opportunity, for he knew I was the doorkeeper. Such was the character with whom I expected to have to deal in this camp, where I arrived on the third day out from Union.

After I had stored everything properly, I was invited into the lodges of the chiefs and leading men, to partake of a dish of pounded buffalo meat and marrow grease, as is their custom. In one of the lodges, where several Indians had assembled, I was informed that Iron-eyed Dog, whom they call in their language Shonkish-ta-man-zah, had gone to the fort, but was expected back that night, and would be apt to make much trouble, and very likely kill me; but they thought I might be able to reconcile him by talking to him and making him a little present, as usual on such occasions. Knowing the Dog of old, I invited the principal chief to my lodge and gave him what he thought was sufficient; he started off, saying that he, with the others, would do their utmost for me. This was some consolation, but did not go very far toward making me feel safe.

That night, when the liquor trade commenced, the very devil was raised in camp. Iron-eyed Dog, who had arrived, and all the other dogs, including my life preservers, soon got drunk. There was I, with only four other men, among about 300 drunken Indians, with no alternative but to trust to luck. One stout, fine-looking Indian whom I had never seen before, and who suspected something, took his seat by my side, holding a large war-club between his knees, and kept very quiet the whole time. At first I did not know what he was there for, but soon found out; things were as I suspected and feared. Suddenly in came Iron-eyed Dog in great fury, saying, "Here you are! Do you expect to live through this night—you who would not open the door for me when my brother was killed? Did I not say I would kill you?" He went on like this at a tremendous rate, and then rushed out again. But it seemed to me that he did not like the looks of the man with the war-club, who now and then pressed his hand on my knee, as much as to say, "Be not afraid." Then came two more drunken Indians; one of them named

Cougher, and the other an individual who had killed his own father; both had plotted with others to murder me in the lodge and plunder my outfit. But it happened that I had a good old friend in camp, whose name was The Haranguer, and who made such a fine speech that they abandoned the idea. This is about as near as I can interpret it: "What is it that I hear? Brothers and kindred, do you think you will need your trader no longer, now that spring is come and trade is over? You have your fill of everything, and now talk of killing your trader. Where will you go? Go north and starve? Give away your hunts for nothing? Why kill this poor white man? What has he done to you? No, brothers! have pity upon him, upon me; spare his life." On his saying this, which they understood to be the conclusion of his speech, a young man got up and handed him his knife, as a sign of approval, and so the idea was given up. My war-club man all this time said never a word, but the repeated applications of his hand inspired a sense of safety in my badly frightened heart.

After that came the One Who Killed His Father, and Mr. The Cougher, when all the liquor was gone, wanting absolutely to get some more, saying, "If you have none, make some. You whites are strong medicine.

You can make fire-water." Seeing, however, that I was not "medicine," they insisted on my giving their squaws some trinkets, and off they went, saying that they would soon be back. Then in popped the Dog again, and came at me with his pipe, saying, "Smoke! smoke! Why don't you smoke? I'll make you smoke—you dog, you." This Indian knew I seldom smoked, and only during some of their ceremonies, so he kept running in and out in this manner, and never left the lodge without threatening to kill me.

At last this night, so long to me, wore away; when day came all was quiet in camp, and I felt as though I had been on board a vessel in a gale which had subsided in a perfect calm. After such a storm my appetite was not very sharp, but we had to get breakfast early, before any Indians came loafing in. A strong cup of coffee was soon ready; this revived me, but the dread of seeing the mad dog again was still heavy on my mind. My war-club man was gone, and I saw no one about me that would be likely to take my part. Iron-eyed Dog soon made his appearance with about 20 of his young men, all armed and painted, and I thought then surely I was gone up. The Dog was quite sober, and said to me, "It was a good thing for you that I got too drunk to come to your lodge once more last night, for I did intend to kill you. Now you must give each of my young men some ammunition, tobacco, and vermilion, a knife, and a looking glass; and give those," he continued—pointing to four or five—"a breech-cloth apiece." This being done, he ordered them to go away; "and now," said he, "give me my present." So I gave him 50 rounds of ammunition—the usual allowance for a big man—eight small plugs of tobacco, one knife, one palette of vermilion, and a breech-cloth. To his squaw who was present, I gave a cotillion of cloth, some beads, and other trinkets. He went off without saying another word and I never saw him again; but what became of him will be made known in the sequel.

The trading being nearly over, I sent to the fort for horses to bring in my returns, and five days afterward eight men arrived with 32 head of horses. Mr. McKenzie advised me by letter to be very cautious on my return, as a party of young men had gone up my way with the intention of stealing the horses; to stand strong guard each night, and, if possible, get some good Indians to come with me. I had all my returns ready to be loaded, and next day we got under march with 35 packs of robes, besides some small furs. The second night we reached Big

Poplar River Camp

Muddy River, about 30 miles from Union. This being a place which I thought dangerous, and likely to be my last camp, I stood the first guard, with one-half of my party. I had taken with me one of the first chiefs of the Indian camp, with three of his most reliable soldiers, which made our party rather strong. About eleven o'clock I discovered the gentlemanly horse thieves coming straight into camp; they shook hands, seemed glad to see us, and after smoking a while laid down to sleep. Seeing us so well on our guard, they gave up the idea of robbing us; early in the morning they took their leave, and glad we were to see them off. The morning was fine and warm, which enabled us to get an early start. We expected to encamp at the Little Muddy, ten miles above Union; but arriving there about two hours before sunset, and not liking the idea of another night's guard, we concluded to push on to the fort. After smoking a pipe we resumed our march, and entered the fort a little after dark. The fort was full of drunken Indians, as usual. Mr. McKenzie was extremely glad to see me back, and began to tell me how things had gone on during my absence, saying he was at a loss how to get through with all those drunken Indians, with the traders he had in that shop. Finally he said, "Larpenteur, I am forced to ask you to finish this trade, although I know you must be tired. I have been frequently tempted to go and trade myself, but you know that would never do." Finding the old gentleman in such trouble, although much fatigued I went into the shop after a good supper, traded all that night, finished the business, and got the Indians off next day.

This [1845–46] winter's trade convinced the New York firm of Fox, Livingston and Co. that it was a losing game to oppose the American Fur Company; they came to the conclusion to sell out, and we were again left masters of the country.

Chapter 13

FORT LOUIS AND THENCE TO ST. LOUIS

EARLY in the spring [of 1846] Mr. McKenzie left on a Mackinaw boat for St. Louis. Nothing of importance took place after his departure until the Company's steamer again arrived, at its usual time, Mr. Honoré Picotte in charge. Mr. Culbertson, who went up a previous summer [in 1844], had burned down Fort Chardon, and gone on with his outfit, according to understanding, to build another post. He had selected, for that purpose, a site five or six miles above Benton, on the south side of the Missouri, named it Fort Louis, and left Mr. Clark in charge. From what motive I cannot say, Mr. Picotte wanted him removed, and on that account arranged with me to go up with the outfit and take charge. I was then getting $600 a year, which he increased to $700. On the 8th of July [1846] I found myself on board a keel boat called the *Bear*, with 30 men on shore, the tow cord on their shoulders, going at the rate of about 1½ mile an hour, with upward of

800 miles before us. On board were one steersman, two bowsmen, two cooks, and one hunter, who had two men with him and three horses. The boat was well rigged for sailing in case of fair wind, and supplied with sweeps and poles. Though we started at the rate I have said, few know what slow progress is made in such navigation. The banks of the Missouri are lined with thick rosebushes and bull-berry bushes, which are thorny, and sometimes attain the height of 12 feet. Such thickets being impenetrable, men must be sent ahead of the cordelle men, as those who tow the boat are called, to prepare a path for them. Besides this, snags and other incumbrances must be chopped down to clear the cordelle, poling is always slow work, and there are rapids to be overcome, of which I will speak when we reach them. It takes Canadian French boys to do all this, on meat alone, or only lyed corn, when meat cannot be obtained.

At this slow rate we finally reached a place called Amell's island, a little below the [Picotte's] rapids, where I stopped to make a Mackinaw boat to lighter up the rapids, and also to enable me to keep on to Fort Louis, as the river was very low. A few days after I commenced my boat two men on horseback appeared on the opposite shore.

They were sent for and on landing informed us that Harvey had arrived at the mouth of the Yellowstone with a large steamer in opposition, and was making a Mackinaw boat to go up to trade with the Blackfeet. Those men had been sent with a letter to me, requesting me to send them on post-haste to Fort Louis with a letter to Mr. Clark to engage all such freemen as he thought might be of service to Harvey. They were dispatched immediately, and a few days afterward Mr. Clark unexpectedly made his appearance. As I had not sent his letters, he thought that I was coming to take the charge, and that he would have to serve under me; and after reading his letter from the Company, observed that he would not have served under me had he been ordered to remain, for the reason that he had been a long time with the Blackfeet and thought himself entitled to the charge during the absence of the owner. This Mr. Clark had been educated at West Point, and was extremely punctilious. The next day he started back to Fort Louis.

In about a week my boat was finished, we were under way again, and soon came to the rapids. Our lightener did not avail us much, for the river was so low that both boats had to be completely unloaded, and the goods to be carried 400 or 500 yards over the rapids, on the men's backs. The boats were pried over by main force, after clearing the channel of rocks; but this was done with the intention of throwing those rocks back into the channel, so as not to let Harvey overtake us.

Under such slow progress I reached Fort Louis 70 days after my departure from Union. But I must remark that I had great sport hunting. The points above Milk River being cleaner of rubbish than those below, I commenced my hunt from that river, and the boat was so slow that I had plenty of time. I killed 35 deer and 15 elk. On arrival at Fort Louis I met with Father De Smet, who was again on his return from the Columbia to the States. In about three days Clark left in a skiff with two men, and then I remained in full charge. The fort was a good one, well arranged for the time which had been spent on it. I was pleased, and getting along so finely that, had my family been with me, I should have been perfectly contented; but I had left them at Union.

One fine Indian summer day, about the last of October [1846], Mr. Clark unexpectedly made his reappearance, having received orders at Fort Pierre to return to Fort Louis, and take charge. I felt mortified at having my charge taken away from me, and not even receiving the scrape of a pen from any one. Feeling myself slighted and remembering what Clark had said to me in regard to his charge of forts, I remarked that I supposed he would be willing to admit that the rule should work both ways. "I am not willing to serve under you," I said; "I have been in this Company's service ten years longer than you have, and I think that ought to entitle me to a charge—or, at all events, to justify me in not serving under you. So I am going to Fort Union." Upon which he remarked that he had nothing to say in the matter, and if I made up my mind to go, he was willing to supply me with the means for my trip.

All the men were displeased with the way I had been treated, and angry to see Clark in charge; for they disliked him as much as they had Harvey. They proposed my remaining in charge, and assured me they would see me through all right, if I would say the word. But I thanked them, and the second day after Clark's arrival I left on horseback with a first-rate guide named Joseph Howard, one of the oldest hands. Our journey was a pleasant one, but with nothing worth mentioning, and on the 15th of November [1846] we reached Fort Union.

My reception by Mr. James Kipp, who was in charge at the time, was rather cool— "Well, Larpenteur, what brings you down here?" On my relating to him the circumstances, said he, "I am sorry for all that, but I have nothing to do with it. Mr. Picotte engaged you, this is all his doing, and you must see him about it. My arrangements are all made for this winter. I cannot give you employment." Thus finding that I should not be a pleasant subject in the fort this winter [1846–47], I made up my mind to leave, bag and baggage. So I immediately got some buffalo hides to make a bull-boat, and in two days after my arrival was under way for some lower post, hoping to be able to reach Fort Pierre. This was about the 20th of November [1846], altogether too late for such a journey; but the weather was fine and I thought I might reach some point where I could pass the winter, and thus keep out of Fort Union, where I did not think myself welcome. But the weather changed suddenly, and the next morning after leaving Union, full of ire at finding that I could not proceed any farther, I was obliged to return.

I must say that Mr. Kipp was fair enough with me. He furnished me with a room for myself and family, and provided my firewood and water, which had to be hauled from the river, all free of charge, and also allowed me to trade all the dried meat I wanted, charging myself what was thus expended. This enabled me to pass a half-pleasant winter; but, doubting that I should ever be re-engaged, I made up my mind to leave the Company, and take my family to the Flathead Mission,[57] of which Father de Smet had so favorably spoken to me. So I made arrangements with Mr. Kipp to build me a boat, in which I was to leave early enough to reach the States in time to get off with the Mormon emigration.

According to agreement the boat was ready, and on the 5th of April [1847] I left Fort Union with my family, consisting of six children, accompanied also by Mr. Latty, son-in-law of Mr. Laidlaw, who had come up in the fall for his health, and two men. We had a pleasant trip, excepting some high winds, which sometimes caused us to remain as much as three days camped in the willows, and one fright from a war party of Rees.

When we stopped at Fort Clark, Mr. Des Hôtel, who was in charge, told us that a party of 22 Rees had gone to war on the Sioux in 11 bull-boats, two in each boat; but

[57] In the Bitterroot Valley, near Stevensville, Montana.

remarked that there would be no danger for us, as the partisan was a young man friendly to the whites. "This partisan is the son of Old Star," said he, pointing to the old man, "and there is Old Star himself"; and a very fine looking fellow he was. The following morning we left, expecting to meet them on that or the following day, as they had started the day we arrived; but it was not till the second day, about noon, that we discovered the party. Although we had been well armed at the fort, and were not in much danger for ourselves, we could not feel entirely safe, on account of my family of Assiniboines, who were deadly enemies to the Rees; for I knew the latter to be worse than any others, in taking revenge on women. But we were soon discovered by them, and on we had to go. As soon as we came near they commenced to yell at a great rate, and in a moment our boat was surrounded. All those that could get hold grasped our boat; but this appeared to be done in good humor. As we thus drifted along with the current, they gave us some of their provisions, which were little balls made of pounded parched corn, mixed with marrow fat, and some boiled squashes; in exchange for which we gave them some fine fat buffalo meat. Ahead of us there was a boat which we afterward found contained the partisan, who, having given his orders, had gone on to find a suitable landing; and in a little while his party, who held us prisoners, landed us in his presence. He was a very fine-looking young man, and had his pipe ready for a smoke; but he understood so few words of Assiniboine that I could make out little of what he said, and was anxious to be out of the clutches of his party. I got out what tobacco I had, a good bundle of dried buffalo meat, and some sugar, of which I knew they were fond, and after this made a sign that I wanted to proceed on my journey; upon which he gave me the sign to go, charging me not to let any one at Fort Pierre know they were under way. Under such fair promises we took our leave of the gentlemen, having fared much better than we expected.

On we proceeded again, quite jovial, and praising the partisan, who we hoped might exchange his boats for horse-flesh, as that was what the party were after, and take some Sioux scalps, if these could be obtained. As we went along I began to think of what kind of a reception I should have from Mr. Picotte at Fort Pierre, which I somewhat dreaded to enter. But as I was a free man, who owed the Company nothing, I did not think there would be much danger in approaching him; and if he would not let me come into his fort, I could very well sleep outside, as I was used to it by this time.

At last we came in sight of the fort, and as ours was the first boat down this spring, many persons came to the landing to see who had arrived, and to learn the news. A little before landing, I saw Mr. Picotte at the head of the crowd, who had made way for him to be the first to receive us. He looked very pleasant, and I supposed he was glad to see Mr. Latty, who handed him the mail; but I soon found him well disposed toward us all. He shook hands with me in a very friendly manner, and invited me up to the fort, saying, "Never mind your baggage; I will send the wagon for it, and for your family." This was rather a surprise to me, who expected anything else but such a kind reception. We walked up to the office, where he opened the letters, read several, and after a while said, "Larpenteur, come to my room." I could not think what this private invitation meant, and supposed it would end in a scolding; but as he had been so kind as to invite me into his fort, and send for my family, I did not think it would be a very serious one. There was no one else in his room, where he bade me be seated, and then asked abruptly, "What made you leave the

Company?" I replied that I had not left the Company; that I had left Clark only. After I had related the particulars he smiled and said, "It is true, Larpenteur, that I ought to have written to you; yet you did wrong—you who have been so long in the Company should have overlooked that, knowing how much we thought of you; and it would have been better for you, if you did not want to serve under Mr. Clark, to have remained at Fort Louis until the arrival of Mr. Culbertson, who you knew was to be up in the fall." To which I remarked that probably that would have been better, but that it would have been very disagreeable for both of us. "Now then," he continued, "I am told that Mr. Kipp treated you badly last winter. Did you have any words with him?" I then told him such reports were false; that I had no complaint to make against Mr. Kipp. "Well, now, here is a draft of $200 on your friend Johnson in St. Louis, in favor of the Company; what is that draft for?" "It is for provisions which I got during the winter," I replied. He then tore the draft to pieces and threw it into the fire. "Now," said he, "how much did you expect to save of your wages this year?" I told him that according to arrangements I had made with Mr. Denig, the clerk of Fort

Union, I expected to save $300, if not more. "Well," said he, "come to the office; I will get the bookkeeper to make you out a draft on the Company for $300."

While the clerk was making out the draft supper was announced, and well was I prepared for that. After supper we all retired to the office, where most of the conversation was on the great discovery of gold in California, this being the first that we had heard of it; for the news had just reached Fort Pierre, and some could scarcely credit it.[58] Mr. Picotte then said to me, "What are you going to do with your family? Are you going to settle below?" After telling him that my intention was to go on to the Flatheads, in company with the Mormon emigration, he said I should be too late for that; but, if I wished, he would give me a letter to Bordeaux, the person in charge of Fort John on the Platte, where I could remain all winter and proceed on my journey early in the following spring; or, better than that, I could engage with the Company for another year, make arrangements with them to take me up as far as Fort Benton, and go from

[58] There is one evident error here. Gold was discovered in California on January 24, 1848. If the news came to Fort Pierre in the spring, it was the spring of 1848 instead of 1847 as here indicated.

there to the Flatheads. This was very kind of him. Being prepared to go either by the Platte or by the Missouri, and convinced that I stood fair in the estimation of the Company, I left Fort Pierre next morning in great glee, holding Mr. Picotte high in my esteem.

On reaching the settlements, I learned that the Mormon emigration had gone, and that I was too late. So I went down as far as St. Joseph, Mo., where I left my family, and immediately proceeded to St. Louis, where I arrived in time for the Company's steamer to the Yellowstone. I made arrangements to serve one season, and they were to bring up my small outfit for the Flatheads the following summer. Everything being thus arranged to my satisfaction, I took my family on board at St. Joe, and after a pleasant trip of six weeks we reached Fort Union on the 27th of June [1847].

Chapter 14

(1847-49)

FORT BENTON AND ELSEWHERE

A FEW days after my return to Fort Union I was reinstated in my former department; but as some of the clerks had gone to the States, and were not to return till the fall, I had an addition to my duties, having the retail store and the men to command, besides the trade. All went on smoothly, excepting that a war party of Sioux attacked the men at the hay field, wounding one, and killing four oxen which had been hitched to the shafts of the carts, in Red River fashion. The men came running, out of breath, to report the attack, saying they thought the oxen were all killed. I then took two Spaniards, mounted the best horses in the fort, and went to see how matters stood. On our arrival at the spot, ten miles from the fort, we found three carts turned over, the animals dead in the shafts, and the fourth ox standing in a ravine with several arrows in him, mortally wounded.

The usual time for the fall express arrived, and on the 15th of October [1847] Mr. James

Fort Benton and Elsewhere

Kipp and suite made their entrance into Union, including Mr. James Bruguière, his nephew, who had formerly charge of the retail store and command of the men. So I was relieved and had only to attend to the Indians. For some time after Iron-eyed Dog had so much troubled me, young men who called at the fort on their warpaths would ask me how I liked my comrade, the Iron-eyed Dog; to which I would very imprudently reply that I had made my medicine for him, that I thought would be as strong as theirs if not stronger, and that they would find it out before the summer were over. Should anything happen to him after I made such a declaration my chance to escape unhurt would be small. To my great astonishment, a party of Blackfeet happened to surprise the Assiniboines during the summer and shot the Dog through the back. This was a bad shot for me, although I must confess that I was not sorry to hear of it, but the scamp was not killed. This news kept me somewhat uneasy. Harvey's Opposition boat having been icebound 18 miles below Union, he concluded to winter there; so a trader had to be sent from Union to oppose him, and I was chosen, for Mr. Kipp did not like to send his own dear nephew. So, toward the last of October [1847], I was dispatched

with an outfit to build in opposition to
Mr. Husband, that being the name of the
gentleman in charge. I dreaded going to this
place, for we had learned before arrival of
the Opposition that the Dog had been killed
by the Rees. At this time a good strong
peace had been made with the Assiniboines
by the Gros Ventres, Mandans, and Rees,
and in the fall they would visit and trade
corn. Mr. the Iron-eyed Dog was a great
gambler; he had won a large quantity of
goods from the Rees, and was returning to
his camp well packed, when a small party of
Rees overtook and shot him. My medicine
was strong! Now his brother was in the
camp where I had to go and build, on the
bank of the Missouri, and the Dog had been
killed about three weeks before. If I had been
uneasy before, imagine how I felt now.

On my arrival in camp I was invited by
the chiefs and most of the leading men into
their lodges, as usual. After accepting many
invitations, I returned to my own lodge,
which I found well lined with visitors. A
little while after I had taken my seat, hoping
that invitations were all over, a little Indian
boy came in, saying, "He invites you."
Indians do not like to mention each other's
names, on which account there is often
trouble to get at the right name. At last one

said, "He is the brother of the one who was killed by the Rees—look out for him!" "Now," said I to myself, "here is another scrape"; but knowing the Indian character, and understanding their language, I thought I could get out of it. So I followed the boy to the lodge. On entering, I saw a great six-footer, in full mourning—that is, daubed all over with white clay, legs full of blood, head full of mud, and hair cut short; indeed, he did look like a monster. On my entering, without shaking hands he bade me sit down, and then commenced to light the pipe without saying another word. During this time I did my best to assume a sad countenance, to correspond with his own. At last he got through with the preparation of his pipe, lighted it, and having handed it to me, said, "I suppose you have learned of the misfortune I have met with." I then answered, "Yes, we have, and on learning this sad news we were all very sorry. It is true your brother was troublesome when in liquor, but this we always overlooked, knowing it was not his fault, and, aside from liquor, he was a good man—a good robe-maker, whom the chief of the post thought a great deal of. I have heard my chief say that he thought the Dog would become the chief of the band of the One who Holds the Knife [Gauché];

and indeed I was of the same opinion." The poor fellow, or the villain, thinking by my talk that he had lost a greater brother than he had supposed, burst into a tremendous lamentation, which I did not know how to take; but it did not last long. During my confab a small wooden bowl was placed before me, filled with pounded buffalo meat and a few pieces of marrow fat; but I had already been to so many feasts that I could not partake of this. When I thought the mourning ceremony over, I told the monster my reason for not eating, said that I would take it to my family, and asked him to send his little boy with me for the pan. This is customary with them. The little boy followed me to my lodge. Having shaken hands with him, I gave the boy a large plug of tobacco, put some hawk-bells, some vermilion, a knife, and various small trinkets in his pan, and sent him back. My success was so great that I got all this man's trade during the winter, and he remained my best friend. So much for having buttered him so well!

During this winter [1847–48], myself and James Bruguière, who each had an Indian family, formed a partnership to open trade with the Flatheads. We sent down our requisition and were to go up in the keel boat to Benton, where we were to proceed to the

Flatheads with a wagon and pack-horses. Mr. Culbertson had moved Fort Louis down the previous spring [of 1847], this being the season after Fort Benton was built.

The steamer, which never failed, arrived on time [in the summer of 1848], bringing up our requisition. Being put in charge of the keel boat I started on my second trip to the Blackfeet. Unfortunately for us the river was even lower this season than it was last and we were 90 days on our trip. The Flatheads had news that we were coming, and as they were at peace with the Blackfeet, a party had come to Fort Benton, thinking it was about time we arrived. They had been disappointed, but left word where we could find them, saying they would assist us over the mountains; but we were frustrated in this good thing.

A band of Blackfeet, called the Little Robes, after the name of their chief, instead of following the rest of the tribe north after trade was over, remained on the south side of the Missouri. Some of Little Robe's young men happened to have a fight with the Flatheads; some one of each party was killed and horses were stolen. So the peace was broken, and the Flatheads returned to their country as fast as they could. This was bad news for us, as the peace had been an inducement for us to undertake this trade.

Still, go we must, and horses must be had, which could not be procured without going to Little Robe's camp to trade them; and there was some risk in that. At this time Mr. Clark was in charge of Benton, and I must say he did all he could for me. He lent me horses to go to the camp and also sent his interpreter with me; a very good one he was, and had he not been with me, it is doubtful whether I should have returned. The second day after we left the fort we came to the camp; it was yet early, and the horse trade soon commenced. This was going on finely, when an old rascal commenced a harangue, in which he said, "Why do you trade horses to that stranger? He wants them to take arms to trade with your enemies. You had better take what he has, and send him home," and a great deal of other bad talk, which at last induced them to take back their horses, for which, however, they returned to us very nearly the correct payment. All this was owing to my interpreter, for, had any other than him been with me, they never would have brought back anything, and most likely would have taken our pile. At last he said, "We had better pack up and leave; the longer we stay the worse it will be for us." Taking his advice, we packed up and went away, leaving the old scoundrel still at his harangue, and having been able to retain but two horses out of eight which we had traded. After this bad luck, we reached Fort Benton next day.

As the season was far advanced, we had no time to wait for the return of the Indians from the north, nor did we think it advisable to do so under the present circumstances. Through the kind efforts of Mr. Clark, we were furnished with two wagons, two carts, and eight pack-horses, besides the four horses to each wagon, and two to each cart; also, with ten men, and a good guide —at least, one who was thought good. It was about the end of October [1848] when we left Fort Benton again. As our horses were not well broken to harness, we had some trouble for the first few days, after which we went along about half right. On the fourth day out we reached Sun River early. My hunter had been in luck, having killed three grizzly bears, and he brought to camp the meat of the cubs, which, at this season, are very fat. It was but fun for this hunter to kill them. He came into the mountains at the same time I did, with Robert Campbell [in 1833], and had remained all this time in and about them; he had been hunter for Captain Stewart, who came out from England two seasons in succession to hunt in the Rocky Mountains.

While the fat cubs were boiling we dug the bank of Sun River to make a crossing place, mine being the first spade ever sunk in this ground by a white man, and my wagon the first to cross this stream, in the year 1848. After a good dinner we hitched up again; the river was fordable, with a good gravelly bottom, and our crossing was made without much trouble. We camped a short distance below the ford, where we had plenty of grass and wood. Our guide, who was a young Piegan Indian, had not been seen since breakfast, as he knew we were acquainted with this part of the country. We thought he might have gone in search of deer or bighorns, and were not uneasy about him till it became dark, when some began to think he had deserted us; at bedtime he had not made his appearance, and in the morning we found ourselves without a guide. Now what to do was the question. No one knew the way to the Flatheads, even by a foot path. I thought of my hunter, who was accustomed to travel through mountains, and proposed to take him with me, and try to find the Flatheads.

The next morning we started, thinking we had given our guide sufficient time to make his appearance. Expecting to find game, we took nothing with us but a little sugar and coffee; but we were mistaken in that, for when one gets in the mountains he is out of the range of game, as I found out afterward. On the fourth day, when on the summit of a mountain, there was a heavy snow, and we had eaten but one partridge and two ducks since the day after we left camp. After this fall of snow, having found no practicable wagon road, nor even any fit one for pack animals, we concluded to turn back.

At this time we had already been three days without eating. Now the fine dreams of well-set tables commenced, with no conversation at noon or at night camp, and this lasted three days longer. On the morning of the sixth day of our starvation my hunter found a mare and colt. Having traveled about two hours, we perceived a party of warriors; but, fortunately for us, we saw them first, turned back a few steps, and then struck for the roughest part of the mountains to hide and select a good place for defense, in case we should be found. During this rambling I thought of a dried buffalo sinew which I had in my bullet pouch to mend moccasins. I pulled it out and cut it in two, offering my hunter a part of it, which he refused, saying, "Eat it all; I believe I can starve better than you." So, without asking him a second time, I soon demolished the sinew, which I found excellent, except that it was too small. We at last found a good hiding place among the rocks, where we remained concealed till near sunset, scared and mighty hungry. The mare was a fine, fat one, but she had gone lame in one of her hips. My hunter, being by this time perhaps as hungry as I was, went out of our hiding place, and very soon I heard a shot. He came back, saying, "We shall have plenty to eat now." "What have you killed?" I asked. "I have shot the old mare," he replied. We both got a piece of the liver and some ribs, went to a place where there was wood, near by, made a small fire, and began to cook. The liver we threw on the embers, but the coals of tamarack pine turned it so very black that, at first, I thought it impossible to eat any. On digging pretty well into it, I found some of it eatable; but this was laid aside when the fine fat ribs were roasted. The fat tasted excellent, but the lean part was rather insipid, and appeared to need a great deal of seasoning to make it palatable. As bad luck would have it, we had forgotten our salt at last night's camp;

so I tried sugar, but that was worse than without. However, we made a fine supper, and grew a little more talkative. In the morning, having looked around as well as we could, to see if we could discover Indians, and found no signs of any, we made up our minds to get under way again, and did so, taking with us a good supply of mare meat. We now traveled without fear of starvation, though our great uneasiness regarding enemies rendered the journey very unpleasant; but we were so fortunate as to reach camp the next day, having seen nothing alarming. We found them all right in camp, but without much to eat, meat being all out. I offered them some of the meat I had, but when they found out what kind it was they declined, saying they thought they could hold out a while longer. As I did not have much left, and had got used to it by this time, I was not sorry for their refusal, now that I had pepper and salt. I can assure the reader that horse meat makes excellent steaks.

Finding no road, winter advancing, fear of war parties—all those things taken into consideration induced us to make up our minds to turn back and winter at Benton. This move, which was the best I could make under the circumstances, was anything but consoling to me. I knew that I was a ruined man. Aside from the danger apprehended on our return to Benton, my situation was an awful one; but there was no alternative. Next morning we got under way for Benton. On the following day, in the afternoon, we discovered Indians on the other side of the Missouri, yelling with all their might and making signs for us to come to them. This gave us a great fright, the women and children crying and going on at a great rate, knowing that we could not reach timber in time should the enemy rush on us. Yet nothing better could be done than to try to make the timber. Had it not been for the women and children, we would have stood our ground behind our wagons, but on their account we made for timber. In the meantime we saw the Indians going up the Missouri, not appearing to want to cross; and, applying the whip pretty sharply, we finally reached the so-much-desired timber, where, losing no time, we forted the best we could, expecting an immediate attack. Night came without further alarm, and arrangements were made for a good strong guard. Just after we had retired a tremendous croaking and cawing of crows was heard, which brought all hands up again, much frightened. The women and children being as well secreted as we could, every man stood to his gun, awaiting the attack; but, when an hour or more passed and nothing happened the fright subsided, and all came out of their hiding places—I mean the women folks and children. Then the talk was that it was a bad omen to hear crows croak at night, and my Canadians had a long sitting up, relating their superstitious stories. I thought that the crows might have been frightened by Indians, who, seeing us thus put on our guard, had concluded to delay the attack until morning. So the same guard was continued, and after a little all was quiet again.

Morning came and all was right. My hunter, who had got up earlier than the others and gone to see what he could discover, soon returned, saying that he had found out why the crows made such a noise last night. The party of Indians we had seen had passed through the timber, where they had killed two elk, taken most of the meat, and gone on their way. The crows had feasted on part of it, when Mr. Bruin, coming for his share at night, had frightened the birds away from their repast. This was the whole cause of their alarming noise. Luckily for us there was more meat than the bear and all the crows could eat, and my hunter brought enough of their leavings to make us a good breakfast. We were soon hitched up and ready to start, hoping to reach Benton the next day, provided we met with no accident on the way. Our hopes being realized, we entered Benton, all safe and sound.

Upon arrival we were informed that the Indians we had seen were those who had killed the elk we had found. They were a party going to war on the Flatheads, and had left the fort shortly after we did, having been told that we were on our way to the Flatheads, and warned not to trouble us if they saw us. They were Piegans—good Indians, who promised not to harm us; and we afterward learned from a couple of them that they had seen us and made signs for us to come after meat; but, seeing that we were frightened, kept on their way.

At the time we returned to Benton, the Indians had commenced to arrive from the north. Among them was a small Indian named Sata, a half-breed Flathead and Blackfoot, who had guided Father De Smet and others from the Flathead Mission. He said he could find a wagon road, and if I wished would show me the way. Having been inspired with confidence in him by the people of the fort, and being anxious to see the Flatheads, wagon road or no wagon road, I determined to try that famous guide.

Fort Benton and Elsewhere

The third day after my return to Benton I was on the way again, taking one of my men who understood the Blackfoot language well. I was mounted on a fine stuball[59] horse, much fancied by Indians, well dressed and well equipped; my man was also well arranged, and we felt sure this time of seeing the Flatheads. The first evening, about camping time, we fell in with a small camp of Blackfeet, who invited us to stay over night with them, and we willingly did so, saving ourselves the trouble of making camp. But it was not long before I repented of having accepted the invitation. I soon felt a crawling in my underclothes, and by morning it seemed as though I were being raised clear out of bed. I never before felt so miserable in my life, and in spite of all I could do, I could not get rid of the lice till I returned to Benton.

Our next encampment was at the Great Falls of the Missouri. The noise was so great that we could scarcely hear each other talk, but I could very well feel the graybacks hunting for their suppers in my shirt. Sata happened to kill a fine buck and we had a glorious supper. Having traveled for two days without any unusual occurrence, pretty much on the same kind of road as on my

[59] That is, piebald.

235

former trip, we reached the base of the mountains. Sata remarked that we had best try to get some meat, as game was scarce in the mountains, and now was the time to provide for ourselves. Thinking myself somewhat of a hunter I went a little ahead of the party next morning, and soon saw some objects crossing a small brook, at so great a distance that I was unable to distinguish whether they were men or game. Hoping they were deer, I slipped the cover off my double-barrel, and went after them. When in the act of shooting, I discovered on my left, behind a small hill, an object which I could not make out, but thought was probably a wolf. Sata and my man, who had come up by this time, asked me, "What have you seen?" I replied in Blackfoot, "Matahpey," meaning "people." On our advancing a few steps, fifteen naked Indians, with guns, bows, and arrows rose up before us, ready to shoot; but Sata cried out, "My brothers! my brothers! don't shoot! It is I." Hearing this they put down their arms, came up, and shook hands. They said, then, that they had discovered us, taken us for beaver trappers, and had made arrangements to kill us. As to myself, whom they took to be the chief, they had me killed already in imagination; one was to have my stuball horse, one my sky-blue coat, another my gun, and so on in the partition of my effects. The object I had taken to be a wolf was one of the Indians, who remarked himself that he had got a little nearer me than the balance of his party, and that I might be glad his gun was hard on the trigger; for he had aimed well at my breast, and I surely would have been a dead man, had he got his gun to go off. On learning where we were going, they told my guide that it was impossible for us to cross the mountains; that they had had great trouble to return, and that our animals could not get over. Thereupon, my Sata gave up the idea of going any farther, and concluded to turn back with them.

So there was another trip for nothing, except gathering an awful crop of graybacks, which I thought would devour me before my return to Benton. The Indians were delighted to see us turn back, immediately struck out on a hunt, and at the place agreed upon to encamp, came in with three fine deer, of which little was left in the morning. This was a party of young men, full of fun and mirth. I could not have been better treated than I was by them. On arriving in camp my place was prepared for me; the best spot was made as soft as it could be, by pulling and cutting small willows on which

to spread my bedding. Then the best pieces
of meat were cooked in various ways, and
given to me first of all. There were roast and
boiled meat, liver and guts broiled on the
coals, blood pudding—in fact, all that was
considered eatable of the animals. They kept
this cooking going on almost all night—
it is incredible what a quantity an Indian can
eat. With the exception of such feasts nothing took place on our return worth mentioning, and on the fourth day after falling in
with this party we entered Fort Benton again.

Although all my efforts had been in vain,
I did not yet abandon the idea of the undertaking, which I intended to put through
early in the spring. Eight or ten days after
my return, I was taken with a pain in the
breast, which I laid to my starvation and exposure, and the failure of my undertaking.
I could not help taking my disappointment
to heart, and this, I believe, was the cause
of a great derangement of my nervous system, from which I never completely recovered. Mr. Culbertson, who had returned
from the States, treated me extremely well,
and I passed as pleasant a winter [of 1848–
49] as could be expected, situated as we were.

During this winter the whole tribe of the
Blackfeet learned that our intentions were
to proceed to the Flatheads in the spring,

and remonstrated against it. The leading chiefs advised us not to go, saying that it would not be good for us, even if we succeeded in getting there safe; that we would not be safe when we got there; that there would be war parties constantly about the Missouri; and that the tribe would not go north as usual, but would remain south of the Missouri, with the intention of carrying on war with the Flatheads.

This information, from such sources, induced us to abandon the project. We sold out to the Company, and early in the spring [of 1849] went down to Fort Union with Mr. Culbertson. We left Benton in a large Mackinaw boat. Having started so early, we were sometimes ice-bound, and suffered a great deal from cold. The water was very low, and frequently we had to jump into the river to get the boat off sand bars, while there was ice running. I was generally one of the first in and last out of the water. Twenty days out from Benton we landed at Union.

On my arrival I was offered $1000 a year to take charge of Fort Alexander,[60] which, at that time, was considered the most

[60] For Larpenteur's account of the erection of this post in 1842, see *ante*, 146–49. It was on the Yellowstone, about twenty miles above the mouth of Big Horn River.

dangerous post the Company had. But, wishing to take my family to some place where I could open a small farm, on which they could remain, should I return to the Indian country, and feeling sick besides, I refused the offer.

While at Union I learned that the Company wanted to sell Vermilion Post. So I concluded to go down and see what I could do in that line. I procured a small canoe, hired one man, and started for the States. There I was, again on the march, in a hollow log, for the distance of 1200 or 1500 miles. Luckily, this time I reached Trading Point [61] without any accident, and remained there awaiting the arrival of the Company's steamer to return to Union. On my way down I stopped a few days at the Vermilion Post, but was not pleased with it, and abandoned the idea of making any arrangements there.

At last the steamer arrived. I went on board, where a letter was handed to me from my father, saying that he had sold his farm near Baltimore, and gone to St. Paul with my brother Eugene, to assist him to settle there, and also to see his grandson, A. L. Larpenteur. He was then to proceed to France, which he wanted to see once more

[61] In southwestern Iowa, opposite Bellevue, Neb.

before his death, and then to return and die in America with his children. He urged me strongly to leave the Indian country and settle near the rest of the family, where what property I might have, with what he could do for me, would enable me to live more comfortably than I could while wandering in the Indian country, exposing myself to the risk of losing my scalp.

Situated as I was, this news was well calculated to revive my hopes; but being born for bad luck, my agreeable expectations were not of long duration. Yet I had some pleasant moments, thinking that I should meet my old father again, whom I had not seen since 1838, and be united again with all the family after a separation of upward of 20 years; and I began to think that perhaps it was well for me not to have reached the Flatheads.

On reaching the Vermilion I was informed that a gentleman had just arrived from St. Paul, across the country, to take the census of the Santee half-breeds; and, at the same moment, the person himself came on board. After being introduced I asked him if he was acquainted with A. L. Larpenteur, to which he replied, "I know him very well." I then asked him if he knew whether Mr. Larpenteur's grandfather had come from

Baltimore. He answered in the affirmative, but added that he had bad news for me; which was that the old gentleman had died the third day after arrival at St. Paul, and that he, my informant, had attended the funeral.

I will leave the reader to imagine my feelings, and to sympathize with me, if there is any sympathy in him. The steamer is pushing off, and I must resume my journey, as well as my story.

During my short stay at the Vermilion, on my way down, Mr. Culbertson had overtaken me there, also on his way to meet the steamer; but, learning that there was cholera on board, he made up his mind to go no further, and to return to Fort Pierre. His reason for going to meet the boat was that they apprehended difficulty with the Indians at Crow Creek Agency, in case their annuities were not on board. So Mr. Culbertson told me, privately, of his writing to Mr. Sarpy, who was in charge, to tell him, in case the annuities were not on board, to send a dispatch to Fort Pierre, and he would come down and help to pass the boat; but, if they had the annuities, it would not be necessary for him to be there. At this time Major Hatting, their "father," a young man of about 26 or 27, was on board.

Fort Benton and Elsewhere

Five or six days after we left the Vermilion Post we arrived at Crow Creek, or as it was called, the Collins Campbell houses.[62] After the boat landed, three barrels of hard-tack were put ashore, with some sugar and coffee, and given to the Indian soldiers; after which the men were sent to take in wood, which was all ready for the boat. In the meantime the Indians, who had not been invited on board, as was customary, took offense, and knocked the heads out of the barrels of hard-tack, which they threw into the river; then they horsewhipped the men away from the woodpile, and placed a guard at the line; after which the chiefs, without invitation, came on board. After they had seated themselves one got up and said, "It is customary, when the boat arrives, to invite us on board, to shake hands, and tell us the news. What is the matter with you this year? Do you think that we have got the itch? Is that the reason you don't wish to shake hands?" Being told that their father was on board, they asked if their annuities were also on the boat. On being answered in the affirmative, they said, "Do you intend to take them to Fort Pierre?" Having been told that was the intention, the Indians remonstrated,

[62] About twenty miles above present-day Chamberlain, S. Dak.

saying they had been promised that the annuities were to be distributed at this place, and that they would have them left here; for they had nothing to do with the fort. The agent, giving no decided answer in this regard, went and sat down near the chiefs, who were all holding their heads in expectation of some reply from their father. Things were thus at a standstill for some time; but at last a tall, robust Indian got up, saying, "I am not a chief; but I am a soldier. I see that my chiefs all hang their heads down, as though they did not know what to say or do. But I know what to do." With that he struck a heavy blow with his tomahawk on the table, and then, addressing himself to the agent, said, "Hold up your head—when you speak with chiefs or soldiers, look them in the face. You are young, but we suppose you must have some sense, or our great father would not have sent you up here. My chiefs have spoken, but it seems that they have not been heard. I am a soldier; I tell you that those goods were promised us here, and they will not go any farther. I know that all the chiefs are not here yet; but we have sent for them. If you think that we want to distribute the goods during their absence you can put them in the store, and keep the key until they come; but we will not go to the fort. Do you hear that? That is what I have to say as a soldier."

The Indians were perfectly correct. I was on board the boat last season, when Major Matlock, at this very place, made them the promise and made up their requisition for the goods now on board; the Indians were then well pleased, and the major said he would throw in a box of sugar as the tail, which was 500 pounds.

During this great debate a cup of coffee and a hard tack had been presented to all who were in attendance, and as soon as the soldier and speaker was through, they all took leave. Upon consultation among the authorities it was agreed to unload the annuities—a very prudent forced move; and the following morning we were permitted to depart. Those Indians had been much displeased, the year before, with the behavior of the agent; they had shot at him while on board, but missed him, and killed one of the hands instead. We reached Union early in July [1849].

Chapter 15

(1849–55)

WITH the intention to proceed to St. Paul I got all my family on board, and shipped for St. Louis, and thence for St. Paul. On examining affairs it was found that my father had not had time to accomplish his will properly. I went to Baltimore, applied to the Orphan Court, and had the will broken. All being arranged to my satisfaction I was ready to return. Being still sick, I applied to a physician, Dr. John Buckley, who said that a sea voyage might prove beneficial to me. So I embarked on a small merchant ship, and in 45 days landed in New Orleans. I put up at the St. Charles Hotel, where I remained a week; but the climate did not appear to agree with me, and I took a steamer for St. Louis.

About the latter end of February [1850] I arrived in St. Louis, where I had to remain until navigation opened to St. Paul. During my stay I made arrangements with the Company to take charge of the Vermilion

Post,[63] on condition that, if I chose, I could purchase it at a certain stipulated price. About the 15th of March I left for St. Paul. When the boat reached Galena it was learned that the ice on Lake Pepin was still too strong, and we had to remain a few days longer. At last the captain concluded to start. On arriving at the lake, it was impossible to get through, and as it appeared to the captain that we would be likely to be detained there long, he preferred to return to Galena. After waiting there a week we again started. The ice was still strong, but by main force, cutting the slushy ice like an old ram, the boat succeeded in getting through. I believe it was on the 8th of April that she landed at St. Paul, being the second boat up that season.

I remained in St. Paul until a St. Louis boat arrived, which was on the 15th of April. Next day I got all my family on board for St. Louis. On my arrival there, the Company's steamer was not yet ready to start; so I took my family up to St. Charles to await her arrival. On the 10th of May the steamer arrived, and I went on board, bound for the Vermilion Post.

[63] In 1843 Vermilion Post was about ten miles below the mouth of Vermilion River. Whether Larpenteur's post of 1850 was at this site, or some distance up the river from it, is uncertain.

About a week after we got under way cholera broke out among the men below, and grew so bad that we boxed up three and four in a night. The boat at last stopped. We put everything out, aired and limed the boat well, and about eight days afterward started again. The disease abated, though there were a few more cases, among which was my woman; but she recovered. Finally we reached the Vermilion Post, where I was deposited for one year, very glad to get out of that steamer.

The post, the country, all pleased me well enough, but I found there was nothing more to be made in the Indian trade, and the place was too much exposed to hostile Indians for me to remain there as a farmer. The Indians robbed me of all my corn, as well as all the half-breeds who were settled near the post; they were obliged to abandon their places and most of them went to settle at Sergeant's Bluffs.[64] Had my health been good, I should have enjoyed myself well that winter [1850–51]. Trade was not bad, and there were good hunting grounds. One young Indian went out turkey hunting by moonlight, and returned in the morning with 14 fine large turkeys. I traded six

[64] In Woodbury County, Iowa, half a dozen miles below Sioux City.

of him, among which one weighed 24 pounds.

Finding that the Vermilion Post would not suit me, and learning that there were good claims to be had cheap down about Little Sioux River, I sent my clerk to see how it looked there, and if possible to purchase for me a certain claim which, from the description given, I thought would be likely to suit me. The situation was about 85 miles from this place [Fort Vermilion]. On his return he said that the claim was a good one, but that it had not been represented correctly; for, in order to have it right, I must purchase a part of the neighboring claim, and that being the case, I had better go and see for myself. A few days afterward I went down, made the purchase to suit me, also arranged to have a ferryboat built, and then returned to my post. At the time I am speaking of there was no settlement between Sergeant's Bluffs and the place I bought—a distance of 50 miles.

About the 15th of May [1851], when Mr. Honoré Picotte came down from Fort Pierre in a Mackinaw, I embarked with him, bound for Sergeant's Bluffs, from which place I intended to go down to my claim by land. We had had a great deal of rain; the Missouri, as well as all other streams, had overflowed their banks, and the bottoms were all inundated. I had to remain about 15 days at Sergeant's Bluffs, waiting for the roads to become practicable. I purchased four Indian ponies, two French carts, and hired a guide, at $2 a day, to pilot me through the water, for there was very little dry land to be seen between this and my place. About the last of May or first of June, my guide said he thought he could get me through; so we hitched up and started. The fourth day, after traveling through mud and water, we reached a place called Silver Lake.[65] Our ponies were then nearly broken down, although they had not made over 35 miles during the four days. As this was the best part of the road, my guide said that it would be impossible for us to reach my place with the carts; that we still had 25 miles to make; "and," said he, "you have not seen anything yet; wait till we get near the ferry." He advised making horse travailles, which consist of two long poles, tied about three feet apart and extending eight or ten feet at the far ends, which drag on the ground, with crossbars fastened to them behind the horse, so as to make a kind of platform on which plunder is loaded.

[65] Near the village of Whiting in Monona County, Iowa.

The travailles being thus prepared, and the children loaded on them, we proceeded on our journey. Having made about 10 miles, we camped at Laidlaw's Grove, which was afterward called Ashton's Grove, and goes by that name still. We were then 16 miles from my place, which we had to reach next day or camp in the water, as there was no dry place to be found. We could have made that distance easily in a half day had the road been good. We rose early, and having placed the children to the best advantage on this kind of conveyance, got under march, not expecting to stop to lunch, as there was no fit place. On we went, my guide taking the lead; I behind him, leading a pony, and my woman behind me, also leading one. The nearer we came to the ferry, the deeper the water became, and the sun was already approaching the western horizon. Finally it came up to the armpit of my guide, and the children were dragged almost afloat on their travailles, crying and lamenting, saying, "Father, we will drown —we are going to die in this water—turn back." At times the ponies were swimming, but there was no use of turning back; the timber on dry land ahead was the nearest point; there was nothing to be seen behind us but a sheet of water, and the sun was nearly down. So on we pushed—on, in spite of the distressing cries of the children, whom we landed safely on dry ground just at dark.

We had not eaten a bite since morning; but the children were so tired, and had been so frightened, that they laid down, and, in spite of the mosquitoes, which were tremendously bad, went to sleep without asking for supper. This was certainly one of the most distressing days I had ever experienced; but we old folks felt like taking a good cup of coffee after such a day's work. A fire was immediately made, the coffee was soon served, and no time was lost in turning in for the night. Next morning we did not rise very early, but took our time, got up a good breakfast, and then called out for the boatman. Mr. Condit and Mr. Chase, the gentlemen of whom I had purchased the place, came to ferry us over, and in a little while I was in my log cabin, about 15 feet square. As I had left the carts and my effects at Silver Lake, I left the ponies on the other side, intending to return next day; but as it seemed impossible to bring my stuff through that deep water with my ponies and carts, I arranged with Mr. Chase to meet me with a yoke of cattle hitched to a large canoe. With that understanding, I started next morning with my guide; we pushed the march, and reached Silver Lake about ten at night. Then a tremendous dark cloud rose in the west, and just as we were going to take supper—about the hour of eleven— it blew a hurricane, or, rather, a whirlwind [cyclone], which took our lodge clear up in the air, and then blew the fire into the baggage. It was all we could do to save our plunder, and the lodge we did not find till next day. The latter was so suddenly taken up that we felt like two fools for a moment, not knowing what had become of it. Our supper, as you may say, was good as gone; but, fortunately for us, it was all wind. When we got up in the morning we found that a great many things were missing from our baggage, and much time was lost in searching for lost articles which had been blown so far off by the hurricane. Having succeeded in finding them, and made ready for a start, we saw a wagon coming from above with four yoke of cattle, and I found it was my old friend, Théophile Bruguière, an old Indian trader, and the first settler at the mouth of Big Sioux River. On his approach he cried out, "Hello, Larpenteur! what in the devil are you doing here? You're in a pretty fix, aint you?" "Yes," said I, "and I'm mighty glad to see you." "You are, hay? Well, put some of your stuff in my wagon—bet you I see you through." Bruguière was one of those plain, good-hearted sort of men, who would help anyone out of such a scrape. Having thus arranged matters, we got under way, and camped that night at Laidlaw's Grove. Early next morning we again got under way, and, being so well fixed, had little difficulty in reaching the ferry. I must not omit to say that we met Mr. Chase, who had been as good as his word, about four miles this side of the ferry, coming to meet me with his oxen and canoe; but we did not need his assistance, and left him to follow us empty. We reached the ferry in time to cross, and, all this trouble being over, I was soon safe in my cabin.[66] We had as good a supper as our means could afford, and after much talk over the eight days out from Sergeant's Bluffs we retired for the night.

Although there were a few Mormons scattered in this part of the country, it might still be considered an Indian country. It was occupied, at the time, by Omahas, and frequent parties of Sioux went back and forth to war on the Omahas and Ottos. After I

[66] The site of Larpenteur's new home was near the southern boundary of Harrison County, Iowa, about four miles above the mouth of Little Sioux River.

had arranged with Mr. Amos Chase to get me out logs for a house, and provided for my family, I started for St. Louis to raise what funds I had in the Company's hands, and also to procure some groceries. On my return I found most of my family down with the ague. Mr. Chase had gotten all the logs out, and I immediately began to build, but, as there were no mills, I had to hire a sawyer to work with a pit saw.

About November [1851] I got into my house. But a short time afterward a small party of Omahas came to trade, who had the smallpox, unknown to me. In a couple of weeks my smallest child, a beautiful little boy, took the disease and died the third day. His mother fretted so that she never fairly got over it.

During the winter I made arrangements with Mr. Peter H. Sarpy to go up to Running Water, to take charge of his trading post for the Poncas. In the spring [of 1852] I rented my place, left my family on it, and early in April started for the Niobrara, or Running Water. The post, a very poor establishment, was situated immediately on the bank of that river, about a quarter of a mile from the Missouri. I had but three laboring men, and one cook. That summer I had no other pastime but that of fishing, and had to smoke away mosquitoes every evening.

In September [1852] the news came that all my children had died. I did not think this possible—some might have died, but not all. Not long afterward I received a letter from Mr. Sarpy, saying that I had lost two of my children. No end to bad luck for me!

The Poncas were a small tribe, who made but few robes. Having been accustomed to large tribes of Indians, and to big trades, I did not pay much attention to them, and have nothing to relate except one little incident which happened in the early part of the winter [of 1852–53]. After Indians have gone on their usual hunt, more or fewer loafers always remain about a post, instead of following the main camp, and become a great nuisance. Just such a set remained here—about six lodges in all. There were six able-bodied men among them; we were but five, all told, and as the laboring men had to be out, only myself and the cook remained at the post. The Indians became such beggars that I was obliged to refuse them a great many things; and they appeared so regularly at meal times that I became disgusted, and sometimes told the cook not to give them one mouthful to eat. One morning they came into my room, after my men had gone to their work. They took their seat on the floor, and I could perceive that there was some dissatisfaction in the assembly. I called to the cook to come in. This cook was a Frenchman from St. Louis, named Louis Ménard, about six feet three, weighing about 130 pounds; but though he had no belly he looked as though he might swallow the biggest Indian of the lot. He was an old voyageur, who had been with Frémont on his trip to California. Just after he came in an old Indian, who had not appeared with the first ones, entered and bolted the door inside. I observed this, but said nothing. Several of those Poncas could speak Sioux, and one of them got up to make a speech, which, of course, was to find fault with my way of treating them. By the discourse I began to see that they intended to take advantage of there being none but us two in to force me to give them eatables. I had a small squaw ax under my bed, which I took out and handed to Louis. I then drew my pistol from under my pillow and placed my gun near at hand. Surprised to see these maneuvers, without saying another word they immediately rose and left the room, somewhat faster than they had entered it. This put an end to their begging and loafing, and I afterward gave them a cup of coffee only when I thought proper. Some days after this incident they came and made an apology, requesting me not to say anything about it to the chief when he returned from the hunt.

The Poncas, at that time, were divided into two bands, one led by a chief called The Whip, who kept on this side of the Running Water, and the other named The Drum, who remained on Ponca Creek. Those two chiefs were jealous of each other, and it was thought that they would become hostile.

This winter's trade was small, and we were now so close to settlements that it did not pay to keep up the post; so it was abandoned. I was thus the last person in charge of the Vermilion, and at the Ponca. I had great sport hunting deer at this place. The Indians being out on their winter hunt, I remained the only hunter at this place. We had a great deal of snow, which brought the deer into the wooded points along the river, where they were so plentiful that I killed five in one day with small shot.

Early in the spring [1853] I returned to my farm. The individual to whom I had rented it died in the summer; but he had done well, and I had 40 acres well broken and fenced. During my absence the travel had greatly increased, and settlers were now coming in fast, so I rented my farm and devoted my attention entirely to the traveling community. Notwithstanding the increase of the settlements, the Omahas continued to hunt in their old grounds, and I always kept a few trinkets for their trade. All went on quite smoothly through the summer—good crops, plenty of travel.

About midwinter a party of Sioux, who had gone to war on the Omahas, killed four of them, and stolen some ponies, passed my place on their return. The day they arrived being extremely cold, they concluded to camp on the river bank near my house. While camped there some of the young men went out hunting, and killed a deer in the timber below my field. They brought in a part of it, and one of them told my woman where he had hung the balance in a tree, a short distance from the house, saying that they did not want it, and if she chose to go after it, she was welcome to do so. Early next morning the party left; toward noon the weather moderated, and she remarked that she had a mind to go after that meat. I told her to do as she pleased about it, and she finally concluded to go. Wrapping up warm in her blanket, and taking her daughter along, she started in quest of the meat. As I was building a bridge at the time, I was

259

left alone at home, my men being all out
getting out timber. She had been gone but
a little while when a party of six Omahas
came in. From their daubed appearance I
soon found out that they were in pursuit of
the Sioux, and became alarmed about my
woman; for, although they knew her well,
and were aware that she was an Assiniboine,
and therefore belonged among the deadly
enemies of the Sioux, yet they looked upon
her as a Sioux, as she spoke that language.
I did the best I could to induce them to stay
long enough to give my woman time to return, but they appeared in a great hurry,
and soon started. Just as they were stepping
off the entry I saw her coming home, about
300 yards from the house. When she saw
them approaching she exclaimed to her
daughter, "My daughter, we are lost!" She
knew who they were, knew their customs,
and rightly judged that her time had come.
On meeting her they shook hands; but the
next thing was the report of a gun, and she
fell dead, shot through the heart. One among
them then wanted to shoot her daughter,
but he was not permitted to do so, being
told, "We have killed her mother—that is
sufficient." This deed was done as quick as
lightning; then, throwing away some of their
little effects, they ran off as fast as their legs

would carry them. The alarm was given, but to no purpose. My wife never said a word, having been instantly killed. She was also struck across the face with some kind of blunt weapon. Her daughter was about 18 years of age. One year afterward I married again.

Chapter 16

(1855-61)

ALL this time the travel increased fast, and as I built considerable, I found myself a little in debt in the crisis of 1857. Seeing no show of getting out of debt without making too great sacrifices, I concluded to engage to the firm of Clark, Primeau, and Co., to go and take charge of Fort Stewart, 35 miles above Fort Union. This fort was built during the time of the firm of Frost, Todd, and Co., who, having been too extravagant, were obliged to give it up.

On the 7th of June, 1859, I took passage at Sioux City on Captain Throckmorton's steamer, whose name I have forgotten. On the 24th of the same month I was landed at my post, and again among the Assiniboines. I found this fort in a very bad condition, but in the course of the summer I got it in order, and had very comfortable quarters. I had not seen the Assiniboines during the last six years, and believe I was about as glad to meet them again as they were to see me. As I was now working for the Opposition, against the "big house," I had to use all my knowledge and experience to draw them to my side. In order to effect this I had to dress some of the big chiefs, and make presents to some of the leading men. On the first arrival of any Assiniboine I would make inquiries about such a one, and about that other one, whom I had known, saying that I had made up my mind to make these individuals some little presents. I knew this would flatter them, and at the same time, they must have the presents they expected or my inquiries would not have the desired effect. So they would come to me, in the best of humor, and, after some conversation, would say, "Is that so? I understood you have made inquiries about me." And I could observe that every Indian was delighted to find that I had asked after him. I proceeded in this way through the whole tribe, and soon had them bound to give me almost all their trade.

This [1859–60] was the pleasantest winter I ever spent with the Assiniboines. We had great dances and talks, which always ended with a treat of a large kettle of mush sweetened with molasses. Although my name was White Man Bear, in their language Mato Washejoe, the buffalo dance was my favorite, and we also sometimes danced the bear dance. What had brought me very high in their estimation was that, buffalo being very plentiful, during summer and winter they made surrounds, in which they killed plenty of meat within 300 yards of the fort. My trade this winter was very good, consisting of 300 robes, beside a great many other skins; but the firm, fearing the American Fur Company, consolidated, and as they needed but few clerks or traders, I was thrown out of employment. I was not very well pleased with Mr. Clark, who had promised to take care that I should have a good place. Those gentlemen, seeing that they had the country to themselves, reduced the number of their clerks, and the wages also; they even cut down on their men and Indians.

On my way down the Missouri I found, at Fort Berthold, Jefferson Smith, an old trader, who, like the balance, was out of employment, and who had about $4000. There I also met a young man by the name of Boller, who said that he could raise $2000 from his father in Philadelphia. I felt sure that I could obtain my share from Mr. Robert Campbell in St. Louis. Under such an understanding we agreed to meet in St. Louis. My plan for taking up our outfit was to go around by the way of St. Paul, thence on to Pembina, and through part of the

British possessions, with the view to avoid the Sioux. This was a road which no one of us had traveled. As those men had to wait for the return of Mr. Chouteau, who had gone up to Fort Benton, it was not till the last of July [1860] that we met in St. Louis. I had arrived a few days before, and had informed Mr. Campbell of our project, of which he approved, and readily advanced me my portion of the outfit. I also informed Mr. Kenneth McKenzie, who knew something of that country; he said that my plan was a good one, and wished me success, adding that he was sure I would do well. One of Mr. Campbell's clerks by the name of Robert Lemon joined the company. A few days after the arrival of the other two partners we went into operation, Mr. Boller having obtained by telegraph the amount required. Our opposition move was soon reported to Mr. Chouteau, who said that it would prove an abortion; that we would never reach our intended points. I was to go to the Assiniboines, at the same place as last winter [1859–60]. Smith and Boller were to winter at Berthold. Our equipments were soon ready and shipped to St. Paul, where we were to purchase our cattle.

On the 5th of September [1860] we left St. Paul with eight wagons and eleven men.

Our train, at this early time, attracted the attention of many as we went along; we were often asked where we were bound, and on telling our destination, the answer would be, "Why! you are going a roundabout way to the Yellowstone! You will not get there this winter." We could have taken Governor Stevens' route,[67] which would have been somewhat shorter, but this would have taken us among the Sioux, whom I wanted to avoid, as well as all other Indians, hostile or friendly, as I knew such meetings were always expensive and bothersome. We had some little trouble at the start, as our cattle were not well broken; but it did not last long. The weather being fine, we traveled well. We crossed the Red River of the North at Georgetown, and thence struck for Pembina. This part of the road was quite level, well watered, and sufficiently wooded. About the middle of October [1860] we reached Pembina. There we crossed on a very poor bridge near the mouth of Pembina River.

[67] Governor Isaac I. Stevens of Washington Territory, subsequently a major general in the army and killed at the battle of Chantilly, Sept. 1, 1862. He was given charge of the survey of the northern route for a Pacific railroad, and in 1853 explored the route from St. Paul to Puget Sound. His two-volume *Report* of this exploration was published as a government document.

Next day we proceeded 30 miles up this river to a small village called St. Joseph, at the base of Pembina Mountain, inhabited by Canadian French half-breeds. Many of my acquaintances who had been on the Missouri had settled at this place, where I almost felt myself at home and had no trouble in procuring such a guide as I wanted. I told him that I wished to avoid all Indians, if possible—my friends, the Assiniboines, as well as all others; and to find a good practicable route for my wagons, even if it took us out of the most direct road. Upon which he replied that he could take me exactly as I required, and that he knew all the camps we had to make from the start, for he had the map in his head. Being asked what his charge would be, he said that he should want two buffalo horses, meaning runners which can overtake buffalo. This price agreed upon, we left next day.

The weather was fine, the roads were good, and we traveled well till our cattle began to get tenderfooted, when we had to go slow. When we reached Mouse [or Souris] River [68] they got so lame that we had to shoe them in some manner or other; so we thought of the iron bands of our trunks, examined the thickest, and with these made shoes which

[68] Near the town of Minot, N. Dak.

helped us considerably, though they wore out fast, and detained us much on our march. When we arrived on a little river called the Elk Head, Smith and Boller, with their four wagons, left for Berthold.

I kept on with my old guide and Mr. Lemon, with our four wagons, for the Missouri or Fort Stewart. At the last crossing of Mouse River our guide remarked that we had better take on all the dry firewood we could find, as we would not have any more till we should come near the Bad Lands of the Missouri. Having acted upon his advice, and done some more shoeing, we again got under way, driving at the rate of about ten miles a day. On leaving this point our spirits rose, and though we traveled slowly we still hoped to reach our destination in good time. According to the camps which our guide could count up, we should not be much over eight days. Although our guide knew the way well, he missed one camp. When we neared the Missouri one evening, the old man, who had gone ahead, returned to camp saying, "Good news! You need not spare your firewood; I have seen the Missouri." At this news a cry of joy burst through our little squad, who threw up their hats and jumped about like crazy men. Good fires were made, and in the morning the last stick was burned; we were glad of it, and left camp fully expecting to reach the Missouri early. But we were disappointed in that; we traveled the whole day without wood or water, and it was dark when we reached a small stream, nearly dry, and without wood, and we had to gather buffalo chips to make fire. No Missouri having been seen, there was great discontentment in camp that night, for we knew not exactly where we were. The old guide was much put out; but, knowing that he had not been much mistaken, got up early, mounted his horse, and very soon returned, saying, "Those who believe that I have not seen the river can come with me, and I will make them see it." Thinking we were lost we had camped within ten miles of Fort Stewart, which we reached a little before sundown on the 9th of November, 1860, all safe and sound, having lost on the whole journey nothing but one ax, which we forgot in our camp on Mouse River.

Thus this great journey was performed, being the first ever made with such wagons. I had been informed that Fort Kipp, which was within 200 yards of Fort Stewart, had been burned down by the Indians, but was in hopes to find Fort Stewart still standing. In this I was disappointed; it had also been burned, and I found myself obliged to build. As all the chimneys of Fort Kipp were still standing, and this was a great item, I concluded to build on the same spot, and next day commenced operations.

On the following day two men and one Indian came up from Fort Union. They were much surprised to find me there, and said that Mr. Clark and the Indian agent were on their way up to Poplar River to invite the Crows, who were camped there, to trade at the fort; and that there would be no going out to camps this winter. From this man I learned some particulars of Fort Union. He observed that Clark thought himself a king, being a member of the American Fur Company, in charge of Union, with no opposition, and that he had made himself quite comfortable, but had reduced the men's rations, particularly their biscuits, which had become very small. For his part, he said he was mighty glad I had come, and added, "How glad they will be when they hear that at the fort!"

Clark and the agent, who had taken the ridge road, about two miles back of the fort, came on to our tracks. On examining them, finding that the wheels were iron-bound, they thought that the party could not have been half-breeds, but might have been whiskey peddlers; but as such would have been contrabands, they put spurs to their horses after us. On learning that the agent of the United States was Major Schoonover, whom I knew well, I hoisted a small American flag. On discovering this, they could not make out who we were, but very soon found out. Clark, on approaching me, turned as pale as a corpse, saying, "Larpenteur, I'm glad to see you, in one sense, but, in another, I'm d——d sorry." Thinking that we might not be acting according to law, he then remarked, "I presume you are well prepared to carry on trade?" I observed, "The major already possesses the necessary documents." "All right, all right!" was his answer. After which he asked in a light manner, "Would you not like to sell out?" I replied that I had come to sell to the Indians, not to the Company, and that I thought I could sell to them to as good advantage as I could to Mr. Chouteau. Finding that there was no chance to make a purchase, he observed that he would turn back immediately, and send men to build at Poplar River. Knowing that this river was a good place for Indians to winter, and that it would suit them better than if I stayed at Fort Kipp, I concluded to abandon this point, where I had not done much in the way of building.

My wagons being still loaded, we were under way again next morning. We had about 25 miles to make, which we accomplished early next day; and I don't believe that Lafayette was more cheerfully received in the United States than I was in that camp. Next day I selected a place for building, and began operations at once. I was favored by good weather, and succeeded in building quite a neat little establishment.[69] In a short time Mr. Clark came here to build, intending to oppose me himself the coming winter [of 1860–61]. I was not sorry for this, for I knew him to be very unpopular with both whites and Indians.

My equipment was not large, but well selected for the Indian trade. I made a small reduction in prices which satisfied the Indians, and I knew that if I sold out, even at this reduction, I would do well. This gave me the first run of the trade. Clark, in the meantime, had made great calculations on the number of robes the Indians already had in camp, besides the many more they would acquire before the season should be over. He did not think it worth while to make much effort, as he thought also that my four wagon loads could not last long. But he happened

[69] The author was again on the scene of his trading operations described in Chap. 12.

to be mistaken in his calculations. Out of my four wagon loads I traded upward of 2000 robes, besides a great many other skins and hides, and the consequence was that he found himself badly beaten in the spring.

This winter was mild, and it would have been a very pleasant one to me, had it not been for Jeff Smith, who proved to be a sharp trader, and Boller a young blatherskite. They wrote letters to Mr. Lemon against me, even requesting him to keep an eye on me, saying that they believed it was my intention to take my robes around by St. Paul, and cheat them out of that trade, and much more to that effect. As Mr. Lemon was a new hand in the country, he did not know how to take such stuff, which made him look and act quite cross at times. I also received letters from the same parties, in which they used up Lemon about as badly as they did me. Thus matters stood until near spring [1861] when, one day, after a few sharp words, the secret cause of our ill feelings toward each other came out. We then compared letters, upon which everything was explained, the doings of my two partners found out, and harmony re-established between Lemon and myself. I thus found out that Smith had sent two men up to bring down the cattle, to prevent me from taking away the robes. The letter which those men had brought made that request, but I did not wish to risk cattle on that trip, to be stolen or killed by the Sioux, nor did I want to part with them.

Besides putting up my little fort I got all the saw logs I needed to make a large Mackinaw boat, to take down the returns, and also a skiff for Mr. Lemon and Boller to go down as soon as navigation opened. They being the financiers, and myself and Smith the traders, we were to remain at our respective posts till the returns went down. Boller, who was not over 23, and had been but two years in the country, took it upon himself to write long letters from Berthold about what I was to do and not to do, and, above all, warned me not to be extravagant in building—as though I had just come into the country!

As I had not sent the cattle down, Smith concluded to send Boller up to see how matters stood. About the middle of March [1861] Boller arrived, and, as it was at night, he had to knock at the door of my extravagant improvements. His supper for himself and man was gotten up, and then it was so late that little was said. In the morning I showed him my store and warehouse, both full of robes, all my fine logs, timber to make the skiff, about which he had written to me so often, and also the cattle, which were in first-rate order for the time of the year, remarking at the same time, "They will do first-rate to take a trip to St. Paul." After I had showed him the establishment inside and out, at which I saw he was astonished and pleased, particularly at the sight of the pile of robes, I remarked, "Do you think I have been extravagant? I have scarcely room enough." To which he replied, "I am really surprised. You are well fixed here. We live more like hogs than like people with old Jeff Smith, and I have had a mighty disagreeable winter of it." I then asked, "What were all those letters written for—that one, in particular, about my taking the robes and peltries to St. Paul, to cheat you two gentlemen out of them? All you see here belongs to Robert Campbell till we have a settlement with him; after which, if there is anything to divide among ourselves, each will get his share. Every hair of this goes to St. Louis, not to St. Paul." All his reply was, "Let us bury the hatchet."

The river was ready for navigation on the 3d of April [1861], and on the 5th the two great financiers departed for St. Louis. On their arrival at Berthold Mr. Smith, instead of remaining at his post like myself, got in the skiff and went to St. Louis. Mr.

Campbell, astonished to see him, asked what brought him down. Not liking the reception he was given by Mr. Campbell, or from some other cause, he went to Mr. Chouteau. Mr. Lemon, who could not get a steamer with an outfit, as he had expected, was obliged to go up again, to assist in bringing down our returns. Not knowing that Smith had hired to Chouteau, Lemon looked for him in all such places as those where he generally kept himself, but Smith could not be found. He had gone up to some place on the river with the intention of returning to Berthold with Mr. Chouteau. Mr. Lemon made arrangements with Mr. Chouteau to take passage with him, and also to bring down our returns.

On the 19th of June, 1861, we learned by an Indian who came from Union that Mr. Chouteau had arrived there with two steamers, and, on making further inquiries, found that Mr. Lemon was on board one of them. The second day after that an individual by the name of Louis Dauphin—a renowned hunter—made his appearance, and from him I learned that Mr. Lemon was coming up on the *Chippewa*, that the other steamer, the *Spread Eagle*, had turned back from Union, and that the *Chippewa* would be up this far to-morrow or next day. On reaching Dauphin houses, about six miles below my place by land, but double that distance by water, Mr. Lemon got off to come ahead of the boat to give me the news. After the greetings usual on such arrivals were passed, he remarked: "Larpenteur, I have bad news to give you. In the first place, I came up with Mr. Chouteau, having made arrangements with him to take down our returns, but the boat is burned up. I had been off her but a little while when I saw her all on fire, and immediately heard the report of the explosion. In the second place, war is declared; the United States are in a great revolution, and there is no sale for anything. In the third place, old Smith has deserted us, and won't let us have his robes. I have other news, but I hate to tell it to you." On my insisting, he said, "All your improvements are burned down. Your house caught fire in the middle of the night, and not even a stitch of clothing was saved." On saying this he paused, and I exclaimed, "Is there any more?" "Is that not enough?" said he. "Yes," I replied, "it is more than enough to lose my home at Little Sioux. But it is no use to cry over spilt milk, and it is under such circumstances that a man is tried."

It was a little before sunset when Lemon arrived, and just at dark we learned the particulars of the accident. The boat was set on fire by one of the hands, who had gone down into the hold to steal liquor. Some of it having run upon his clothes while he was drawing it, the candle came in contact with the wet parts and ignited them. He was burned badly, and then the boat took fire. Immediately upon the alarm being given the boat was landed, and she was abandoned as soon as all passengers and hands were ashore. Nothing could be saved for fear of an explosion of the magazine, in which there was a great quantity of powder. After being abandoned she drifted about two miles, and then exploded on the south side of the river. Owing to this accident we sold our cattle and wagons to very good advantage to some gentlemen who resided in Bitterroot Valley, one of them a merchant named Warren, and others going to the Columbia.

Not expecting any steamer to take down our returns I had pushed work on the boat so well that, six days after Lemon's arrival, it was completed; she was 65 feet in length and 11 feet in breadth of beam, being thus large enough to take my returns and those of Smith. The bursting of the *Chippewa* set my men almost crazy, thinking they would get a fortune out of the wreckage. They did not like the idea of rowing my boat down, although they were engaged to do so; and besides, they feared the draft, on account of the rebellion in the United States. I was therefore forced to give $100 for the trip. I had engaged a pilot for $300, but he at last refused to go. At last I succeeded in getting a crew, consisting of four to row and one pilot, and on the 2d of July, 1861, we left Poplar River. On the fourth day after our departure we reached Union. At the same time Mr. Rider came from Berthold with two of our wagons and four yoke of our cattle, Jeff Smith having made some arrangement with the company. This accounted for his having sent for the cattle I had; for he wanted to dispose of them to his own private interest. Mr. Lemon having demanded pay for the cattle, a check on Mr. Chouteau for the amount agreed upon was given, which was so much saved. Smith had no idea that we would fall in with the cattle where we did.

We remained at Union about two hours, and pushed off again. On the fourth day out from this place we landed at Berthold. We called on Smith for the robes, but failed, after all our efforts, having been able to get nothing more than the buffalo tongues. Without any accident we went on well, and a little below Nebraska City met the steamer *Emilie*, Captain Nicholas Wall, bound for

Omaha. We made arrangements with him to take down our robes, and waited for his return. It was still considered dangerous to travel down the river, though not nearly so much so as it had been, and when the boat returned there was a company of soldiers on board from Omaha, bound for St. Louis; but no bushwhackers were seen, and on the 4th of August we reached the port of St. Louis, all safe.

Chapter 17

FORT STEWART AGAIN: FORT GALPIN

AS Mr. Lemon had reported, there was no sale for robes. The best part of our robes had been stolen. No longer had I a house to live in. Now what to do? Mr. Campbell, who saw what a plight we were in, said, "Gentlemen, I cannot sell your robes, except at a great sacrifice, which I see no necessity to make. If you wish to return I will furnish your outfit. Now make up your minds and let me know." Having consulted upon what to do we made up our minds to return. Smith, of course, was out; we allowed Boller a small share, but he was to remain out of the country.

Our outfit was soon ready and shipped again by St. Paul, where we bought our cattle. This time we adopted Burbank's way of freighting. We bought light wagons and put but one yoke to each. In this way one man can drive two wagons, and it is no trouble to get through swampy places, as each wagon takes only from 18 to 20 hundredweight.

We left St. Paul on the 14th of September [1861], with seven wagons and eight men, bound for Poplar River. We traveled well, but I was so sick most of the way that it was feared at one time I was going to leave my bones in the prairie. The weather was also very disagreeable. The previous trip I walked the whole way, nearly 900 miles, except two days; but this time I rode more than half the time. We went pretty nearly the same route; the only difference was that we struck direct for St. Joseph instead of Pembina. We had provided ourselves with ox shoes, and got our cattle shod on arriving there. I got another first-rate guide, by the name of Louison Vallée. This guide was one of the best hunters I ever saw for buffalo, as well as for small game; he was near fifty, about six feet three, built in proportion, a very powerful man, and a tremendous walker. He made us live on ducks and geese at the start, and, when we got in among buffalo, on the fat of the land. His killing so many fine fat ducks I believe saved my life. In coming in with a load of ducks he would exclaim: "Monsieur Larpenteur, c'est bon pour la moustache," for he could not speak English. He was as good a guide as my first one; he took us farther north, but managed to get us through without seeing Indians, except the day previous to our arrival.

When we came near the Missouri he observed that he had never been up to Poplar River; he could put us on the Missouri, but not take us direct to the spot. That did not make much difference with us, as we had a man by the name of Joseph Ramsay, who had been the hunter for Fort Union for 20 years, and said he knew the country well. So the remainder of the journey was left to Ramsay. We did not, at the time, consider ourselves more than two days' travel from our destination. In the morning Ramsay took the lead, and the guide went ahead of the teams, in his own direction toward the Missouri, expecting to fall in with us from time to time. I remained with Ramsay, going ahead of the teams. After traveling about an hour I observed that I thought he was going too far north. "No," said he, "I am on the direct way. You see that big hill yonder, with that pile of rocks on it? From there you can see the Missouri." When we came near the hill, being anxious to see the Missouri, and, at the same time, thinking that my man was lost, I started ahead of him. But, when I reached the top of the hill, the Missouri was not to be seen, nor any sign of it. As Ramsay came up I asked him to show me the Missouri. He looked around, very much surprised, not knowing what to say, and I saw plainly that he was lost. I then pointed out a direction, went back to the wagons, and changed our course. We had gone but a little way when we saw an Indian coming after us at full gallop. On approaching us he asked: "Are you going to Woody Mountain?" Ramsay had taken quite a northerly direction.

This Indian was Broken Arm, the chief of the Canoe band of Assiniboines; he said that they had come across our tracks, and made sure whose they were. Many of his people wanted to follow him, but he did not allow them to do so, as he knew I would not like it. He then asked me where I was going to winter. I told him at my former place. He remarked that it was not so suitable as Fort Stewart, where all his band intended to winter; that I had better change my plans; that there were no Indians as yet on the Missouri, but they would all come to my place as soon as they should learn that I had arrived. This was all a lie, for I found out afterward that most of the Assiniboines were at Fort Charles, about 50 miles by land above Fort Stewart.

Owing to his report I consented to go to Fort Stewart; the Indian guided us, saying

we would get there the next day. It was late
at night when our guide Vallée came to the
camp, quite angry with Ramsay. It snowed
that night about four inches, and kept quite
cold all the next forenoon, but moderated
in the afternoon. A little before sunset we
were at Fort Stewart, strange to say, again
on the same date as last year—the 9th of
November, 1861.

It was a glad set of men who put up the
lodge, not to be taken down till comfortable
quarters were made; and, after a bouncing
supper, we turned in, with the pleasant idea
that there would be no hitching up in the
morning. Had Ramsay taken us in the right
direction, we should have reached Poplar
River the day the Indian overtook us, and
found good quarters already built. My own
had been burned down, but those of Clark
were still up, and would have saved us a
great deal of disagreeable labor.

On rising in the morning we found about
five inches of snow on the ground, and it was
still snowing; but the wind soon changed and
a cold northwester made it impossible to
work. From this time until March [1862]
extremely cold weather continued. Through
the assistance of squaws whom I employed
to heat water and daub the houses, we
succeeded in getting ourselves comfortable

quarters, but no stockade. I made use of the places we prepared the previous fall. Buffalo were so plentiful here last summer that they ate up all the grass; it looked as though fire had burned the prairies. In consequence of this and the hard winter [of 1861–62] I lost all my cattle—20 head. Owing to the severity of this winter my trade was light, after that of the Assiniboines was over. I had but 1000 robes, a great many goods left on hand, and more trade must be made. I knew the Gros Ventres of the Prairie were at war with the Blackfeet—that is, with the Piegans; that they dared not go to Benton; that few traders had been in their camp; and, consequently, that they must have yet a great many robes.

Matters standing thus, I proposed to Lemon to go after the Gros Ventres. I had a man in view for this trip who knew the country, and intended to send him with Lemon. After a great deal of persuasion Lemon agreed to go. My man, whose name was Louis El, was ready. My instructions to Lemon were, in the first place, to do all he could to bring the Indians down with their robes; and, secondly, if he could not succeed in that, to get enough of them to come with what number of horses would be required to take all my goods up to Milk River at Dauphin's old fort, where I intended to remain during the summer, and where I would have a boat ready for him to go down with what returns I should have; but by all means to do his best to bring them down with robes.

Under those instructions and conditions they started afoot, with their rifles on their shoulders and a dog to carry or drag their sugar and coffee, about the 10th of May [1862].

In the meantime I set to work on my boat, which went very slowly, as I was out of provisions and had neither horse nor mule to send after meat. I had traded a horse and a mule, but one Mr. Assiniboine had relieved me of both; and I had to send my men with the cart after meat, when it was not killed too far from the establishment, or to pack it on their backs.

Twelve days after Lemon's departure he returned with a trading party of Gros Ventres, having 450 robes. After this trade was over, I proposed to put my plan into execution; but Lemon objected, saying that the Indians would rob me of all my goods, and that we had better go down together. As he had been quite contrary all winter, and fretful at every little disappointment, I became dissatisfied with him, and determined to have nothing more to do with him. So I went on preparing to go down stream. On the 4th of June [1862], we were ready to start, with oars all shipped, when a steamer hove in sight. We awaited her arrival, and found she was the *Shreveport*, Captain John La Barge, who informed us that his brother Joseph was not far behind, coming up with the *Emilie*, and that he had letters for us from Robert Campbell, also some provisions. When we were ready to push off, he asked us if we had any ice. I told him that he would find some in a barrel. The ice had been so thick that a large cake of it, which we had covered in the sand, had kept until this time. The steamer resumed its way up, and we made our oars ply down stream. We learned by John La Barge that they had formed a company to oppose the American Fur Company, the firm being La Barge, Harkness, and Co. We met the *Emilie* about 20 miles below Big Muddy River. By the letter from Mr. Campbell we learned that robes and all furs and peltries had risen in price, and also that he had sent us groceries of all kinds, as Captain John La Barge had already informed us. I was sorry that Lemon had not consented to let me take my goods up to Milk River; had he done so,

I should have found myself well supplied, and we would have done well in that country. But, as a large company was now organized to oppose the American Fur Company, I did not think it advisable to return with the boat, though I could have done so at but little expense, and most likely would have done so, if Lemon had been the right kind of a man. Taking everything into consideration, I thought best to sell out.

So we sold out to Joseph La Barge. Mr. Lemon went on down to Berthold with the boat to deliver the goods, and await the return of the *Emilie*. I turned back with Captain La Barge, under a provisional understanding, to examine and select a point to build near the mouth of Milk River. Having examined that vicinity, I chose a situation at the head of Moose Point, about 10 miles above Milk River by land and 15 by the Missouri.

I remained there until the return of the *Emilie* from Benton, when I again got on board, bound for St. Louis. At Berthold we took on our robes and proceeded. At Fort Pierre we learned that Smith, who had gone down with his robes in a small Mackinaw, had returned with Mr. Chouteau, whom he had met a little below, and had left his robes at Fort Pierre, in charge of Mr. Charles

Primeau. Mr. Lemon demanded them as our property. Mr. Primeau consented to give them up on our paying him $50 for storage. We gave the required amount, and took them on board the *Emilie*. So we got out our robes at last, though, from what we learned afterward, we supposed Smith had sold them to Mr. Chouteau. They both felt very much surprised, on their return to Fort Pierre, to find the robes gone.

Early in July [1862] we reached St. Louis, where, after a final settlement, I found myself with $1400, from our dividends. This was my all, after two years of hard work, trouble, and exposure. Having made arrangements with the firm of La Barge and Co., which was to give me one-fourth of the net proceeds of the Assiniboine and Gros Ventres of the Prairie trade, I left for my place at Little Sioux.

On arrival I found my family all well, but living in a very poor log house, which was standing about 40 steps from my main buildings, and had escaped the fire. All I could see of my improvements, which had cost me upward of $3000, was a pile of ashes; and I had no insurance.

I went the rounds at once, settled all my debts, big and small, and eight days afterward was again under way for the upper country, having shipped at Sioux City, on the *Shreveport*, bound for Benton, with goods for the Indian trade.

Late in August [1862] we reached Milk River, when the Missouri became so low that the steamer could proceed no further. The next day, while we were taking the goods into Dauphin Fort, a large war party of Sioux gave us a few shots, and stole several head of horses from the Crows. The *Shreveport* left, and I remained in Dauphin until teams came from Benton to take up what goods the company had for that place, and also to move me up to the fort, which I called Galpin.[70] On our way up we left Owen McKenzie about 150 miles below this point, to build a trading post for the Assiniboines.

Here I erected a handsome, good little fort, and might have had a pleasant time. But in consequence of the very mild winter we had no buffalo, and the Indians, who were starving as well as ourselves, became very unruly. At one time they threatened to pillage my stores, and for a while our

[70] Named for Major Charles E. Galpin, a picturesque and well-known character on the Upper Missouri until his death about 1870. In the original edition of Larpenteur's narrative, Coues supplies an interesting description of him.

case looked rather dark; but they contented themselves with stealing a few articles. I tried my men, but they refused to fight, saying they would rather let the Indians take all the goods than expose their own lives. I had a mean, cowardly set of men, many of whom had been hired by Captain John La Barge on his return from Benton, during his first trip. I knew them of old, and had I had my own way about this, they should never have been in my employment.

In spite of all this my trade was tolerably fair this winter [1862–63]. McKenzie did little. Early in the fall he had a fight with the Sioux, in which one man was killed, besides one Assiniboine and several horses. This was a party of about 200 warriors, who attacked our men in their house. The latter immediately cut portholes, and defended themselves through them. Our man was killed in the house by a ball which penetrated the door. The Indians were bold enough to come and shoot through the portholes; but one of them remained there. The fight lasted all day; there were but four white men and six Assiniboines on our side. The next day three Sioux were found dead, and there were signs of several wounded ones, who had been taken away. This fight frightened the Assiniboines away from the post, and was the cause why McKenzie did but little trade—only 350 robes.

Toward spring [1863] we were in a starving condition, game of all kinds extremely scarce, and men afraid to go out for a hunt. For about six weeks I lived on nothing but jerked elk meat, having some salt but being entirely out of other groceries. There is little substance in elk meat. I became so weak that I could scarcely get up the river bank with a bucket of water; my knees felt like giving way. It was only by seeking for coffee in the warehouse, picking it up grain by grain out of the dirt, that I now and then got a cup of coffee, without sugar; but it was a great treat notwithstanding.

On the 11th of June, 1863, Captain John La Barge landed at this place, bound again for Benton, or, rather, for Fort La Barge,[71] which the firm had built in opposition to Benton. Having heard some great stories, all of which he or they believed, previous to seeing me, the firm had made up their minds to discharge me. In consequence of this they abandoned Owen McKenzie's post and brought him up to take charge of Fort Galpin. McKenzie was a great drunkard, not

[71] Fort La Barge had been built by the Company in the summer of 1862, about one and one-half miles above Fort Benton.

at all fit to be in charge of such an establishment; but, without any inquiries, my charge was made over to him. Captain La Barge, not satisfied with this, and being the meanest man I ever worked for, except his brother, told some of the men that I had given him a very bad account of their behavior.[72] This set them against me; and now that I was no longer in charge, one gentleman among them —a bully nearly six feet six inches tall—took it into his head one fine day to give me a pounding. He would have done so had it not been for my son,[73] who was about 20 years of age, and much of a man. He saw me in a quarrel, and, thinking that there would be a fight, went into the house, and got his rifle. By that time we were engaged in the fight. I received a severe blow, which stunned me; and when I recovered I saw my antagonist lying as if dead at my feet.

[72] The severity of this language betokens a personal grievance. Captain Joseph La Barge was living in St. Louis in 1898 and declined to respond to Coues' invitation to present his version of the disaster at the Tobacco Garden which Larpenteur describes in the pages which follow. His account was subsequently given to General Chittenden, his biographer, however, and as published by the latter it takes sharp issue with Larpenteur's recital.

[73] The birth of this half-breed son, August 9, 1842, is related *ante*, 148.

I made sure it was none of my doing, and next saw my son in the act of giving him another blow, saying, "Let me kill the son of a b——h." McKenzie, who had come up, said, "Don't strike him again, Charles; you have killed him." During all this time the men were standing outside near their houses, not daring to approach, and when we left him they came and took him in for dead; but he recovered.

McKenzie now being in charge, my presence was no longer needed at this place. I got a canoe, and, taking my son and a young freeman named Keiser, went down to meet Captain Joseph La Barge, who was coming up with the steamer *Robert Campbell*, loaded mostly with the Blackfoot annuities. Instead of meeting the *Robert Campbell*, which we thought would be the first boat up, we met Mr. Chouteau, on the steamer *Nellie Rogers*, bound for Fort Benton. This was at Fort Kipp, where we got on board to return to Fort Galpin, as we had learned that the *Robert Campbell* was yet far below. About 50 miles below Fort Galpin we met the *Shreveport*, on her return from Benton. We boarded her and proceeded on our way down; but she was to turn back to assist the *Robert Campbell* up with the annuities. At Heart River we met the *Robert Campbell*, and, as agreed upon, we turned back in her company.

The third day afterward we were fired upon by a party of Sioux, while wooding, but no one was hurt. We went on again to a place called the Tobacco Garden, about 100 miles below the mouth of the Yellowstone, where we saw a large war party of Sioux on the south side of the river. The two boats came within 100 yards of each other, and anchored in the middle of the river to see what those Indians were going to do. After the Sioux had all gathered up, they cried out for the boat, saying they wanted to have a talk, and were out of tobacco. There were two Indian agents on board, Major Latta for the Gros Ventres, Mandans, and Assiniboines, and Major Reed for the Blackfeet. I was at the time on the *Shreveport*. The captain and those gentlemen, not knowing much about Indians, thought best to send for the head men of the party, and in spite of all that could be done from our boat to make them abandon the idea, Captain Joseph La Barge would send out the yawl. The first crew ordered refused to go; the mate, not wishing to insist on sending another crew, without further orders, reported to the captain that the men had refused, and was sent back very roughly with orders to send another crew. So seven men were ordered out. One young man of this crew, already in the yawl, caught hold of the steamboat, saying, "I don't want to go—we'll all be killed." The mate threatened to break his fingers if he did not loosen his hold, and he was obliged to go with the crew—never to return. As soon as they started I took my double-barreled gun and ran up on the hurricane deck. When the Indians saw the yawl coming they jumped down the bank, and the moment the yawl landed, discharged a volley, killing three men and wounding another, who, it was thought, would not recover. From the steamboat we fired several volleys, but to no effect. A few shots were afterward fired from the willows by the Indians, also without effect, and about three o'clock in the afternoon we got under way.

The next day, at 10 a. m., we buried the three poor fellows in one grave; the young man Martin was one of them. Two days afterward we reached the mouth of the Yellowstone, where both boats stopped, it being impossible for them to proceed farther.

Although they were on bad terms with the American Fur Company they concluded to ask Mr. Hodgkiss, who was in charge, to let them store their goods in Fort Union.

Knowing that Mr. Hodgkiss was very fond of liquor, they made sure of success, and certainly succeeded.

When we came to the fort we learned that Malcolm Clark had shot Owen McKenzie. Mr. Chouteau had not been able to ascend the Missouri farther than Milk River, where he had to put out all his freight, to be hauled up to Benton with wagons. While he was there McKenzie came down to the boat. McKenzie had disputed with Clark in regard to some settlements of the time of Frost, Todd, and Co. Clark had been in charge for that company, and McKenzie was not on good terms with him. So McKenzie got very drunk and commenced to quarrel with Clark, who, knowing him to be a dangerous man, took out his pistol and shot three balls through McKenzie, killing him instantly. Thus one of Captain La Barge's best kind of men gone, there was no one in charge of Fort Galpin. They put in charge Louis Dauphin, whom I knew to be a regular thief, and who did not know his *a b c* of the business. Finding themselves in a bad fix about Galpin, they had the brass to ask me how I would like to go there again; but I bade them to be so kind as to excuse me, as they could find plenty of better men than myself. Shortly after this Dauphin was killed by the Sioux. A young man named Antoine Primeau was shot by Jerry Potts, a half-breed. My cook, a nice young man, who wanted to display his bravery, was killed by some Sioux near the fort. James Windle was killed by a bull-driver who came down from Benton. All this happened at Fort Galpin shortly after I left, and the goods which the La Barges had brought up were nearly all lost.

The annuities being all stored, we started for the States. A few miles below Sioux City the mate had a quarrel with his hands, in which he stabbed one of them, who died in fifteen minutes. The gentlemanly La Barges, having treated all their clerks about the same as they did me, drew out of the Indian trade. This was in 1863.

Chapter 18

(1864–66)

IN the spring of 1864 I made arrangements with Mr. Charles Chouteau to take charge of Fort Union. As he was not ready to leave St. Louis, I started ahead of him on the steamer *Benton*, in charge of 50 tons of commissary freight, having been appointed as commissary by General Alfred Sully of the U. S. Army. I was to be relieved on the arrival of his fleet, which was to be up during the summer. The main reason of my appointment was that we had 17 barrels of whiskey in this freight.

We left St. Louis on the 26th of March. On arriving at Fort Randall,[74] we learned that 1500 lodges of Sioux were camped near Fort Berthold, determined to stop all navigation, and so placed that they could sink boats by rolling rocks down the bank. Those who knew neither the country nor the Indians believed all this rubbish, and some

---

[74] Fort Randall was established by General William S. Harney in 1856. It was on the Missouri, some fifty-five miles, airline distance, above Yankton, S. Dak.

of the ladies who were on board, bound for Montana, expressed a desire to turn back. We kept on our voyage, which was very tedious, on account of low water.

On the 6th of May we reached Fort Sully[75] with a part of our load, having been obliged to make a double trip. On our arrival Colonel Bartlett, in command of Sully, informed us that, owing to reports of hostile Indians being strongly forted near Berthold, he had just received a dispatch from headquarters, ordering him to prevent any steamers from going farther up till a sufficient number arrived to justify him in sending an escort with them, which was left, in a great measure, to his own judgment. He said that he would let us know shortly what he would determine upon, and requested the captain to call again the next day. Being anxious to move on, and not putting much faith in any such stories as we had learned, we called on the commander. As I was a commissary, and had been for many years with the Indians, he would have me let him

---

[75] Fort Sully was established in 1863 by General Alfred Sully, a few miles below Pierre, S. Dak. Three years later the site was abandoned, and a new fort (also named Sully) was established, about twenty-five miles above Pierre and twenty miles below the mouth of Cheyenne River.

know what I thought about the matter. To which I replied that I thought all those reports, like many others, much exaggerated, and should not be at all surprised if we did not see a single Indian on our journey. For one thing there was no game on the river, and it was impossible for 1500 lodges to remain long in camp together; and as to any place where they could roll rocks down the bank and sink the boat, I knew of none such —at which he smiled. As to danger, I could not say there was none; we might be fired on and some persons might be killed, but as there were nearly 150 men on board, all well armed, I did not apprehend much danger. The greatest danger would be at night, but good care would be taken to always anchor on a sand bar in the middle of the river. Colonel Bartlett then asked the captain when he thought he would be ready to leave; the answer was, "In a couple of days." "Well," said he, "when you are ready, let me know; something more favorable may turn up in that time."

With the consent of the commander we resumed our journey on the 9th of May. The river being still very low, we made but slow progress. No Indians were seen until we came to the mouth of Heart River, where, on the 24th, about 9 a. m. we discovered a few Indians in the broken banks of the Missouri, awaiting our arrival with the American flag hoisted. Being well prepared, we landed, and gave them some few provisions and a little tobacco. They were but 12 in all—a half-starved looking set. After proceeding about 10 miles, we saw three Indians, who desired us to land; we did so, and found that one of them was Black Catfish, chief of the Yanktonais, who showed his papers from General William S. Harney. Having given them a good cup of coffee on board, and a few presents, we again got under way; and those were the last Indians we saw.

We landed safe and sound at Union on the last day of May, being the first boat up this season. We arrived early in the morning and came in sight of the fort unobserved. The doors were all closed, and not a living object was stirring except some buffalo, pasturing about 300 yards from the fort. But the door was soon opened, the flag hoisted, and the artillery fired; to which salute the boat responded. We were informed that the Sioux had been, and were still, so bad that the men dared not keep the doors open. The Indians had at one time made a rush, and shot a squaw through the thigh just as she was entering the fort. The *Benton* left about

3 p. m., having discharged 50 tons of freight, which pleased the passengers very much.

I have omitted to say that, while at Berthold, I was informed of Mr. Hodgkiss' death; this news had not reached St. Louis when I left. Mr. I. C. Rolette was then in charge.

I was not to take charge of Union until the return of Mr. Chouteau from Benton. On the 13th of June Mr. Chouteau arrived with his steamer, the *Yellowstone*, bringing a company of soldiers for the protection of the fort, and of the Assiniboines; it was Company I, Wisconsin Volunteers, commanded by Captain Greer, and Major Wilkinson, the Indian agent, also arrived. The *Yellowstone* left for Benton the same day.

On the 2d day of July the *Yellowstone* returned from Benton, and, after all arrangements had been made, I took charge of Fort Union for the last year of the American Fur Company; but I still retained my position as commissary until the arrival of General Sully's fleet.

Now a few words in regard to that expedition.[76] Previous to my leaving St. Louis

[76] In the summer of 1863 two armies were led into Dakota in a converging attack upon the hostile Sioux, one from Minnesota, led by General Henry H. Sibley, the other from Sioux City, Iowa, up the Missouri, led

General Sully, one day, while at Mr. Chouteau's office, took pains to tell me the route he was going to take to the mouth of the Big Horn. He showed me the map, observing that the route from Heart River, at which point he intended to leave the Missouri and strike for the Horn, was the shortest, and could be accomplished in little time. I had been on the Horn, and had also traveled some on the Little Missouri. I knew the latter to be very rough country, which, further up than I had been, was almost all Bad Lands. This made me observe that I thought he would have a great deal of trouble in getting through with his command; but with a map and some good brandy, in Chouteau's office, one can get through any-

by General Sully. Several battles and much fighting occurred, in which the whites were uniformly victorious, but the Sioux were not conquered. In 1864 General Sully led another army against the hostiles, old Fort Sully below Pierre having been appointed as the rendezvous for the various units of the army. Leaving here on June 24, it established Fort Rice, a few miles above the mouth of Cannon Ball River and then advanced by way of the Knife River country to the Yellowstone. On July 28 several thousand warriors were defeated in a stiff battle at Killdeer Mountain, the white army numbering about 2200, including cavalry, infantry, and artillery. Numerous documents, including General Sully's own reports, are published in *S. Dak. Hist. Colls.*, Vol. VIII.

where. I found him convinced that he would meet with little difficulty; but I was satisfied to the contrary. After this he went on with his talk, saying, "I have a fleet of five steamers, which are going up as far as Union. Among them I have two light ones, intended to bring up all the goods and implements to the mouth of the Horn, where I expect to meet them." This notion I knew would never be realized; he might get to the Horn with his command, but for a steamboat to ascend the Yellowstone that distance I knew to be impossible, and was much surprised at the idea.

Now we will return to Fort Union, and relate what took place until the arrival of the fleet. Captain Greer had not been long stationed in the fort when a war party of Sioux, early one morning, stole all the horses, not more than 40 steps from one of the bastions. He started a detail of 20 men in pursuit on foot; had the Indians been so disposed, they could have destroyed those men with all ease. Two weeks later another party made an attack. It happened that there were a few Gros Ventres of the Missouri at the fort, who, with some soldiers, succeeded in overtaking one of the Sioux; they pretty soon returned with his scalp, ears, and nose, and a great scalp dance followed. After this everything went smoothly till the 20th of November [1864], when a party of 83 miners arrived on their return trip to the States by the *Yellowstone;* they had been frozen in about 20 miles from the mouth of that river, and obliged to abandon their boats. Finding that they could not all be entertained comfortably in the fort, and some wishing to go to the States, half of the party made up their minds to take it afoot. Those remaining would have proved very troublesome, and more dangerous than the hostile or friendly Indians, had not Captain Greer, who was quartered in the fort, kept them quite civil. They were a rough set. Early in the spring [1865] I made them a large Mackinaw, in which they left two days after the ice broke, on the 17th of April. Captain Greer went with them, to meet the steamer *Yellowstone.*

We were not troubled by the hostiles that winter [1864-65], and should have had a pleasant time, had not scurvy broken out toward the end of that season; three soldiers died. As we had seen no enemies all winter, when spring came the soldiers went out hunting in all directions, as though there was no danger, and became very careless. On the 26th of April [1865] two of them returned from a hunt, and said they had found the remains of an elk which had been wounded

and died, and was partly eaten up by a
grizzly bear. The orderly sergeant and those
two men agreed to go early next morning to
see if they could get a shot at Mr. Grizzly,
and gave orders to the guard to awake them
by daylight. The guard did as he had been
ordered, and the three hunters went after
the bear. When they had gone about three-
quarters of a mile, and were passing through
some thick bushes, they were fired upon by a
party of concealed hostiles, about 40 in number, and one of them was shot down. Another
of them shot and killed an Indian. The orderly sergeant, who had had the scurvy,
could not run; the Indians rushed upon
him, shot nine arrows into him, pounded
him with their war-clubs, and then
scalped him, not leaving a hair upon his
head. The young man who fell at the first
discharge was shot with one ball, above his
left breast, and two in his leg. The bushes
were thick where he was lying, and he saw
them looking for him; but as the alarm had
been given at the fort, by the guard, who
had seen and heard the firing, they had no
time to search, and ran away, leaving their
own dead man. In the afternoon a party of
soldiers went to the spot and hung him in
some elm trees where he could be seen
dangling from the Fort.

Nothing worthy of note took place from this time till the arrival of the *Yellowstone*, on the 5th of June. Mr. Chouteau arrived this time in great distress; having been reported as a rebel he could not obtain a license, and was obliged to sell out all his trading-posts, except Benton; all other posts he sold to Hubble, Hawley and Co., of which A. B. Smith of Chicago was the head; it was called the North West Fur Company. This being the case, we immediately set to work taking the inventory. When the post was turned over to the N. W. Co. I made arrangements to take charge of it for this new firm. Captain Upton of the regulars,[77] who arrived to relieve Captain Greer, had instructions to take possession of Fort Union for the United States, and turn all citizens out. So I had to turn out my men, and would have been obliged to leave myself, had not the captain suffered me to keep my own room and my cook. I thus found

[77] This was not Captain (later Major General) Emory Upton (the only officer of this name then in the regular army), distinguished for gallant service in the Civil War and for his remarkable study, *The Military Policy of the United States*. Instead, it was a Captain Upton of the First U. S. Volunteers, which Coues explains was composed of Confederate ex-prisoners of war who had been released on condition of entering the U. S. service to fight Indians.

myself, as it were, under arrest, but this did not last long.

On the 14th of August Captain Upton was ordered away, and I was again in full posession of the fort. Two days afterward Mr. Frederick D. Pease, a member of the Company, arrived to attend the sale of the commissary goods. He asked my opinion in regard to sending after the Crows, who, he thought, had still many robes. I remarked that I would not send; that they could not have much left to trade, as so many boats had been up the river; and, for another thing, that I knew Captain Greer, during the past winter, had created such a jealousy between them and the Assiniboines that if they met it was sure to be war. So I did not think advisable to send; it would be better to wait till the arrival of the agent. But, in spite of all I said or could do, he would send. After the sale he left, and I remained with six men in a place where a company of soldiers had once been thought required for safety.

On the 21st of August Mr. Pease and all the Government officers left Fort Union; I resumed full charge, being left with six working men, one clerk, and one loafer named Conklin, who Mr. Pease said he thought was a government spy, and who turned out to

be a perfect blatherskite. After the departure of all the force which had been stationed
here the men at times became quite unruly,
and threatened to leave, which made it very
disagreeable to me. During the night of September 10th the forerunners of the Crows
arrived, with three white men who had been
in their camps, reporting that these Indians
would be in next day. There happened to be
in the Fort a few young Assiniboines, who
left that same night for their camp, about 20
miles distant. In the mean time the Crows
arrived, with but little to trade, and camped
close to the fort—about 200 in all, men and
women. On their arrival the chief demanded
the annuities, but, as I had not been instructed to give them, I declined, but promised that if the agent did not arrive within
eight days, I would then do as he desired.
He said that was a long time, but finally
agreed to wait; but trade commenced, and
all went on well.

On the 12th of September, 1865, a little
before sunrise, I was awakened by my interpreter, saying, "Mr. Larpenteur—the Sioux!
the Sioux! they have made a rush on the
Crow horses, driven them all off, and are
now fighting." I immediately got up, and
ran up on the gallery; by this time the Indians had got out of sight, but I could hear

the firing. A little while afterward the report came that there were some Assiniboines among them. By another dispatch we learned that they were all Assiniboines, that the Crows had already killed two, and were still fighting. After the battle we learned that there were four Assiniboines killed, two Crows wounded, not dangerously; and that the latter had lost 45 head of horses. It was fortunate for us that no Crows were killed; for, had there been, we could not have saved the Assiniboines who were in the fort at the time; and it was only after a great deal of talk that we pacified the Crows. Then the chief, called Rotten Tail, came to me and said, "You must give me the annuities. You see that we cannot remain here any longer, the Assiniboines will have some more of our horses if we do." The old chief was right; I could no longer refuse him his annuities, and granted his request. But a little while afterward he came in with his soldiers, requesting me to give him the Assiniboines' annuities in payment for the 45 horses they had stolen, and also saying that the Crows must have ammunition. I saw plainly that they meant no good. I told the old Chief that I would give him his annuities, but that I had nothing else to give him, and that if he wanted pay for his horses he would have to wait till his father arrived on the steamer, which I expected would be up in a few days. Seeing that something was wrong, I had my men all well armed, and the cannon loaded. After a little more argument on the subject, the old fellow concluded to take his annuities. I then took him into the warehouse and showed him his pile, saying, "This is yours, just as it was sent up. Here are your papers, calling for so many boxes, sacks, barrels, and bales. You can see that none of them have been opened. Now I will send them out to your camp. You can remain here, to see that they all go, and after that you can divide them to suit yourselves." He then remarked that he would rather have me divide them. I told him I would have nothing more to do with them; that Indians always accused the whites of stealing annuities, which was my reason for refusing to make any division. Then he asked if I would let my "little whites," as the laboring men are called, divide, or help divide. I told him that would be as they chose. Finally the goods were divided, and the next morning, when all were ready to leave, the old chief came to me in the best of humor, saying, "Well, I have come to take breakfast with you before I go, and see if you have any more documents for me to sign." I told him I had some breakfast for him to eat, but no documents to be signed. When the old man was ready to go he shook hands in a very friendly manner, saying, "I am well pleased, but sorry that my friends the Assiniboines have been fools. You can tell them, from me, that I am still their friend, and willing to smoke with them. The scalps which were taken were given to your interpreter to bury and were not allowed to be danced, as we do with those of our enemies." Upon which he put the whip to his horse, and it was good-by, Mr. Crow. This being the result of Mr. Pease's dispatch.

On the 17th of September the *Hattie May* arrived, bringing Mr. A. B. Smith, the Chicago hypocrite, Mr. Hawley, and Mr. Pease. Having found myself slighted, and not liking the proceedings of this new firm, I requested my discharge of Mr. Pease last August; but he then said he could not do that, and I would have to await the arrival of the steamer. On her arrival I was discharged. The steamer on which I went left at noon next day, and was to wait for those gentlemen in the point below Union, where the captain would take on a little wood; but as they did not come at the appointed time, he went down to the Fort William landing, only

2½ miles by land, to wait for them there. While landed there I found that I had forgotten some documents, which I had left with Mr. Thomas Campbell, and wanted to go back to the fort for them. A great many ponies were seen, supposed to be those of Sioux, which had kept those gentlemen at the fort. But I knew that the Assiniboines were camped near by and that the ponies were those of this party, who, on hearing the cannon firing at the arrival of the boat, had come to the fort. Now that it was nearly dark, and those gentlemen had not arrived, the captain, who knew that I wanted to go to the fort, said, "Larpenteur, if you want to go you can; I will not leave to-night." I asked someone to accompany me, but none dared go, saying, "Those Indians may be Sioux"; so I started alone. The fort was locked up on my arrival, and, as my business was with Campbell, who was in a small cabin about 100 yards off, I passed by the fort. There I saw many of my old friends among the Assiniboines, who shook hands with me, saying they were sorry to see me go. Having been satisfied about the documents I started back to the boat. During my absence those gentlemen arrived in a skiff. Not knowing, as yet, that I had gone to the fort, they said that it was a good thing for me that I was not at the fort, for the Assiniboines would surely have killed me; then blaming me for that scrape with the Crows. At this the captain remarked, "Larpenteur has just gone to the fort." "Well," said they, "it is not good for him; we should not be surprised if he does not return." Not long after that I fired off my pistol and the yawl came for me. When the captain told me what had been said, I remarked that, if I had been obliged to leave the country whenever Indians threatened to kill me, I should have been gone long ago.

We left next morning, and, without anything worthy of notice, reached Sioux City on the 4th of October. Having remained at Little Sioux River a week, I started for St. Louis, to have a settlement with Mr. Chouteau. He received me like a gentleman, being pleased with the winding up of his affairs at Union. We settled up satisfactorily to both parties, and then I returned to pass the winter at my place.

Chapter 19

(1866–72)

O N the 29th of April, 1866, I received an appointment from Governor Edmond as interpreter with the Peace Commissioners for the Assiniboines. I started immediately for Yankton, went on to Randall by stage, and then by land to Sully, at which point I boarded the steamer *Sunset*, and reached Fort Union on the 11th of June.

On my arrival I found that the Assiniboines had been sent for; they soon came in, and I had everything arranged for the treaty on the arrival of the steamer *Ben Johnson*, on which the commissioners were coming. They were Governor Edmond of Dakota Territory, General Curtis of Iowa, Judge Gurnsey of Wisconsin, Elder W. Reed of anywhere, and Mr. M. K. Armstrong, secretary. The treaty, like many others which were never realized, was made for the purchase of all the Assiniboine lands on the south side of the Missouri, and 20 miles square on the north side, directly opposite the mouth of the Yellowstone River. In consideration of this they were to receive $30,000 per annum, for the term of 20 years; and I, for my children, was to get a section of land wherever I chose to take it on the Assiniboine land; but nothing of this was realized.

The following summer General Sully was sent by the department to treat with the Assiniboines. At the council they asked him if he knew anything of the boat which was to fetch them money according to last summer's treaty. He told them he knew nothing about it. They said they thought it very singular, if he came from their great father's house, that he knew nothing about their boat. Then they told him he lied like all the others; that they had been filled with talk up to their throats, and did not want any more. A few annuities were sent them this year, but, as bad luck would have it, the steamer on which the goods were coming sunk, and their groceries were all lost.

General Sully's object was to find out something about the treaty of last summer, and to show them what could be done without an Indian's having Ely Samuel Parker[78]

[78] Ely S. Parker was a full-blood Seneca who was born on the reservation at Tonawanda, N. Y., in 1828. He obtained an education, became a civil engineer,

as an example, and Father De Smet to inspire them with a conviction that the truth was spoken. I will say nothing of what remarks the Indians made. General Sully's commission was the most useless one I ever saw in the country, and the great Peace Commission was a complete failure.

On the 19th of July we left Union. On reaching the landing at Buford we learned that the Sioux had fired on the traders whom Mr. Gaben had sent from Union to them, after obtaining permission of the Peace Commissioners to do so. One was shot in the back with an arrow; and at least one ball glanced off the other, having struck the brass mounting of his belt. The fort was set on fire last night; but as many were moving about, it was discovered in time, and no injury was done. Having stolen many goods the Indians made their escape. The boat took on all that was left, and we proceeded down river.

As the treaty had not been made coming

and lived for a time at Galena, Ill., where he gained the acquaintance and friendship of General Grant, whose military secretary he was during the latter years of the Civil War. In 1867 he attained the rank of brigadier-general in the army, and from 1869 to 1871 served as Commissioner of Indian Affairs. His biography, by a great-nephew, comprises Volume XXIII of the Buffalo Hist. Soc. *Publications*.

up, the Commission had to stop at Berthold, which we reached on the 21st of July. The council was held next day. As the interpreter, Pierre Garreau, could not speak good English, I was appointed to interpret from his French into English. As the Gros Ventres did not feel inclined to sell their lands —at least, the portion the Commissioners wanted—the council lasted a long while. In some of their speeches the Commissioners remarked that they had treated with all the neighboring tribes, who would all be well off, and the Gros Ventres alone would remain poor; even some of the Sioux, who were considered hostile, had made peace, and now would listen to their words. The chief said: "I like to see you all. You look well—very nice-looking men indeed; but we think you lie, like all the others. One reason why we don't wish to sell you the land you want is that we have been much deceived. When we make treaties·for a long time, we get pretty well paid for a while; but it tapers off to a very small point, and then we see how completely we have been cheated. It is plain that you don't know what you are talking about when you say the Sioux are going to listen to your words; the Sioux are dogs—wolves—liars; and you will find it out ere long."

The Peace Commission

Not more than an hour after the Indian's speech the alarm of "Sioux! Sioux!" was given, and in less than half of a minute not a man was left in the council lodge—every Indian flew to his gun or bow and arrows, and was off in pursuit of the Sioux. About sunset they returned with five scalps, which they exhibited in front of the store to the gaze of the gentlemanly commissioners. Some of the Indians also had Sioux feet and hands tied around their horses' necks, while old squaws were dancing and jumping upon the scalps. They also took nine horses, but most of them died, having been overfed. "Now," said they, "here are your Sioux; see how well they listen to your words! They are the very same Sioux with whom you have just been making peace. We finished them with the fine new guns you gave them, and scalped them with your own knives. They are the very ones; and you will see some more of them at Fort Rice."[79]

The treaty was finally concluded, resulting in the purchase of 15 miles square at Snake River, 16 miles below Fort Berthold, where Fort Stevenson is now standing.

[79] Fort Rice was built by General Sully in the summer of 1864 on the right bank of the Missouri, half a dozen miles above the mouth of Cannon Ball River.

On the 28th we left Berthold, and next day reached Rice, where we found, as the Indians had said, the partisan of the war party, who had been at Berthold; they were 22 in number. Further down we stopped at the Santee Agency, at Running Water [the Niobrara]. The commissioners had a long sitting with these Indians, who requested them to tell their Great Father to give them a better place, for they could not stand it here—no wood, and subject to overflow. They were afterward removed lower down. On the 5th of August we reached Sioux City, where ended the great Peace Commission, and whence all went to their respective homes.

On the 12th of September I lost my daughter—25 years of age. On the 14th of February [1867] my son Charles died, 23 years of age. In the spring I went to St. Louis and made arrangements with the firm of Durfee and Peck to take charge of Union, in opposition to the North West Company. We reached that place on the 19th of June, 1867.

According to the request of the gentlemen of this Company, and contrary to my knowledge of the affairs of the concern, I erected an adobe store, 96 by 20 feet. During the summer Colonel Rankin, commander of Fort Buford, purchased Fort Union, to use the materials in building Buford. The North West Company then moved down and built at Buford. Finding that all the business of the country would finally be done at Buford, I abandoned my adobe store and erected one there of logs, 120 feet in length.

At this place I had to oppose the military sutler and the North West Company. In spite of this I traded 2000 buffalo robes, 900 elk hides, 1800 deerskins, and 1000 wolves', worth, in cash, $5000; but, owing to some jealousies, malicious reports were made against me, and I was discharged on the arrival of the steamer, on the 18th of May [1868].

I immediately went to the States, got up an outfit for Indian trade and sutler business, and on the 18th of August I was at Buford again, on my own hook. Having made some reductions on all sutler goods, I acquired popularity among the soldiers, and did well, considering my small outfit.

On the 3d of June [1869] I went down again and brought up another outfit the following August. All went on flourishing with me till the 1st of February, 1870, when I had the misfortune to break my thigh.[80]

On the 7th of June [1870] I went down to Omaha, to settle with the firm of Richard

[80] He remained a cripple from this time on.

Whitney and Co., with whom I was concerned. I bought them out, and returned to Buford. On this trip I was partly carried by some good folks, who would transport me from one car to the other, and in hobbling on crutches I suffered very much. Notwithstanding this great misfortune, I was getting along pretty well. I had a splendid establishment at Buford, where I was living with my family, having made it my home. But, being born for misfortune, I was ruined by the army bill, which passed Congress the previous July, allowing but one post sutler; this we did not learn till the following January [1871]. My daughter died on the following 14th of February. On the arrival of the new post sutler, Mr. Alvin C. Leighton, my store was closed, like that of the other sutlers. On the 14th of May, 1871, I left Buford, bag and baggage, for the States, and that was the last of the Indian country for me.

At the time those orders came from headquarters, I was a regular licensed trader, having been appointed sutler by General Hancock at St. Paul. Notwithstanding that it was in January, we were ordered forthwith off the reservation, which is only 30 miles square. Through the kindness of Colonel Gilbert, the commanding officer, we were permitted to remain on the reservation till spring, but our stores were closed. A month afterward we were allowed to open again and go on till the arrival of the regularly appointed sutler. On the 22d of June I took possession of my three forties which I had purchased of the railroad, and built a good house. On the 9th of December my little boy Louis, aged 12 years, died of inflammation of the lungs, after an illness of 48 hours.

Forty years ago was my first winter [1833–34] in the Indian country, at Fort William, when the stars appeared to fall. That my lucky star fell is plainly to be seen in this narrative. Whether there are any such stars may be a question, but there is no question of my being out of luck.[81]

---

[81] The autobiography was completed by the author in June, 1872. Considering the recency of the disasters chronicled in its closing paragraphs, the tone on which it ends is one of manly resignation; "written," says Coues, "when he had almost finished the allotted span of life, broken in health, broken in fortune, to die broken-hearted within a year."

Chapter 20

AMONG the Blackfeet the law in regard to adultery is death for the adulteress, and forfeiture of all the property of the adulterer. His lodge is cut into pieces, his horses are either killed or taken from him, and the woman must suffer death.

While I was at Benton an instance of this occurred in a very respectable family—for there are such among Indians. I should have said in two families. The woman was very young and handsome. Contrary to custom they had made it up, and the Indian could be seen with his wife as usual; but, being sensible that he had broken the law, he thought that he was looked upon as a weak-hearted man, and could not resist this tormenting idea. She was handsome; he loved her; he must either keep her or kill her. Tortured by reflections, which he could endure no longer, he took her out to walk, as he had been accustomed to do. They were sitting together, when he took her on his lap, combed her hair neatly—which is a mark of love with all Indians—vermilioned her face beautifully, and told her to sit by his side again. He then said, "My good wife, you have done wrong. I thought at one time I could overlook it, but I am scorned by my people. I cannot suffer you to be the wife of another. I love you too much for that. You must die." So saying, he buried his tomahawk in her skull.

When an Indian sees that his wife makes too free with young men, the penalty for such an offense is a piece of the nose. I have seen several who have undergone that punishment, and awful did they look. After cutting off her nose the husband says, "Go now and see how fond the young men will be of talking to you."

Among the Assiniboines there is no particular law in regard to adultery. This is left at the disposition of the injured individual, who sometimes revenges himself; but, if the relatives of the adulterer are strong, he may be content with a payment. Some give the woman a flogging, and then either drive her away or keep her. Nothing will be said about it, but the woman then bears a bad name—in their language Wittico Weeon, which means a prostitute, but not one of the first degree. A regular prostitute has no husband, and goes about to "lend herself," as they term it, for pay. Such a woman is gone beyond redemption. There are three different degrees of prostitution, one of which is looked upon as legal. This is when she is loaned with the consent of her parents, and then the larger the payment the more honor it is for the woman. When little quarrels arise among mothers in regard to the characters of their daughters, they will say, "What have you to say against my daughter? What did yours get when you lent her? Look at mine—what she got! You are making a Wittico Weeon of your daughter."

The young man who is courting dresses himself in the best style he can afford. His hair, which is the main point of attraction, is generally well combed in front, taking care that his stiff topknot stands straight up, while a long braid of false hair hangs down to his heels. With large pieces of California shells [abalone—*Haliotis*] in his ears, his neck and breast covered with an immense necklace of beads, his face vermilioned, and a fine pair of moccasins on his feet, his dress is complete. His over garment is either a blanket or a robe. Attired in this style, he commences his courtship by standing quite still in a place where he thinks that she will be likely to see him. This may last for many days without saying a word to her. He then makes friends with her brothers, particularly the elder one, who has a great deal to say in regard to the marrying of his sister. Then he watches for her when she goes for wood or water, saying a few words to her, and giving her a finger ring. When he makes small presents to the mother, father, and brothers they discover what he is after; but he never enters the lodge of his sweetheart. At this stage of the proceedings, if the young couple get very much in love with each other, and the young man cannot obtain the means to buy her, they elope to another band of the same tribe. But if he be a young man of means, and has obtained the consent of the woman, he ties a horse at her lodge; if the horse is accepted, the girl goes that night to his lodge; if not, the horse remains tied at the lodge, and the young man sends for it in the morning. If he has other horses, and loves the girl enough, the following day he ties two; and sometimes four or five horses are thus tied—the more horses, the greater honor for all parties. An elopement may also take place when the old folks will not consent, after the girl has been given the refusal of a horse. She is never forced to marry. Sometimes the individual who wants to buy a girl has never asked her whether she would have him or not, but has made very inducing offers to her parents, who then do all they can to persuade her, saying, "Take pity on us, daughter! This man likes us. He has given us a great many things. We are poor; we stand much in need of horses. He is a good hunter; he will make you live well; you need not remain poor." Yet, if the girl does not consent, they will not force her.

After marriage the woman belongs to the man. No one else has any right to her; and if she be the eldest, and have two or three sisters, they are also considered his wives, and cannot be disposed of without his consent. It frequently happens that he will take them all. The son-in-law never speaks to or looks at either of his parents-in-law. When invited to a feast or council where his father-in-law is to be he is duly apprised of it, and he covers himself with his robe and turns his back upon the old gentleman. An Indian who has but one wife will always be poor; but one that has three to four wives may become rich—one of the leading men, if not a chief. The reason of this is that the more wives the more children, and children are a source of wealth, resulting in a large family connection, which gives him power; for "might makes right" with them. An

Indian marries also in this light: When his family has increased with one wife till they find it impossible to get along without help, he buys a servant, as there is no such thing as hiring one; but she also becomes his wife, and is not looked upon as a servant. In all cases the old wife is always looked up to as the mistress of the whole. The son-in-law never keeps anything to himself until he gets a family; everything goes to his wife's relations, and this may continue even after he has a considerable family. From such customs it is plainly to be seen that the more wives an Indian has the richer he is—contrary to what the case may be with the whites. Notwithstanding customs so strange to us, these Indians live as peaceably and contentedly as civilized people do. It is a fine sight to see one of those big men among the Blackfeet, who has two or three lodges, five or six wives, twenty or thirty children, and fifty to a hundred head of horses; for his trade amounts to upward of $2000 a year, and I assure you such a man has a great deal of dignity about him.

The medicine lodge, which takes place once a year, in June, is conducted with the view to show how strong are Indians' hearts, and to beg the Great Spirit to have mercy upon the tribe. This lodge is erected of a size suitable to hold whatever number of spectators may be in attendance. A very large pole is planted in the ground, and many smaller ones are set up against it, in the manner of an ordinary lodge. One half of the space inside is reserved for those who are to undergo the torture, of which there are three kinds. In this half of the lodge pews are made with green bushes about four feet high; those for the women being separated from the others. When all is ready for the services to commence, the supposed strong-hearted persons come in and take their stands. They are painted in all colors, looking like so many devils—men and women alike; the former are naked down to their waists, but the latter are dressed. Holding in their mouths a small whistle made of the bone of a crow or pelican, and looking straight up to the center post of the lodge, they keep whistling and jumping up and down for three days and three nights, without drinking or eating; during which time eight or ten musicians, all blackened over, beat drums the whole night and day.

The second torture is done by piercing a hole through the skin of each breast, just above the nipple, and tying to each a lariat, which is then fastened by the other end to the top of the lodge-pole. Bearing all the weight they can upon the lariat, they trot back and forth outside the lodge, the space allowed each being according to the number of performers. This kind of torture goes on with a piteous groaning and lamentation, and these devotees are also painted in all sorts of colors, like the dancers. The third medicine or torture is performed by piercing a hole in each shoulder, to which lariats are fastened as before, but the other ends are tied to three or four dry buffalo skulls, which the communicant drags over the prairie, sometimes even up high ridges, weeping and wailing. Such performances are a great sight to behold.

An Indian chief is looked upon by most civilized people as a powerful and almost absolute ruler of his tribe; but he is not. Every tribe, no matter how small, is divided into bands, each of which has its chief and roams in a different part of the territory belonging to the tribe. As everything must have a head, a chief is appointed to represent the band in councils with the whites, and be consulted in the way of governing. He is a man who has power to do a great deal of harm, but as a general thing does little good. The soldier is the one who governs the band, and rules the chief, too, with a kind of government which the civilians

do not like; for when the soldier is established, they are under martial law. His lodge,
pitched in the center of the camp, is organized with the view to keep order and regu-
late the camp; mostly to prevent anyone
from going out alone on a hunt, so as not to
raise the buffalo, but also for mutual protection against enemies. When anyone is
caught outside his dogs are shot, his lodge
is cut to pieces, and if he rebels he gets a
pounding—the chief not excepted. Those
soldiers have their head soldier, to whom
each one applies to have his rights respected
or enforced. If anything be stolen, the head
soldier is apprised of the theft; he takes
some of the soldiers to examine the lodges,
and if the property is found it is given
back to the owner, but nothing is done with
the thief. This lodge is supported by the
people, who have to find wood, water,
and meat. Buffalo tongues go mostly to the
soldiers' lodge, and, if there be more than
can be eaten, they are sent to be traded for
sugar, coffee, and flour to make a big feast.
But the regular soldiers' feast is dog, and
when they feel like having such, no poor
old squaw's fine, fat, young dogs are spared.
Take it on the whole, Indians are very glad
when the lodge breaks up, and each one can
go where he pleases. After that the chief

will be left with eight or ten lodges, as they then go by those family connections which make leading men, some of whom actually have more influence than the chief himself —I mean with the people of the band.

All things considered, an educated man will see that their whole system of government amounts to nothing; that they are incapable of enforcing any laws like those of a civilized nation, and consequently not able to comply with treaties made with the United States. But such laws as they have answer their own purposes. As a nation they are kind and good to one another, and live in about as much peace and comfort as civilized people—that is, in their own way. One hears less complaint about hard times among them than among ourselves, except when they make a speech to a white man; then they are all very poor and pitiful, on the begging order. As a general thing the men are not quarrelsome. A fight will take place almost without a word. The women quarrel a good deal, and frequently fight with knives or clubs.

There are men and women doctors among them. They use some kinds of herbs and roots, but their greatest medical reliance is the magic of superstition. When the doctor is sent for, he comes with his drum, and a rattle, made of a gourd or dry hide filled with gravel. He sits beside the patient, and commences to beat the drum and shake the rattle at a great rate, singing a kind of song, or rather mumbling some awful noise. He always finds out what ails the patient. Sometimes it is a spell which has been thrown on him by some medicine man in camp, who had a spite against him. Such spells vary. Sometimes they are cords which have been passed through the limbs; at other times wolf hairs have been put between the skin and flesh, or bird claws of different kinds. But all of these he extracts by his magic, and shows the patient the hairs, claws, cords, or whatever may have been the spell. But some maladies are due to the devil, who has got into the sick person. In a case of that kind the doctor stations three or four boys with loaded guns outside the lodge at night; then he beats his drum at an awful rate, and at a certain sound, which is understood by the boys, they fire off their guns at the ground, as though they were shooting at rats running out of the lodge. These are supposed to be the devils whom the doctor has driven out of his patient. Should he continue sick, the treatment is repeated until he is cured or given up. Indians spare nothing to have their families or themselves doctored; they will give their guns, lodges, horses—everything they possess—to a doctor who will cure them. I have seen some completely stripped of all they had to pay the doctor. When a child dies the parents give everything away to mourners; and if the family is rich there will be a great many mourners, particularly among the women, who come to shed a few tears for the sake of plunder. It is thought, "She cries; she loved my child; she must have something." The mourning lasts for a year, unless some relation kills one of their enemies; then the family blacken their faces, which does away with the period of mourning. After this, someone will give a gun, another a horse, some other a lodge, and thus the Indian will get a start again.

Medicine men who are thought able to lay spells are much in danger, and sometimes lose their lives at the hands of the relations of one who dies by such magic. I myself saw a young man kill a fine-looking Indian for having, as he said, laid a spell on his father, who died of consumption. The young man shot him at night, about twenty steps from the fort. We went to see him in the morning; he was lying dead, the ball having penetrated his heart. The young man was there, laughing and whirling his tomahawk over him, saying, "That doctor will lay no more spells."

Indians have no words for swearing or cursing, like whites, but they have a way to express wrath a great deal more scornfully than a white man can in words. This is done by gathering the four fingers against the thumb and letting them spring open, at the same time throwing out the arm, straight in one's face, with the body and face half turned away, saying, "Warchteshnee," which means, as nearly as I can interpret it, "You villain!"

The Indian idea of futurity and immortality of the soul is something about which I never could find out much. All Indians believe in a Great Spirit, the ruler of all they see and know, but of any future existence, in which the wicked are punished and the good rewarded, they know nothing. They believe in ghosts, who live again in an invisible form, thinking that their dead relations come to see them; and that the only way ghosts make themselves known is by whistling, mostly at night, but sometimes by day, in very lonesome places. In consequence of this belief, they make feasts for the ghosts, consisting principally of dried berries, which they would not for anything omit to gather. They boil these berries with meat, or pound a quantity of buffalo meat with marrow fat, with either of which they go to the place where the dead is deposited, say a few words to the departed, hold the eatables up for him or her to partake of, and then divide the feast among the living who are in attendance. Anyone is allowed to attend this ceremony. But whether the ghosts are in a state of happiness or not, they do not pretend to say, nor do they know what distinction may be made between the good and the wicked. To themselves it makes no difference; they feed both good and bad alike.

On being very hard pressed for a statement expressing their ideas regarding resurrection, most Indians would finally say that they thought once dead was the last of a person. In conversation with them I found much pleasure in hearing their stories, which they relate with great eloquence, using a great many figurative expressions. I had some books printed in their language, which I brought with me from St. Paul. These were religious books, gotten up by missionaries of Minnesota, containing Noah's Ark, Jonah swallowed by the whale, and other miracles; at which they would laugh heartily when I read to them, and then say, "Do the whites believe all this rubbish, or are they stories such as we make up to amuse ourselves on long winter nights?" They were very fond of having me read them such stories; that big boat tickled them, and how could Noah get all those animals into it was the question. Then they would say, "The white man can beat us in making up stories." Telling stories is a great pastime with Indians. There are many among them who are good at it; they are always glad to see such come into a company, saying, "Here is such a one; now we'll have some stories told."

The Indian is born, bred, and taught to be a warrior and a hunter; he aspires to nothing else. There is no regular habit of husbandry among them; they always live from hand to mouth. During the 40 years I was in their country I saw no disposition on their part to ameliorate their condition. They are still in the same state. They have no intellectual invention. In regard to their "medicine," one performance which has attracted my attention I do not attribute to magic but to skill. This is the way in which they bring a band of buffalo into their pens. Such a pen is constructed of poles, and bushes, and any other combustibles they can obtain to make a kind of fence, which is by no means sufficient to keep in the buffalo. This inclosure is made of different sizes, but is generally capable of containing 200 or 300 buffaloes. It is made round, and a pole is stuck up in the middle, with scarlet cloth, kettles, pans, and a great many other articles tied to the top. Those are sacrifices to the Great Spirit, made by the individual who is to go after the buffalo. When this pen is finished two wings are made extending a great distance from the entrance, like an immense quail net. These wings are made either of snow or of buffalo chips, gathered at intervals into small heaps sufficiently large to conceal a person. As the pen must be made where there is little wood, it frequently happens that the buffalo are discovered two or three days' march from the spot. When all is ready, the medicine man starts after the buffalo. When the people of the camp see him coming, they all surround the pen, except those who are stationed at intervals along the wings, each hidden behind a pile of snow or chips. The buffalo follow him, and when the last one has passed, the herd being completely within the wings, the people all rise from their places of concealment. The buffalo then rush into the pen. Then the people who surround the pen also rise up, and are joined by those who were behind the wings. The buffalo, being frightened, keep away from the sides of the pen, running around the pole in the middle; though it sometimes happens that, the pen being too small or too weak, they break through in spite of all the Indians can do. With their bows and arrows the Indians begin the work of destruction, and go on till all the buffalo are killed. It is a good sight to see that one Indian bring in a large band of buffalo, which has followed him for two or three days. He is considered a great medicine man.

Chapter 21

BEFORE offering some suggestions I wish to make in regard to future rules and regulations for Indians and their country, I will introduce all the Indian agents I have personally known on the Missouri.

In 1832 Major Sanford took from Union to Washington three chiefs—one Assiniboine, one Cree, and one Chippewa. The Assiniboine was the son of the chief of the Rock or Stone band, named Wan-hee-manza (the Iron Arrow-point). He was a fine-looking man about 30 years of age, named Lya-jan-jan (the Shining Man). All the manners and other good things which he brought from Washington, to show his people what an advance he had made in civilization, was a white towel, which he used to wipe his face and hands, and a house-bell, which he tied to the door of his lodge. His people said that all he had got from the whites was a gift of the gab. After his return he passed himself off for a great medicine man, and said that no ball could penetrate his skin. He had a strong connection, and was much feared. But the next summer a certain individual thought he would try the strength of his medicine, and shot a bullet through his head. The ball was harder than his head, and went through in spite of the strength of his medicine. He was brought to Fort Union, and buried after their own way in a tree. In the summer a requisition for Indian skulls was made by some physicians from St. Louis. His head was cut off and sent down in a sack with many others. Which of them came out first is hard to tell; but I don't think his did. This is the whole amount of good that chief did. As he went down during President Jackson's administration, his name, with the whites, was Jackson. The Cree chief never amounted to anything, nor did the Chippewa.

Major Sanford was very much of a gentleman, but cared more for the interests of the American Fur Company than for Indian affairs. He afterward married Mr. Pierre Chouteau's daughter, and one can judge in whose favor his reports would be likely to be made.

Major Ferguson, the greenest of all agents I ever saw, was paid $1500 for a pleasure trip from St. Louis to Fort Union. He came up in the steamer, saw no Indians, and left what few annuities he had to be divided among them by the Company. What report could that agent make in regard to his Indians? None, of course. That was the last of him.

Major More was a great drunkard, who came up to Union in the steamer, remained 24 hours, and returned to Fort Pierre. It was reported by a person whom I believe, that the Indians there kicked his stern, taking him for a dog, when he was crawling out of the room where they had been sleeping, and laughingly said they were very sorry that they had kicked their father.

Major Matlock was a drunken gambler. The last I saw of him was at Trading Point, opposite Bellevue, where he was drinking and gambling, and kept several Mormon women. I was informed that he died, shortly afterward, in poverty.

Major Dripps was, I believe, a good, honest old beaver trapper. He was sent to examine the trading posts, to find out about the liquor trade. He sent his interpreter ahead to let us know he was coming. On his arrival he looked in all places except in the cellar, where there was upward of 30 barrels of alcohol. The major was afterward equipped by the American Fur Company, and went on the Platte, where he died.

Major Hatting was a young man about 27 or 28 years old, a drunkard and a gambler, almost gone up by the bad disorder. He was of no earthly account. I could say much more, but decency forbids.

Major Norwood, instead of being with his Indians, kept himself about Sergeant's Bluffs, attending balls and parties given by whites and half-breeds, and was finally killed by William Thompson, who knocked his brains out with the butt of a rifle. This was the last of the major.

Major Redfield went 50 miles up the Yellowstone, on his way to the Crows, was taken sick, and returned to the States in the fall; his goods were left to be divided by the Company. I knew nothing regarding his personal character.

Major Vaughan was a jovial old fellow, who had a very fine paunch for brandy, and, when he could not get brandy, would take almost anything which would make drunk come. He was one who remained most of his time with his Indians, but what accounts for that is the fact that he had a pretty young squaw for a wife; and as he received many favors from the Company, his reports must have been in their favor.

I have but little to say about Major Schoonover, who remained one winter at

Union, powerless, like all others, being dependent on the American Fur Company.

Major Latta was a pretty fair kind of a man, but the less said of him the better. He came up to Union, put the annuities out on the bar, and next day was off.

Major Mahlon Wilkinson came as near doing the right thing as was in his power, but he was too lazy to do much of anything.

Major Clifford was a captain of the regular army, which rendered him unfit for such an office, not caring a fig about Indians. I could say a great deal more if I felt so disposed. From what I have been able to learn I fully believe that all the Indian agents were of the same material; and had those men been ever so well qualified to fill their office, they could not have done it under the existing rules and regulations. Once in the Indian country they came entirely under the influence of the American Fur Company, and could not help themselves.

Those gentlemen were appointed by the Indian Department not only as agents, but as fathers to the Indians; to remain with their children, and to make true reports to their Great Father at Washington of the behavior of the Indians and of all transactions in their country that come to the agent's notice, thus keeping the department

well posted. The question is, Was that done?
No; evidence shows the contrary. In consequence of this bad state of affairs, the department remained ignorant of the true
condition of the country, and could never
hold the proper kind of council with the
Indians; and, finally, war broke out. Of all
the councils I attended, I never saw one
properly held, according to my knowledge
of Indian character and customs.

I will mention one, which was the most
absurd I ever heard of—though gotten up
by men who should have known better. This
is the Laramie treaty of 1851.

David D. Mitchell, who had been an Indian trader, was the superintendent of Indian
Affairs at St. Louis. I suppose speculation,
as in the case of all other treaties, was the
cause of this one.[82] It was gotten up with

[82] The purpose of the Fort Laramie council and
treaty of 1851 was to establish peaceful relations between the several tribes and between them and the
U. S. government. A good account of the negotiation,
together with its ultimate results, is given by General
H. M. Chittenden in his *Hist. of Early Steamboat
Navigation on the Missouri River* (New York, 1903),
II, 359 ff. The author presents a more understanding
account of the situation than does Larpenteur, but his
final conclusion that the entire governmental system
of dealing with the Indians was fundamentally wrong,
coincides with the opinion, less temperately expressed,
of the latter.

the intention of making a general peace between all the tribes on the Missouri and the Platte. For this purpose two or three chiefs of each tribe were invited to the treaty. Anyone who has the least knowledge of Indian character ought to know that they are not capable of keeping such a peace. Of course any Indian, for the sake of presents, will say "How" to any proposition made to him; but, after that, what assurance have you to rely upon that this Indian will comply with the stipulations of the treaty? None at all. You may say that, if he does not comply, he shall forfeit a part of his annuities. But if you make him forfeit his annuities it will be worse; for, although this will have been explained to him, he will think that he had a right to do as he did. He will say that his young men had no ears; that he did all in his power, but could not control them; and still think himself entitled to the annuities. He will surely find some excuse.

The result of the Laramie treaty was that the Indians fought before they got home; war was carried on among them the same as before, and afterward war with the whites.[83]

[83] The peace with the whites was broken in 1854 over the slaughter of a detachment of soldiers, precipitated by the theft by an Indian of a stray cow. In 1855 General Harney severely punished the hostile

At the time of this treaty, did the Crows think the Sioux would be permitted by the Government, after all the promises made them, to drive away their traders from the Yellowstone, and that they themselves would then be driven out of their own country? Did Crazy Bear, chief of the Assiniboines, expect his people to be removed from their country into that of their enemies? "No," they said, "the whites have lied to us. They have taken our country. They say they bring soldiers to protect us; but, when they come, they bring the Sioux with them. Loads of provisions come out of their garrisons for the Sioux, who are on our own lands, and we can get nothing. Do they give rations to the Sioux because they are afraid of them, or is it because the Sioux drive away their cattle and kill their soldiers? We cannot understand those whites. We had a good country, which we always thought they would save for us; they have given it

Indians in the battle of Ash Hollow, and a new peace of seven years' duration was established. In general, it may be said that the white race was bent on taking the Indian country from its red owners, the latter resisted to the best of their ability, and a generation of more or less constant warfare followed, the last military action being the battle of Wounded Knee in 1890, since when the Indians have lacked the power to challenge the white man on the field of battle.

to our enemies. Fort Union, the house built for our old fathers,—in the heart of our country,—the soldiers have pulled it down to build their Fort Buford, where we are scarcely permitted to enter."

It is plainly to be seen that treaties made with Indians have never amounted to anything, and never will. The Government must manage them; but, to do so, must be well acquainted with their wants. They are called children, and must be treated as such. The father should know his children; but how can he know them if he is not with them? And if he be a worthless father, how can he bring up his children right? My suggestions will show the proper way to manage Indians. I think I have plainly shown errors in the Indian Department. Treaties, councils, and expeditions have not had the desired effect.

One not acquainted with Indians might say that the army has been the means of bringing them under some subjection. I know that the chief motive for yielding was not the sword, the bullet, or the bayonet, but hunger and the prospect of starvation. Had the Indians continued to possess the buffalo which were theirs 25 years ago, a different display of armed forces would have been made. Hunger has somewhat tamed them, much against their will. When I first came into the country few Indians liked coffee, and they looked at a white man's eating pork as we did an Indian's eating dog.

It must be borne in mind that the Indian is wild, and that any attempt to tame him is going entirely contrary to his nature. The question remains with me, can it be done? From what I have seen, and knowing him as I do, I would say it cannot be done; yet there is nothing like trying. The following suggestions are those I propose for the trial. In the first place, much of the Indian country is not capable of large settlements, on account of the insusceptibility of the soil for agriculture, and the scarcity of timber. I would divide the tribes into agencies according to their population, and establish regularly surveyed boundaries to each of those agencies. In all tribes in which there were more than one agent, I would have a superintendent, who should be called the governor of the tribe. All agents should be obliged to remain nine months in the year at their agencies. They should keep a regular diary of all transactions, and a regular list of chiefs and leading men of the tribe, stating their characters and giving all such other information as would tend to bring them to the acquaintance of his successor. In tribes where there was but one agency, this agent should be the governor of the entire tribe, and have the power to issue a license for trading with Indians or whites to any American citizen, without bonds. This agency should be the point where all business should be transacted. No traders or storekeepers should be allowed to establish themselves more than 500 yards from the agency, and under no consideration should they be permitted to go among the Indians to trade. Every trader and storekeeper should be provided with the rules and regulations of the agency, and, should he violate any of them, his store should be closed, and himself ordered out of the country, never to be allowed to trade again in any of the Indian countries. No white man should be allowed to live with a squaw for a wife, unless lawfully married; and such marriage should entitle him to the same privileges as an Indian. The agent should be allowed 25 laboring men, two carpenters, one wheelwright, one blacksmith, one engineer, and one sawyer. All laborers should be enlisted for the term of two years, under military rules and regulations, but allowed to dress as they pleased. A laundress should be provided by the department for the benefit of the men, her wages to be $30 per month. The amount of washing allowed at this rate to each man per week should be two shirts, one pair of drawers, two pair of socks, and two handkerchiefs; all fine linen shirts to be paid for extra. Laborers should receive $30 per month, paid every two months. No house should be frame, but all built of sawed or hewn logs, roofed with earth, having pine floors, doors, and casings for windows and doors.

The agent or governor should have full control over the territory said to belong to his Indians. To give him power to enforce rules and regulations and to police his territory well, I would recommend a military post of one or more companies, according to the Indian population, to be established not over half a mile from the agency. The troops should be cavalry, as infantry avails naught in the Indian country. The commander of such a post should have nothing to do with Indians, being only stationed there to assist and protect the governor, and should never be permitted to act without the latter's consent.

This governor should be provided with all kinds of agricultural implements, to be distributed to his Indians. He should furnish them with timber to build and allow them each a certain sum in payment for every panel of fence any Indian might put up, besides furnishing him with material to make it; and so much an acre for breaking his land, let it be with the plow or hoe. All fences should be horse-high, bull-strong, and hog-tight. Hogs, cattle, and chickens should be distributed, and there should be an agricultural fair annually, as in the States. Every three months inspect the Indian houses, and give premiums to the first, second, and third best housekeeper. Hold monthly meetings with chiefs and leading men, and as many others as the house can hold. There are many other regulations I could suggest, but the above are the main ones. Agencies being established in this manner, the agent cannot fail to be well posted on the state of affairs in his territory, and can thus govern with due care.

In regard to schools and missions I think that the Indians are still too wild for any such establishments or institutions. They must first be turned to agriculture, be taught habits of industry and economy, and thus become gradually accustomed to the ways of the whites. It would be better, in my opinion, to postpone the institutions for a few years. Teach them the Ten Commandments, and try to make them obey them— which I leave for the governor to do if he can. There are two strong obstacles to success—the wild nature of the Indians, and the sterility of their soil.

To secure an agent or a governor fit for such an office would require a salary of at least $3000 a year, instead of $1500.

After all, whether agencies be established in this manner or not, I see no use of the military posts now on the Missouri. I do not propose to abolish them with the view of saving expense to the Government, but rather to apply the military to the work of ameliorating the condition of the Indian. Supposing agencies established as I have suggested, what would be the use of Randall, Sully, Rice, Stevenson, and Buford? To my knowledge they have never been of any use. They have reservations 30 miles square, upon which no one is allowed to remain but themselves, their sutler, and contractor; and that land is generally taken from the best part of the Indian country. Thus stationed, far apart, with infantry only, what good do they do? Whom have they to protect but themselves? From Berthold to Peck, a distance of at least 500 miles, there are no agencies, nor traders. Buford is situated about the middle of this distance, with three or four companies of infantry. What are they there for but to do nothing on the best of the land at the greatest expense?

Indian Agents and Agencies

Stevenson is perfectly useless. Rice is situated where no Indians go, 125 miles from Stevenson, and about the same distance from Grand River agency; of what use is it, with its four companies? None. Sully is in sight of the Cheyenne agency, with one or two companies, and all the organized agencies below. I pronounce it of no earthly use. Randall ditto. The country will not support such large garrisons. The scarcity of grass and fuel will not admit of such forts, which destroy the best locations on the river and displease the Indians to no purpose. Buford has one of the best locations, which would answer for a very extensive Indian reservation; there is not another such point on the river between Randall and Benton. It is now spoiling that fine country for the mere sake of living there.

On these large military reservations no licensed Indian traders are allowed; but the sutler is allowed to trade with Indians, and they are permitted to come on the reservation. If a licensed trader wishes to establish a post he cannot do so nearer than 15 miles from the garrison, much too far to receive any protection, and this gives the sutler the monopoly of the Indian trade. As the soldier trade is well secured, it is plainly to be seen that the military rule the Indian country.

But my suggestions would put the control of the Indian and his country where it properly belongs.

If the Indians should commit depredations requiring punishment, would those garrisons, organized as they are now, be able to pursue and chastise them? Surely not; and, if they had absolutely to be punished, the government would have to send a different force after them, and let the garrisons eat their pork and beans uselessly, as usual.

A few days after writing my remonstrance in regard to the garrisons on the Missouri, I saw in the *Sioux City Journal* a report made by a gentleman named A. D. Rodefer, in reference to the pastimes of the officers of Fort Rice. During his stay at the post he participated in a deer-hunt with the officers. There are sixteen hounds at the fort, and a number of experienced hunters; and what with the hunters and the hounds, the officers' tables are constantly supplied with game. The amusements at Rice are numerous and varied. Two nights in the week the post is entertained by amateur theatrical and minstrel troupes. One night is devoted to dancing, and the rest to epicurean parties, etc.

Such reports, I think, show the uselessness of these garrisons. Why do the soldiers not

358

amuse themselves by running after this famous Sitting Bull, who, the same reporter says, is bound to take Fort Peck this winter? No; they would freeze. It is best for them to dance all winter, and let the United States send somebody else after Sitting Bull when the grass grows in the spring.

Ta-tang-ah-eeoting's or Sitting Bull's ideas in regard to the whites were expressed in my presence at Fort Union in 1867. He remarked: "I have killed, robbed, and injured too many white men to believe in a good peace. They are medicine, and I would eventually die a lingering death. I had rather die on the field of battle"—or, as he put it— "have my skin pierced with bullet holes." "And, for another thing," he continued, "I don't want to have anything to do with people who make one carry water on the shoulders and haul manure." He has frequently invited the Sioux and Assiniboines to join him, telling them not to stick so close to the whites, getting as poor as snakes, eating nothing but bacon and hard-tack. They had better leave, he thought, and do as he did—go into the buffalo country, eat plenty of meat, and when they wanted a good horse, go to some fort and steal one. "Look at me," he said; "see if I am poor, or my people either. The whites may get me at last, as you say, but I will have good times till then. You are fools to make yourselves slaves to a piece of fat bacon, some hard-tack, and a little sugar and coffee."

Index

Index

ABEL, Annie H., edits Chardon journal, 114.

Adams Prairie, Fort Alexander built, 138, 146–49.

Adultery, Indian punishment of, 326–27.

Ague, traders suffer from, 126–27.

Amell's Island, Larpenteur camps at, 208.

American Fur Company, organized, xvi; Western Department established, xviii; employs Larpenteur, 11, 300–309; traders oppose, 12, 44–50, 151, 185–87, 198, 288–89; operates distillery, 46, 60–62; builds Fort Clark, 65; enters trade of Upper Missouri, 91–97; quarrel with partners, 137; employs Alexander Harvey, 142–46; Major Dripps, 345; trading methods described, 199; competition feared, 264; controls Indian agents, 344–47.

Andrew, interpreter, ill, 156; dies, 180.

Annuities, controversy over, 242–45; payment, to Indians, 311–14, 345–47; lost, 318.

Antelope, on Upper Missouri, 121–22.

Arikara (Ree) Indians, language spoken, 65; threaten traders, 114; warfare with Assiniboine, 115; with Sioux, 213; encounter of Larpenteur with, 213–15; kill Iron-eyed Dog, 222.

Armstrong, M. K., secretary of Peace Commission, 317.

Army posts, uselessness of, 356–58.

Ash Hollow, battle of, 349–50.

Ashley, William H., organizes Rocky Mountain Fur Company, xvi; fur-trade operations, 9–12; employs James Bridger, 181.

Ashton's Grove, Larpenteur camps at, 251.

Assiniboine, on Upper Missouri, 51.

Index

Index

Index

Bonneville, Captain, post, on Green River, 26.

Bourbonnais, Augustin, love affair of, 98–102.

Bordeux, ——, fur-trade employee, 218.

Brazo, John, flogs culprits, 101, 135–36; shoots Bourbonnais, 101–102; in smallpox epidemic, 111; in hunting contest, 127–29; gives Indian alarm, 130.

Bridger, James, reputation, 14; career, 181; at Fort Union, 181–85.

Broken Arm, Cree (Assiniboine?) chief, Larpenteur visits village, 160–66; deceives Larpenteur, 284.

Brugière, Jacques (James), nephew of James Kipp, as fur-trade employee, 126, 221; as drunkard, 138; as partner of Larpenteur, 224–39.

Bruguière, Théophile, befriends Larpenteur, 253–54.

Buckley, Dr. John, advises Larpenteur, 246.

Buffaloes, meat, as food, 20–22, 48, 56–57, 65–66, 138–39, 158, 161, 168, 178, 214–15, 229–30, 351–52; lightning kills, 24; boats made from hides, 25, 34, 212–13; cattle shod with hides, 40; scarcity, 47–48; hides taken by traders, 51, 136, 151, 162, 165, 204, 264, 273, 286–87, 323; fight over, 141–42; dance, 263; abundance, at Fort Stewart, 264, 286; hunted, 282, 340–42; dispute over ownership of hides, 279–80; market for, destroyed, 277, 281; prices rise, 288.

Bull-boats, traders make, 25, 34, 212; Indians use, 213.

Burbank, ——, system of freighting, 281.

Bushwhackers, danger from, 280.

CABANNÉ, John P., career, 137.

California, gold discovered, 218.

Campbell, Robert, career, 10; fur-trade operations, 12–53, 198, 264–65, 275–76, 288; kindness to Larpenteur, 13, 15, 28–29, 51–54; misadventure of, 40; dealings with Gauché, 44–47; sale of interests, 28–29, 50; employs hunter, 227.

Campbell, Thomas, at Fort Union, 315.

Canadians, employed at Fort Union, 85–86; Blackfeet friendly with, 93–94; as keelboat men, 208.

Index

Index

Crazy Bear, treatment of rival traders, 153–54; mentioned, 350.

Cree Indians, visit Fort Williams, 92; language of, 132, 156; Larpenteur trades with, 155, 160–66.

Crow Creek Agency, controversy over payment of annuities at, 242–45.

Crow Indians, friendly toward traders, 36–38; Fort Cass established, 38; traders visit, 84, 93, 193; relations with James P. Beckwourth, 89; language spoken, 149; alarm traders, 232; warfare with Sioux, 291; with Assiniboines, 310–14; Major Redfield as agent, 346; government mistreats, 349–50.

Culbertson, Alexander, commands Fort Union, 138, 145–46, 150–55, 165–80; commands Blackfoot outfit, 192; settles with Alexander Harvey, 197; builds Fort Louis, 207; abandons, 225; kindness to Larpenteur, 238–39; fur-trade activities, 217, 242.

Curtis, General, as Peace Commissioner, 317.

Cyclone, overtakes Larpenteur, 253.

Dances, at Fort Stewart, 263.

Dauphin, Louis, reports arrival of steamboats, 276; commands Fort Galpin, 298; slain, 298–99.

Dauphin, Louise, as mate for Larpenteur, 8.

Dauphin's Fort, Larpenteur plans sojourn at, 287.

Davenport, Col. George L., career, 6–7.

Deer, abundance, at Ponca Post, 258.

Deerskins, traders take, 323.

Denig, E. T., as surgeon, 102; Larpenteur visits parents, 123–25; as drunkard, 138, 156–57; on trip to Woody Mountain, 155–57; quarrel with Wounded Leg, 170; in fight with Sioux, 183; leader of fur-trade employees, 193–94; at Fort Union, 218.

Deschamps, François, Jr., plot to slay, 72–75; slain, 81–84.

Deschamps, François, Sr., slain, 72–75; evil character, 74.

Deschamps, Mother, in family feud, 80; slain, 82; buried, 84.

369

Index

Index

Index

Index

Fort Vermilion, Larpenteur visits, 120–21, 240–42; commands, 246–49, 258.

Fort William, history, 40; built, 42–43, 49–50, rebuilt, 58–60; trading activities, 44–55; shelters half-breeds and free trappers, 64, 72; smallpox victims, 111; Deschamps family slain, 62–64, 72–76, 80–84; opposition to American Fur Company, 153–55; mentioned, 314.

Fox, Livingston and Company, opposes American Fur Company, 148, 151–206.

Frap, ——, buys fur-trade interest, 28.

Frederick (Md.), Larpenteur visits, 123.

Free trappers, Indians harass, 50; misconduct at Fort Union, 63–64; competition for services, 209; mentioned, 257, 295.

Frenier, Antoine, horse stolen, 131–32.

Friday, ward of Thomas Fitzpatrick, 14.

Frost, Todd and Company, builds Fort Stewart, 262; mentioned, 298.

GARDEPIE, Baptiste, feud with Deschamps family, 65, 72–75, 80–84; in fight with Sioux, 184–85.

Galena (Ill.), Larpenteur visits, 247.

Galpin, Major Charles E., Fort Galpin named for, 291.

Garreau, Pierre, sent to Canoe Assiniboines, 104–108.

Gauché (Cohan, Hurry-up, Meenohyaukenno), trades with whites, 44–47; raids Blackfeet, 76–78; visits Fort Union, 110–11; successor of, 223.

Georgetown, route via, 266.

Gervais, ——, buys fur-trade interest, 28.

Ghent, W. J., biographer of Thomas Fitzpatrick, 14.

Gilbert, Colonel, kindness to Larpenteur, 324–25.

Gold, discovery of, 218.

Gooding, Capt. George, widow remarries, 5.

Government, among Indians, 333–35.

Grand River Indian Agency, mentioned, 357.

Grant, General U. S., befriends Ely S. Parker, 319.

Index

Index

Hatting, Major, in annuity controversy, 242–45; as Indian agent, 346.

Hawley, ——, member of North West Company, 309, 314.

Heart River, Indians encountered, 302–303; route via, 305; mentioned, 115–17, 295.

Henry, Andrew, as organizer of Rocky Mountain Fur Company, xvi.

Herbs, in Indian medical practice, 335.

He Who Fears His War Club, befriends Larpenteur, 169–70.

Hodgkiss, ——, commands Fort Union, 297–98; death, 304.

Holmes, George, bitten by wolf, 30; death, 33–34.

Halsey, J., in smallpox epidemic, 109–10; as doctor, 126.

Hooting Owl, befriends Larpenteur, 106–107.

Horses, stolen, 85–89, 103, 131–32, 139–41, 146, 176, 194, 287, 291; recovered, 104–105, 133, 194; Indians attempt to steal, 205; sell, 226–27; as food, 229–31; as payment for wife, 329–30.

Howard, Joseph, as guide, 211.

Hubble, Hawley and Company, purchase trading posts, 309.

Hudson's Bay Company, method of marking blankets, 55; rivalry with North West Company, 90–91.

Hydrophobia, mad wolves inflict, 33–34.

Ice, blocks navigation on Mississippi, 247.

Immortality, Indian conception of, 338–40.

Independence (Mo.), as limit of Missouri River settlement, 121.

Indian Agents, characterized, 343–48.

Indian ponies, purchased, 250.

Indians, hostility to whites, 32, 35–36, 248; in smallpox epidemic, 109–12; threaten traders, 114–17, 121, 138, 166–69, 291–92; fear bears, 147; rivalry for trade of, 185–87; dispute over annuities, 242–45;

Index

Index

Lice, afflict Larpenteur, 235–37.

Liquor, drinking sprees, 6, 46–47, 63-64, 80, 105–107, 134–35, 150, 159–62, 165, 201–203; traders smuggle, 46; drinking, by fur-trade employees, 25, 27–28, 58–60, 136–38, 156–57; by Blackfeet, 77; by Indian agents, 345–47; Crow Indians abstain from, 37; as payment for horses, 104–105; fondness of Francis Chardon for, 120; as present to Indians, 153; in Sully campaign, 300.

Little Frenchman, in Deschamps family feud, 72, 75–76.

Little Blue River, traders cross, 20.

Little Missouri River, mentioned, 305.

Lake Pepin, frozen over, 247.

Lisa, Manuel, fur-trade activities, xv.

Little Robes, warfare with Flatheads, 225–26.

Little Sioux River, as home of Larpenteur, xix, 249–55; home burned, 277; Larpenteur visits, 290, 316.

Lorimier, Louis, career, 23.

Lya-jan-jan, Assiniboine chief, visits Washington, 343.

McConnellstown, Larpenteur visits, 123–25.

Mackinaw boats, traders use, 51, 136, 144, 149, 151, 198, 207, 209, 239, 278–79, 288–89; described, 278; built, 274, 278, 283–88; miners use, 307.

Mackenzie, Alexander, relative of Kenneth McKenzie, 90.

McKenzie, Kenneth, fur-trade activities, xviii, 45, 50, 52–54, 56–58, 61–62, 87–88, 122, 137, 193, 198–206, 265; career, 38, 90–97; builds Fort Union, 55; rôle in half-breed feud, 81; affair with Bourbonnais, 98–102.

McKenzie, Owen, as messenger, 193–94; commands Assiniboine post, 291–92; Fort Galpin, 293–95; slain, 298.

Mal de Vache, malady, characterized, 22.

Mandan Indians, visits of early explorers, xiii; sell corn, 46; warfare with Assiniboines, 65–67; make peace with, 222; mentioned, 296.

Index

Mitchell, David D., career, 104; fur-trade activities, 113, 126–33, 137; sentences murderers, 135–36; as Superintendent of Indian Affairs, 348.

Moncrèvie, ——, misconduct of, 58–60; discharged, 63.

Montana, settlers bound for, 301.

Moose Point, as site for trading post, 289.

More, Major, as Indian agent, 345.

Mormons, feud with James Bridger, 181; migration of, 213; as early settlers, 254.

Mosquitoes, as pests, 252, 256.

Mouse (Souris) River, traders reach, 267–68; axe lost, 269.

Mules, traders use, 10, 16, 18, 23–26, 41, 103; frozen, 163; stolen, 287.

Murray, ——, commands Fort Van Buren, 138; Fort Alexander, 148.

NAPOLEON I, rescue planned, 4.

Nellie Rogers, on Upper Missouri, 295.

New Orleans, Larpenteur visits, 246.

Niobrara (Running Water) River, Ponca Post at mouth, 255; as boundary, 258; Santee agency at, 322.

North West Company, rivalry with Hudson's Bay Company, 90–91; Larpenteur opposes, 322–23.

Norwood, Major, as Indian agent, 346.

Nose, cut off, as punishment, 327.

Nute, Grace Lee, report on Larpenteur manuscript, xxi.

O'FALLON, Benjamin, career, 6; recommends Larpenteur, 11.

O'Fallon, Dr. James, career, 6.

O'Fallon, John, career, 6.

Old Star, father of Arikara war-chief, 214.

Omaha, mentioned, 280, 323.

Omaha Indians, attack traders, 121; on Little Sioux River, 254, 259; transmit smallpox, 255.

One Who Guards the Whites, slain, 199–200.

Index

Index

Index

Sioux City, as terminus of French exploration, xiii; first settler, 253; General Sully leaves, 304; mentioned, 262, 299, 316, 322.

Sioux Indians, warfare with traders, 182–85, 220, 291–92, 296–303, 306–308; with Assiniboines, 194, 199–200; with Omaha and Oto, 255, 259–60; with Gros Ventres, 320–22; language spoken, 257; traders avoid, 265; campaigns of Sully and Sibley against, 300–306; relations with Peace Commission, 320–22; government favors, 350–51; career of Sitting Bull, 359–60.

Sitting Bull (Ta-tang-ah-eeoting), attitude toward whites, 359–60.

Skiff, Larpenteur builds, 274–75.

Smallpox, epidemic of 1837, 109–12, 115; Larpenteur's son dies, 255.

Smith, A. B., heads North West Company, 309, 314.

Smith, Jedediah S., fur-trade activities, xvii.

Smith, Jefferson, as fur-trade partner, 264–80; characterized, 273; misconduct, 276–77, 279–80, 289–90.

Snake Indians, boy adopted, 14; traders visit, 28.

Snake River, explored, xvii; reservation ceded, 321.

Snow, traders encounter, 156–62, 166–67, 258, 285.

Soldiers, Indian, powers of, 333–34.

Souris River, see Mouse River.

South Pass, discovered, xvii; traders reach, 25.

Spain, owns Missouri country, xiv. See also Isidoro.

Spells, medicine-men lay, 337–38.

Spread Eagle, at Fort Union, 276.

Squashes, as food, 214.

Steamboats, on Lower Missouri, 13, 122–23; on Upper Missouri, 50, 63, 109, 121, 137, 191, 198, 207, 209, 240–45, 262, 317; on Yellowstone, 306; affray on, 196, 299; cholera on, 248; burned, 277–78; sunk, 318.

Stevens, Gov. Isaac I., surveys railroad route, 266.

Stuart (Stewart, Steuart), Sir William Drummond, tours America, 17–18, 228.

385

Index

Index

Wyeth, Nathaniel, career, 61; visits Fort Union, 61–62.

YELLOWSTONE, on Upper Missouri, 304, 307, 309.

Yellowstone River, Fort Manuel established, xv; explored, xvii; traders descend, 39–41; Fort Union established at mouth, 92; adventure of horse thief on, 141–42; as objective of traders, 266; General Sully reaches, 305; mentioned, 297, 306, 317, 346.